Cover and Title Pages: Nathan Love

www.mheonline.com/readingwonders

Send all inquiries to:
McGraw-Hill Education
Two Penn Plaza
New York, New York 10121

ISBN: 978-0-02-141787-2
MHID: 0-02-141787-3

Printed in the United States of America.

5 6 7 8 9 LWI 20 19 18 17

Wonders

Program Authors

Diane August

Donald R. Bear

Janice A. Dole

Jana Echevarria

Douglas Fisher

David Francis

Vicki Gibson

Jan Hasbrouck

Margaret Kilgo

Jay McTighe

Scott G. Paris

Timothy Shanahan

Josefina V. Tinajero

Mc
Graw
Hill
Education

THE BIG IDEA

Eureka! I've Got It!

4

 Go Digital! http://connected.mcgraw-hill.com

UNIT 2

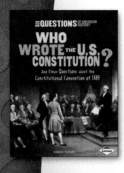 
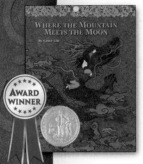

Go Digital! http://connected.mcgraw-hill.com

UNIT 3

THE BIG IDEA
Getting From Here to There

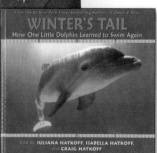

 Go Digital! http://connected.mcgraw-hill.com

THE BIG IDEA

IT'S UP TO YOU

 Go Digital! http://connected.mcgraw-hill.com

UNIT 5

THE BIG IDEA

What's Next?

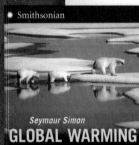

Go Digital! http://connected.mcgraw-hill.com

THE BIG IDEA

Linked In

(b) Image Source/Getty Images, Martin Ruegner/Photographer's Choice RF/Getty Images

One Hen

by Katie Smith Milway
illustrated by Eugenie Fernandes

Kojo tugs the knot tight and hoists a bundle of firewood onto his head. Since his father died, he has had to quit school and help his mother collect wood to sell at the market. It is the last load of the day, and he is tired and hungry.

Kojo and his mother live in a mud-walled house with an open fire for cooking. Beside it is a garden where they grow their own food. They never have much money or much to eat.

As Kojo nears the house, he can smell his mother's *fufu* cooking, their main meal made from cassava and yams. He begins to walk faster.

Kojo and his mother live in a village in the Ashanti region of Ghana. None of the twenty families in the village have very much money, but they do have a good idea. Each family promises to save a bit of money so that one family can borrow all the **savings** to buy something important.

One Hen: How One Loan Made a Big Difference written by Katie Smith Milway and illustrated by Eugenie Fernandes used by permission of Kids Can Press Ltd. Toronto. Text © 2008 Katie Smith Milway. Illustrations © 2008 Eugenie Fernandes.

This is the loan that Kojo gets.

The Achempong family is first to borrow the money. They use it to buy two cartloads of fruit, which they sell for a **profit** at the market. When they pay back the **loan**, the Duodu family borrows the money to buy a second-hand sewing machine. They plan to turn the cloth they weave into shirts and dresses to sell.

One day it is Kojo's mother's turn. She uses the loan to buy a cart so she can carry more firewood to market. She also hopes to rent the cart to people who need transport.

There are a few coins left over. Kojo asks if he can have them to buy something for himself. He has a good idea, too.

Kojo's idea is to buy a hen. He and his mother will eat some of the eggs it lays and sell the rest at the market. There is a farmer in a neighboring village with many hens, and Kojo will ask to buy one.

It takes Kojo two hours to walk to the chicken farm. By the time he arrives, he is hot and dusty. He wonders how he will know which hen to choose. There are so many!

Kojo tries to look over *all* the chickens. A white one pecks the ground near his foot. Should he choose this hen? A speckled one flaps her wings and clucks. Perhaps she is the one? All at once Kojo spies a plump brown hen with a bright red comb sitting in her nest and puffing out her feathers. She looks as if she would enjoy laying eggs. Now he doesn't have to think: he knows in his heart that she is the one.

Kojo pays for the brown hen and puts her in a wicker basket. He gently covers the hen with a cloth and lifts the basket onto his head. As he walks home, he dreams about the future and he sees a lot of eggs in it—eggs to eat and, if he is lucky, eggs that he can sell to buy more hens.

That night he puts the basket with the hen beside his bed-mat to keep it safe.

This is the hen that Kojo buys
with the loan he got.

Kojo makes a nest for his hen from an old wash-powder box and checks it for eggs every day. On the first day he finds...nothing. On the second, still no—but what is this? In the corner, under some straw, a smooth brown egg! Kojo is lucky, indeed: his hen does seem to enjoy laying eggs. She lays five eggs the first week. Kojo and his mother eat one egg apiece, and he saves the other three for the market on Saturday.

On market day he walks among the stalls of fruit, vegetables, meats, *kente* cloths and calabash bowls. He finds a good place to set down his small basket and call out for customers. Kojo sells two eggs to Ma Achempong and one to Ma Duodu. He clutches his egg money tightly so he won't lose it. He is about to pack up his basket and go home when he finds another treasure: loose grains and bits of fruit fallen on the ground that can feed his hen.

Slowly, slowly, Kojo's egg money grows. After two months he saves enough to pay his mother back. In four months he has enough to buy another hen. Now Kojo can sell five eggs a week, and he and his mother have more to eat. After six months he buys a third hen, and he and his mother have an egg a day. Kojo is proud of his eggs. And his mother is proud of Kojo. Bit by bit, one small hen is making a big difference.

These are the eggs that Kojo sells from the hen he bought.

STOP AND CHECK

Reread Why is Kojo's mother proud of him? The strategy Reread may help you.

14

One year later Kojo has built up his flock to twenty-five hens. He thinks the sound of chickens clucking and skittering about their enclosure is better than the beating of festival drums. But collecting eggs from so many hens is hard work. His speckled hen tries to hide her eggs. Today he finds one under a cassava plant. And his white hens peck at him when he checks their nests. Then there is his brown hen with the bright red comb—his first and still his favorite. She always seems to have a smooth brown egg for him.

Selling eggs at the market has given Kojo some savings. Maybe he will use his egg money to build a fine wooden chicken coop. Maybe he will buy some things his mother needs, such as a new water bucket and a good knife. Or maybe he can pay for something he's been dreaming of: fees and a uniform so that he can go back to school.

"Your eggs have made us stronger, Kojo," says his mother. "Now go to school and learn...for both of us."

These are the chickens Kojo buys with the money he got from selling the eggs.

Kojo's uniform feels stiff and new as he walks to school. With each step his lips move silently, reciting the ABCs and numbers he learned before his father died.

In school Kojo works hard to catch up with other students on reading and spelling and arithmetic. Later he learns to write essays and solve math and science problems. And he learns about his country's history and its resources and about other countries in Africa and around the world.

There are practical lessons for country life, too: how to filter drinking water with a cloth to remove parasites; how to use chicken manure and compost made from garbage to fertilize soil and grow vegetables. The lessons Kojo learns help him care for his chickens.

His dreams are growing bigger, but now he sees that he will need more education to make them come true. Kojo studies even harder and wins a scholarship to an agricultural college to learn more about farming. His mother will care for his chickens while he is away.

At college Kojo's dreams start to take shape—the shape of a farm of his own.

This is the school Kojo attends with the fees he paid from the money he made selling his eggs.

After Kojo finishes college, he decides to take a big **risk**. He will use all the money he and his mother have saved to start a real poultry farm. He buys a large plot of land and enough wood and wire to build chicken coops. Now he needs hens—nine hundred of them—to start the farm. He needs another loan—and a big one.

This time Kojo goes to a bank in Kumasi, a nearby town. When the banker hears that Kojo wants to buy nine hundred hens, he shakes his head. He does not want to lend money to a young man from a poor family.

This is the farm that Kojo builds using the lessons he learned at college and a loan from a bank.

Kojo does not give up. He goes to the capital city, Accra, and visits the bank's headquarters. Kojo waits and waits to see the bank president. The bank is near closing when, finally, the president agrees to see him. But not for long. He is a busy man.

Kojo tells the banker that he has schooling and will work hard. The banker has heard such stories before and frowns. Then Kojo tells him about the small loan and the brown hen and the egg money he has used to build his flock.

The banker sits back in his chair. He taps his fingers together. This is not a story he hears every day. He smiles and nods—Kojo will get his loan. The banker and Kojo shake hands.

Back home Kojo buys his hens. Soon there will be eggs—so many eggs that he will need helpers to collect them all.

Kojo's hens are good layers. There are more than enough eggs for his village, so he travels to Kumasi to sell to the shopkeepers there.

STOP AND CHECK

Reread Why does Kojo go to the bank in Accra after he goes to the bank in Kumasi? Use the strategy Reread to check your understanding.

This is the family Kojo raises on the farm he built with money he made.

One shopkeeper is called Lumo. Kojo knows him well. This man grew up in the same village that Kojo's father did and was his good friend. Kojo always goes to Lumo's shop last and sometimes stays for supper. He likes to hear stories about his father. And he likes the peanut stew and palm oil soup that Lumo's daughter makes.

Her name is Lumusi, and she is a teacher. She has many stories about boys just like Kojo once was—boys who want to learn and who have big dreams. Kojo loves these stories, and he visits more and more often. He wishes he could hear Lumusi's stories every day. One day he asks if she will be his wife.

Lumusi is proud to marry Kojo and join him on the farm. Soon Kojo and Lumusi are to be parents. As the years go by, they have three boys and two girls, all strong and clever. With the money from Kojo's eggs they build a bigger house of cinderblocks and stucco. Kojo's mother comes to live with them and tend the garden. She will never have to sell firewood again.

19

These are the people Kojo hires to work on the farm he built.

Before long, many people are working on Kojo's farm. Men come to feed the chickens and clean the coops. Women collect the eggs and pack them in boxes. Still other workers drive the eggs to markets in Kumasi and Accra.

The workers have families. In all, one hundred and twenty people depend on the **wages** from Kojo's farm. Families like the Odonkors have enough food to eat and money for their children's school fees. Ma Odonkor can buy medicine when her daughter Adika falls ill. Pa Odonkor can rebuild the walls of their mud home with cinderblocks and buy wood-stamped *adinkra* cloths for special occasions.

The workers on Kojo's farm can even **afford** livestock of their own. Some families buy a goat, others a sheep, and some start with one brown hen.

STOP AND CHECK

Reread How does Kojo's farm help other families? Use the strategy Reread to help you.

20

Kojo's farm is now the largest in Ghana. And his town has grown, too. Some people come to find jobs on the farm and build homes for their families. Others come to the town to open shops and sell wares to the workers.

One day, as Kojo tallies the accounts, he hears a knock at the door. Adika Odonkor, all grown up now, is there. She greets Kojo and then holds out a small sack of coins.

She tells Kojo that she has saved her wages. With just a bit more, she says, she could buy a mechanical grain mill and start a small business helping families turn their grain into flour. Would it be possible to have a small loan?

Kojo knows Adika's family well—they have worked on the farm many years. He likes this idea. But he makes Adika promise that one day she will loan money to another family.

Adika agrees and, bit by bit, as one person helps another, the lives of many families in the town improve, and so do the lives of their children. More children have enough to eat, more children go to school and more children are healthy.

This is the town that grows as Kojo sells his eggs and pays his workers.

21

This is the country that grows as businesses like Kojo's and Adika's prosper.

As the years pass, Kojo's poultry farm becomes the largest in all of West Africa. He is older now and a proud grandfather. His grandchildren visit often and help collect eggs. "Where will this one go?" they ask. "And that one?"

"To Bamako in Mali," Kojo replies, "or to Ouagadougou in Burkina Faso." Kojo's workers pack thousands of eggs a day, and Kojo feels proud each time an egg truck pulls away to take food to families in neighboring countries.

By now Kojo has paid many taxes to the government of Ghana. So have his workers and the shopkeepers who sell his eggs. The government uses the tax money to build roads, schools and health clinics across the country. It uses the money to improve the port at Accra where ships from many countries come to trade.

One more egg truck drives away, and Kojo looks down at his youngest grandson. The next time the boy asks Kojo where an egg will go, Kojo will say, "To your future, my child."

This is the way that one young boy named Kojo, with one small loan to buy one brown hen, eventually changed the lives of his family, his community, his town and his country. It all started with a good idea and a small loan that made it come true. It all started with one hen.

And it all started with one small loan to buy one brown hen.

About the Author and Illustrator

Katie Smith Milway lived and worked in Africa for almost ten years. While there, Katie fell in love with the African people and their rich language and storytelling tradition. In her writing of *One Hen* she tried to capture the simplicity and rhythm of traditional African languages. She hopes that her work shows children that they have the power to help themselves and others.

Eugenie Fernandes says that illustrating books about faraway places is like taking a trip. Whenever she illustrates a place she hasn't been she does research to learn all about it. She likes to find out what kind of food the people eat, what their clothes look like, and where they live. Then she brings the setting to life in her illustrations.

Author's Purpose

Katie Smith Milway describes how one small loan can make a big difference. How does the author's way of organizing events help you see the change in the community?

Respond to the Text

Summarize

Use the important events from *One Hen* to summarize how Kojo made a difference in his community. Details from your Story Map may help you.

Character
Setting
Beginning
↓
Middle
↓
End

Write

How does the author help you understand how Kojo changes and how he changes the lives of so many people? Use these sentence frames to organize your text evidence.

> Katie Smith Milway starts and ends the story . . .
> She uses cause and effect to . . .
> This helps me understand . . .

Make Connections

Talk about how Kojo and his community got what they needed. ESSENTIAL QUESTION

What are other ways people in a community help each other meet a need? TEXT TO WORLD

Compare Texts
Read about how banks help people get what they need.

Banks:
Their Business and Yours

Have you ever tried to save your money to buy something special? You may have used a piggy bank to keep your money safe. Every time you placed some coins or dollar bills into the slot at the top of your piggy bank, you were helping your **savings** grow.

Did you know that there is another kind of bank that can help you save money? Your community probably has one of these banks. Banks help people keep their money safe and build their savings. They are also the place where people can go to borrow money in times of need.

What is a Bank?

A bank is a business. But instead of making or selling things like computers, clothing, or cars, a bank provides services that involve money. Two basic services that a bank provides are savings accounts and **loans**.

Savings accounts help people save money for things they might need in the future, such as paying for college. Putting money in a savings account is like saving money in a piggy bank. But when you put money in a savings account, the bank pays you extra money, called interest. The interest is a reward for keeping your money in the bank. It also helps your savings grow.

Why does the bank reward you for keeping money in a savings account? The bank uses your savings and the savings of other customers to be able to offer people loans. Banks provide loans for many different purposes. Some people get loans from a bank to help pay for things they need, such as homes, cars, or college education. Other people want to build a small business, such as a store or a farm, but their funds are **scarce**. So, they go to a bank to borrow the money.

When the bank lends money, it isn't *taking* your savings. It's just *using* your money for a certain period of time. Any time you need your money, it's available for you.

Fun Fact

Banks aren't just for people or businesses. Countries use them, too. Many foreign governments keep gold bars in a vault at the Federal Reserve Bank of New York. Governments make payments by having gold bars moved between compartments.

The Business of Banking

Even though a bank does not make or sell things, it is still a business. A bank can make a **profit** on the services it offers. How does a bank do this?

One way a bank makes money is by lending money. Remember that the bank uses your savings to make loans. The bank pays you interest on your savings. When the bank loans this money, the person who borrows it must pay interest to the bank. To make a profit, the bank charges borrowers more interest than it pays to savers.

Banks figure out interest using percent (%). Here's how it works. Suppose the bank pays 2% interest on your savings. That means that the bank will pay you $0.02 for every dollar in your account each year. So if you keep $100 in your savings account, you will earn $2.00 in interest by the end of the year. Banks make money, but you make money, too.

How Do Banks Help Us?

Think about what life would be like without banks. You might still find a safe place to keep your money. But your money wouldn't earn interest, and your savings wouldn't grow as quickly.

Without banks, you might still be able to get a loan. But it would be much harder to find one. Suppose you wanted a loan to buy a home or start a business. You would have to find a person or business willing to give you the money. This process would result in many fewer loans, and people would have a harder time meeting their needs and building businesses.

Thanks to banks, people have a place to go when they need to borrow money. You can see the results all around you. No matter where you live, banks are an important part of the community. They have helped many people buy homes, start businesses, and get a college education. They have helped people meet their needs and change their lives.

Fun Fact

The Federal Reserve Bank System, or "The Fed," is a bank for other banks and a bank for the federal government.

Make Connections

Talk about how banks help people get the things they need. ESSENTIAL QUESTION

How has a person or character you've read about met a need? In what ways could a bank have helped? TEXT TO TEXT

(r) Finnbarr Webster/Alamy, (b) Mark Wilson/Getty Images News/Getty Images

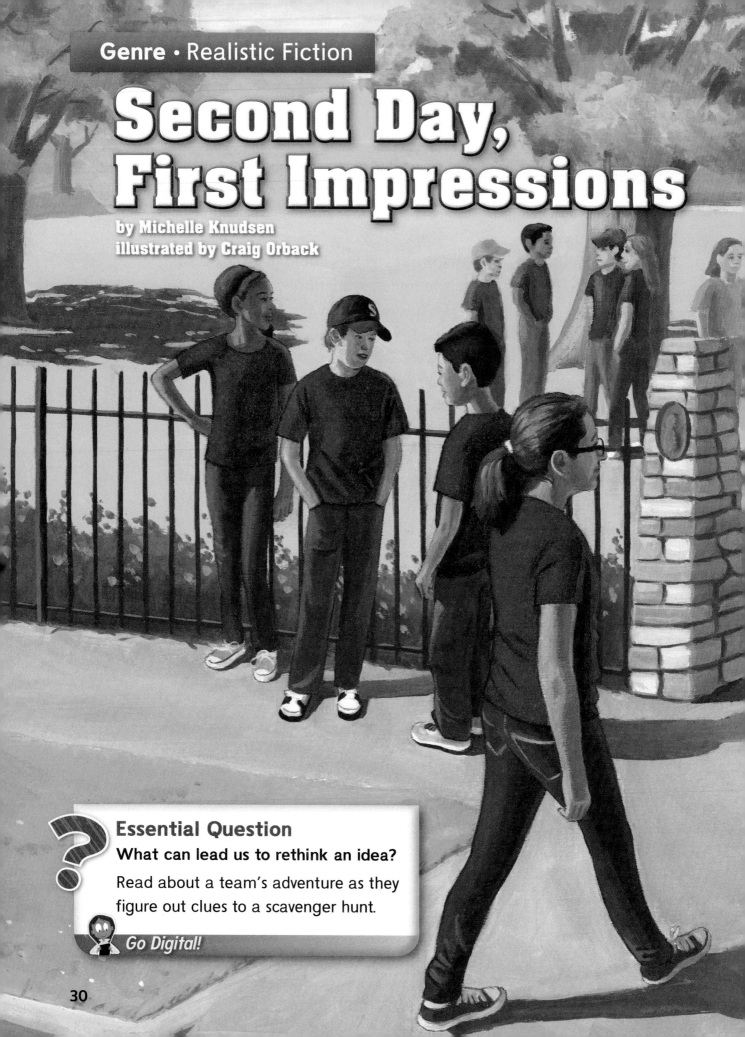

Second Day, First Impressions

by Michelle Knudsen
illustrated by Craig Orback

Essential Question
What can lead us to rethink an idea?

Read about a team's adventure as they figure out clues to a scavenger hunt.

Go Digital!

Luisa hesitated at the park entrance, scanning the sea of strangers for red T-shirts and trying to ignore the butterflies in her stomach. The entire fifth grade of Greenhaven Elementary was spread out before her, along with assorted teachers and parent volunteers, wandering the sun-dappled grass and gathering excitedly in color-coded groups for the morning's event. She finally spotted her teacher, Mr. Martucci, waving at her with a clipboard from the shade of a huge oak tree. She made a beeline for him.

Three of her teammates were already there. Luisa had met them yesterday in class—the boys leaning on the fence were Tyler and Sam, and the tall girl near them was Devon. Luisa hadn't had an opportunity to get to know any of them yet. *Maybe today*, she thought hopefully. This was her first real chance to start making some friends in this new town. She just had to get off on the right foot.

"All right, everyone," announced Principal Goldstein into her megaphone. "I know you are all **anxious** to begin, so please **assemble** with your teams to start the annual Greenhaven Fifth Grade Second-Day-of-School Scavenger Hunt! Remember: you have unique sets of clues, so don't get **distracted** by what your rival teams are doing. The finish line is not marked on your maps—you must figure out the clues to get there. The first team to reach the finish line will be our winners!"

Another boy from Luisa's class, Hailin, dashed over to their group. He was panting audibly as he stumbled to a stop, his sneakers untied, his red shirt inside out, and his hair a crazy mess on top of his head.

"Overslept again?" Tyler asked.

"How'd you know?" Hailin seemed genuinely perplexed as he knelt to tie his laces. Tyler, Sam, and Devon smiled, rolling their eyes.

"Aaand...GO!" shouted Mrs. Goldstein.

Mr. Martucci produced a small, cream-colored envelope and ripped it open. They all leaned in to read their first clue:

> Welcome, Explorers! It's time to begin.
>
> You'll have to be both quick and clever to win!
>
> Think of the one place that has the most letters.
>
> Then go there to go on, Greenhaven go-getters!

Mr. Martucci handed the map and clue to Devon and stepped back. "Okay, Red Team," he said, "go to it! I'm just here to keep you company—it's your job to **decipher** the clues and determine where to go next."

Luisa held back, uncertain, but the others jumped right in. "Maybe the movie theater?" suggested Devon. "That's twelve letters..."

"Greenhaven Public Library has twenty-three," said Sam, pointing at the map.

"Wait, you guys," said Tyler. "It's a clue, right? We should have to, you know, figure something out, not just count letters."

That was a good point, Luisa realized, relieved that she hadn't blurted out something ridiculous before Tyler pointed out they were on the wrong track.

"Oh—*letters*!" Hailin exclaimed, grinning. "Not alphabet letters—the kind you mail! It's the post office!"

They took off for the post office at a run. Luisa necessarily let the others take the lead, since she was still unfamiliar with much of the area. Taped to the stately front door was another envelope, which Hailin tore open to reveal the next clue.

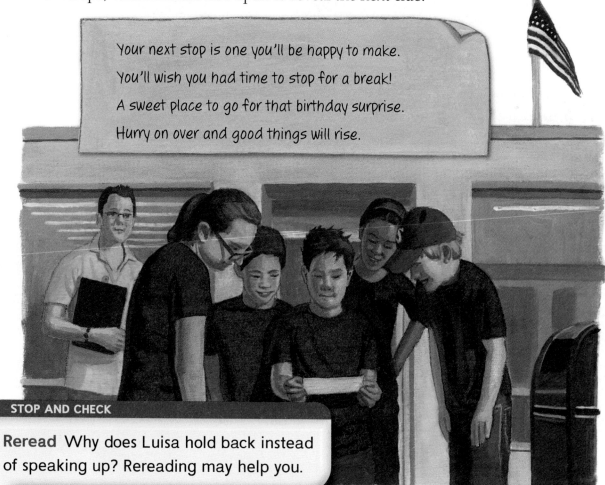

Your next stop is one you'll be happy to make.
You'll wish you had time to stop for a break!
A sweet place to go for that birthday surprise.
Hurry on over and good things will rise.

STOP AND CHECK

Reread Why does Luisa hold back instead of speaking up? Rereading may help you.

Come on, Luisa told herself firmly, *you have to attempt to contribute.* "Maybe—maybe it means someplace with an elevator? Things will rise?"

"No, wait, I've got it," Sam said. "The bakery! That's where you'd get a birthday cake for a surprise party...and cakes are good things that rise!"

Luisa glanced around, embarrassed, but no one seemed to care that her idea had been wrong. And now that she thought about it, Sam and Devon's ideas for the first clue had been wrong too, and no one had teased them or anything. The butterflies in her stomach seemed to be fluttering a little less as she headed toward the bakery with the others.

Through the bakery's front window, they spotted the next envelope attached to the cake display case. Sam darted inside to retrieve it, maneuvering deftly around amused bakery patrons, then read the clue aloud.

Think of our founder, the great you-know-who.

He started this town back in 1802.

Make your way now to his last resting place.

But time's growing short! Pick up the pace!

Hey—I actually know this one! Luisa thought, astonished.

"To the cemetery!" Devon cried.

"No, wait!" Luisa said, stopping them. "That's not right."

"It said his 'last resting place.' That sounds like a cemetery to me," said Devon.

Luisa nodded. "I know. But he wasn't buried in the cemetery. I—I did some reading when my family decided to relocate here. The founder was actually buried near the library. There's a tree with a little plaque with his name engraved on it and everything, right out front."

The other kids looked at each other.

"I've walked by that library almost every day of my life," Sam said. "I never knew that!"

"Good save!" Devon said to Luisa. "We'd have lost valuable time if we'd had to **retrace** our steps from the cemetery."

"We still need to hurry," Tyler reminded them, pointing at a group of yellow-shirted students running purposefully across an intersection.

STOP AND CHECK

Reread What error was the team about to make? How does Luisa help? Use the strategy Reread.

"I know a shortcut!" Hailin cried. "Follow me!"

No one moved.

"No, seriously," Hailin said. "You know how I'm always late? Trust me, I've figured out a *lot* of shortcuts in this town."

The others had to agree that made sense, and so they let Hailin lead them up a tiny side street and across a scraggly patch of grass. A few more blocks, a sharp right turn, and suddenly they were standing in front of the library. Luisa found the clue taped to the plaque honoring the town's founder.

Now go to the place where the pigskin is found.
But don't waste too much time running around!
Center yourselves, then rise to the top.
When you run out of space you'll know it's time to stop.

"Football stadium," Tyler said decisively. "Pigskin, running around...that seems pretty obvious. I don't know what the 'center' stuff means, though."

"Maybe the center of the field? Or the center section of the seating area?" Devon proposed.

"I bet that's it," said Luisa, nodding. "We should find the center section, then go up to the top."

By the time they ran to the high school, home of the town's only football stadium, and up the many, many, *many* steps to the top, they were all out of breath. Tyler plucked the envelope from the aisle seat in the uppermost row.

> You're getting so close! The end is in sight.
> **Accomplish** your goal. Don't give up the fight!
> Look where you've been, see where you are.
> Now **navigate** wisely and you'll be a star!

Devon stared blankly at the map. "That doesn't narrow down the **options** at all."

"Maybe this one's the movie theater? You know," Sam said, "like movie stars?"

"Maybe," murmured Luisa. "'Close,' like a close-up, and 'sight,' because movies are something you watch..."

"It could be a planetarium," said Tyler. "Does our town have a planetarium?"

"Guys!" Devon exclaimed suddenly. "Oh, wow—look at this." She grabbed a pencil from her bag and placed the point at the park, where they had started. As they watched, she traced a line from there to the post office, then to the bakery, then the library, then the stadium. "Do you see what I see?"

Luisa followed the lines with her eyes and got it at once. Their path was forming the shape of a star! They just needed one more line to complete it—a line connecting them right back to the beginning.

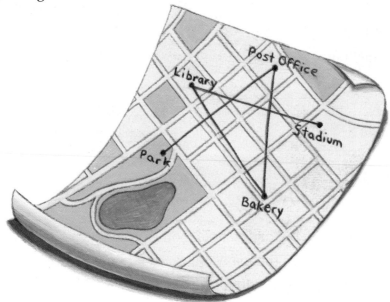

The others saw it, too, and together they turned and raced toward the park. When they reached the final stretch, Mr. Martucci veered off to the side, waving them on and shouting, "Go, Red Team, go!" Luisa could see the finish line beckoning up ahead. They were going to win!

Suddenly the Green Team burst into sight from their left, followed by a blaze of yellow streaking by on the right.

Luisa ducked her head and lengthened her stride, giving it everything she had. She could tell the others were doing the same. They ran faster and faster, arms pumping, feet flying, blurs of yellow and green and now blue and purple too crowding in from all sides. The finish line was growing closer, and Mrs. Goldstein was shouting into her megaphone, and there were other people all around, cheering and yelling words of encouragement.

Finally, the Red Team tumbled across the finish line—just one fateful step behind the Greens. As Mrs. Goldstein pronounced the Green Team the winners, Tyler, Sam, Devon, Hailin, and Luisa collapsed in a big, red, exhausted heap on the grass.

"So...close..." Tyler gasped.

"Yeah," Sam said, sounding even more out of breath, "if only you ran a little faster, we might have won."

Tyler made a face, and they all burst into laughter.

"Nice job, new girl," Devon said approvingly, giving Luisa a high-five. "We wouldn't even have come in second without your help."

"That was really fun," said Hailin. "I hope we get to be on the same team for something else."

"Me, too," Luisa agreed, smiling. Her stomach-butterflies had vanished without a trace. She lay under the trees with her new friends, still trying to catch her breath, confident that today had been only the first of many adventures yet to come.

STOP AND CHECK

Reread How does the Red Team feel about coming in second? Reread to check your understanding.

ABOUT THE AUTHOR AND ILLUSTRATOR

Michelle Knudsen has been writing for as long as she can remember and is now the author of more than 40 books. Michelle enjoys writing everything from picture books to fantasy novels and nonfiction books.

One question readers typically ask her is "Where does she get her ideas?" The answer is that they come from anywhere and everywhere, usually without advance warning! Michelle is constantly scribbling notes about new story possibilities on scraps of paper and sticky notes. She never knows when something around her will spark an idea.

Craig Orback began painting and drawing at an early age. Later, he studied design and illustration at college, and shortly after began his career as an illustrator for magazines, children's books, and school textbooks.

Craig mostly uses oil paint, but also uses watercolor, acrylic, ink, pastel, and computer technology. When he first begins to illustrate a story, he lets his imagination run wild and then sketches his ideas. He says it's his favorite part of illustrating a book.

Author's Purpose

How does Michelle Knudsen use dialogue to make her characters seem like real people? Give a specific example.

Respond to the Text

Summarize

Summarize how Luisa and her team made it to the finish line in *Second Day, First Impressions*. Include events and details from your Problem and Solution Chart.

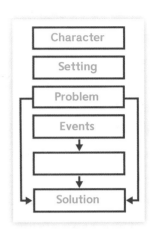

Write

Think about how the author uses repetition. Why does she use the idiom "butterflies in her stomach" at the beginning, middle, and end of the story? Use these sentence frames to organize your text evidence.

Michelle Knudsen repeats . . .
The reason she does this is to . . .
This helps me know that Luisa . . .

Make Connections

Talk about how Luisa and her teammates had to rethink their ideas during the scavenger hunt. ESSENTIAL QUESTION

In this story, each team member suggested answers to the clues. Why is it important to listen to others' ideas when working as a team? TEXT TO WORLD

Compare Texts
Read about a group's adventure when they get separated from their class in a museum.

Lost in the Museum Wings

"James," called Mrs. Roberts. "Please keep up with the rest of the group."

How am I ever going to **accomplish** *keeping everyone together,* she wondered, *when at every turn there's something interesting to see!* As she waited for her **distracted** son to catch up, she peered into a nearby display of gemstones, all the while keeping a watchful eye on her other three charges as they browsed the Hall of Minerals. When James caught up, she gathered Kaitlin, Ian, and Emi and they continued along with the rest of the class and chaperones into the museum's Meteor Maze.

Before they entered, James tapped Kaitlin and pointed behind her. "Look," he whispered. "Butterflies!"

Ian and Emi overheard, and all three turned around to look. Two orange and black butterflies fluttered across the hall and the children giggled.

"What's all the fuss?" Mrs. Roberts asked.

"James just saw two butterflies," Ian explained. "Over there!"

"In here? That's odd," Mrs. Roberts turned to look too, but all she saw was a flood of visitors pouring out of the hall.

Then she noticed the back of a boy's head moving away from the group and immediately recognized it—James! When she looked back, the class was already making their way through the Meteor Maze. She'd have to act fast to get her son and catch up to the class. She gathered the three and said, "Come with me. I've got to get James. Now stay together."

Together they hurried down the hall and caught up with James as he was rounding the corner into the Coral Corridor.

"James, you can't just wander off when you know we must all stay together as a group," Mrs. Roberts chided.

"Sorry—I wanted to get a look at those butterflies," James explained.

The five retraced their steps, but when they returned, the Meteor Maze had now been roped off. A sign read: Last Tour 1 pm.

"Now how will we find them?" Mrs. Roberts wondered aloud.

"I know!" Kaitlin said. "Our teacher said we would visit the Monarchs exhibit next and **assemble** by the bus at two o'clock to return to school."

Mrs. Roberts looked at her watch: 1:15. They would have to hurry.

"Please, where is the exhibit on monarchs?" she asked, approaching a guard.

"Go down the end of this hall," the guard directed, "but before you get to the end, take a right, just past the sign Ancient Dynasties."

They hurried away, but when they reached the next hall, a silence welcomed them. "This is way too quiet for our class. Do you think they've already left?" Emi worried.

The group passed displays filled with jewels, robes, and headdresses, but there was no sign of their class. James stopped suddenly. "Wait! Maybe it's not monarchs as in kings," he said.

"What other **options** are there?" Ian asked.

"Remember the butterflies?" James asked. "I bet we're supposed to see monarch *butterflies*!"

"Well, we won't have much time to find them if we have to hurry back to the guard," Mrs. Roberts said, checking her watch anxiously.

Kaitlin pointed to a wall. "Look—a map! Maybe we can find another way to the exhibit without having to go back."

Ian quickly deciphered it. "Here's an exhibit called Magnificent Monarchs and Stunning Swallowtails—it's just down those stairs!"

They quickly descended the stairs. There, they could see an exhibit, but it was enclosed in glass and had a special entrance.

As they waited impatiently to enter, the group peered into the exhibit. "There they are!" James exclaimed.

"Our class?" Kaitlin asked.

"The kinds of butterflies I saw earlier!" James replied.

"Look," Ian said, pointing to their teacher. "Our class is here, too. We got here just in time!"

Inside the exhibit, they rejoined their class. As butterflies flapped and danced above their heads, the others excitedly blurted out facts they had learned. "I found out that monarchs can travel long distances," a fellow classmate informed James.

"They move together in colonies, or groups!" another chimed in.

James gave his mother a knowing look and said "They're not the only ones!"

Make Connections

What led Mrs. Roberts and the group to rethink their plan to get back to the class? ESSENTIAL QUESTION

How is the problem the group faces in this story similar to a problem in another adventure story you've read? How does rethinking ideas help the characters in each story solve the problem? TEXT TO TEXT

CAMPING with the PRESIDENT

by Ginger Wadsworth

illustrated by Karen Dugan

President Theodore Roosevelt mounted his favorite horse and shook the reins. He and Renown shot out the White House stable door. They galloped straight for the woods on their daily ride. As always, hooves pounded behind them. The President made sure that the Secret Service had to ride hard to keep up with him.

America's twenty-sixth president loved his busy job...except for one thing. He missed what he called the "strenuous life." He wanted to hike alone through the woods, whistling for birds. He longed to chop wood or hunt wild animals.

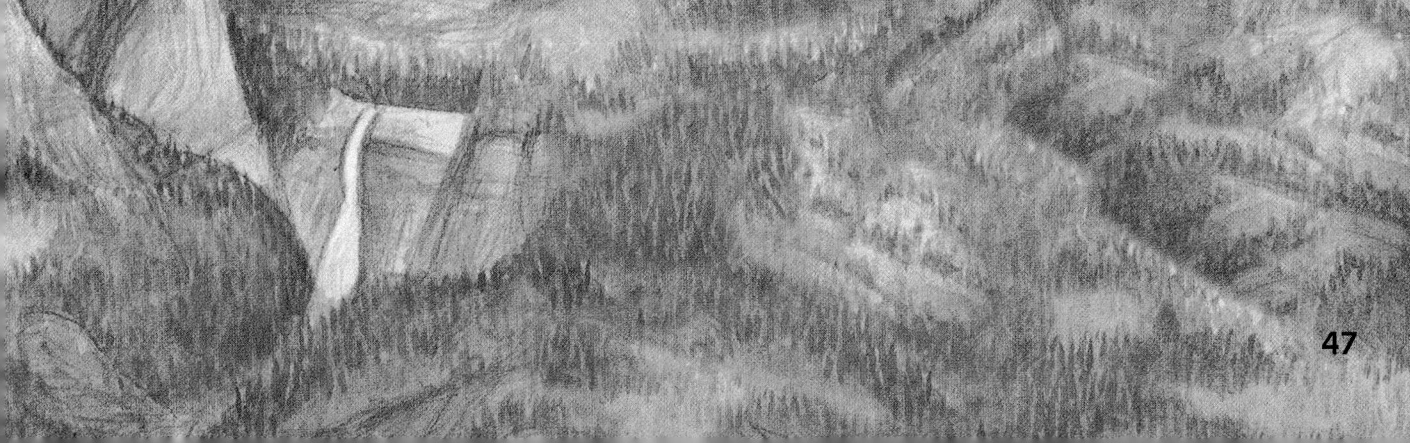

Camping with the President by Ginger Wadsworth, illustrated by Karen Dugan. Copyright © 2009 by Ginger Wadsworth and Karen Dugan. Published by Calkins Creek, an imprint of Boyds Mills Press. Reprinted by permission.

Most nights, he set aside time to read. Some of his favorite books were about nature. One evening in the White House, the President finished John Muir's newest book, *Our National Parks*. The author's descriptions of California's Yosemite National Park fascinated the President. He tried to picture the three-thousand-foot-high walls that surrounded Yosemite Valley. Besides all the waterfalls, there were granite boulders bigger than buildings, with names like Half Dome and North Dome. Distant mountain peaks soared over ten thousand feet into the sky.

Muir's nature essays clearly **indicated** a man with strong opinions about land preservation. Roosevelt enjoyed lively discussions. It would be exciting to talk with the country's best-known expert on conservation *and* explore Yosemite.

But why couldn't he? He was the President of the entire United States, wasn't he?

The President picked up his pen. He wrote so fast that his spectacles danced to the tip of his nose.

Dear Mr. Muir,
I am coming West. I want to go camping with you and no one else...

In his letter, he explained that he had already decided to take a fact-finding trip in the spring of 1903. Roosevelt had never seen the far West, and he was eager to meet the people and learn about the natural resources, such as minerals, trees, and water. This visit would help the President make better decisions about the region in the future.

Roosevelt wrote Muir that he would first visit Yellowstone National Park. After seeing the Grand Canyon and Arizona, he would come to California by train. To wrap up his trip, the President asked Muir to guide him through the Yosemite area. While camping and avoiding dignitaries, they could talk.

The President grinned as he stamped his official seal on the back of the envelope. Camping sounded bully! He especially wanted to see California's giant sequoia trees, the largest living things in the world. Four whole days in the Yosemite wilderness! The President felt giddy with excitement.

He would have to get some Western clothes.

Months later, the President's special train sped southeast across California, from Oakland on the coast, to reach the tiny town of Raymond, at the end of the railroad line.

"I am dee-lighted to meet you," President Theodore Roosevelt said, pumping Muir's hand up and down.

STOP AND CHECK

Ask and Answer Questions
Why does the President want to talk to John Muir? Go back to the text to find the answer.

Soon Roosevelt and Muir were escorted with the rest of the presidential party in stagecoaches some thirty miles up through the foothills of the Sierra Nevada into the Yosemite wilderness. The two men stood in the Mariposa Grove of Big Trees in front of the Grizzly Giant, one of the largest giant sequoia trees in the world. On either side of Muir and Roosevelt, important men, including George Pardee, governor of California, posed for the cameras. *Poof!* Burning white flash powder blinded them.

Roosevelt smiled his famous toothy grin for the cameras. Reporters would write about the Grizzly Giant and the other trees in this grove. But they wouldn't have much else to write about because the President didn't plan on seeing them any time soon!

The President announced that he was "prepared to go into the Yosemite with John Muir...I want to drop politics absolutely for four days...." He punched his fist in his hand for **emphasis**.

Everyone roared with disappointment. But there was no arguing with the strong-willed leader of the United States. He waved away the reporters. All the dignitaries climbed into their stagecoaches. Thirty cavalrymen mounted their dapple-gray horses. They saluted their President.

Finally, the President even ordered his Secret Service men to stay away. Spurs jingled and leather creaked. The President watched everyone head down the zigzagging road to the nearest town.

Three men waited with the pack animals and gear. They were under the watchful eye of government ranger Charlie Leidig. Charlie's family ran a hotel in Yosemite Valley, where he had lived and worked his entire life. He was the perfect man to be in charge of the day-to-day details of the camping trip.

Centuries-old giant sequoia trees surrounded Roosevelt. He reached out to touch the cinnamon-colored bark of the Grizzly Giant. It felt spongy. Twisted tree limbs reached toward the sky, so heavy they didn't even sway in the afternoon wind.

Deep in the forest, a squirrel chattered. Then a bird sang.

The President whistled back, hoping to draw out his first Yosemite bird.

A robin dropped from a branch and pushed **debris** about on the forest floor.

Roosevelt pulled out a pocket-sized notebook he always carried. He wrote down "Yosemite Wilderness, May 1903, robin."

Then the President sucked in a deep breath of brisk mountain air. "Now this is bully!" he shouted. "Boys, let's build a campfire."

When Roosevelt woke up the next morning, he recognized the "wonderful music" of a hermit thrush, one of his favorite birds.

The President was starving! He wrestled the fry pan from Charlie. Before long, bacon-scented smoke drifted into the forest. Then the President scrambled six eggs beside the slab of bacon.

He ate a huge breakfast, happy to be away from the White House cooks who fussed over his diet.

After nibbling on a crust of bread, John Muir picked up a sequoia cone. He shook it. Tiny dark seeds, much smaller than snowflakes, spilled out. Muir explained that, from just one seed, the Grizzly Giant had sprouted about two thousand years earlier. Other trees in the grove were almost as old. Many were hundreds of years old. Sequoias, Muir added, grew on the western slopes of the Sierra Nevada, but nowhere else in the entire world.

Roosevelt's eyes widened with surprise.

Sequoia cone

STOP AND CHECK

Ask and Answer Questions Why is the President surprised? Find details in the text to support your answer.

Moments later, Muir scrambled up a nearby sequoia tree stump like a mountain goat. *He is pretty spry for a sixty-five-year-old,* Roosevelt thought.

The stump's flat top was big enough to hold a dozen men or more. Muir yelled that it had taken several days to saw down this tree. When it crashed to the ground, the tree shattered into splinters. Sequoia wood was of little use, except for fence posts. But lumbermen still continued to cut these trees.

The President shook his head in disgust. How could anyone cut a tree that had been growing for so long? For fence posts! What if future **generations** never saw a giant sequoia tree?

He and Mr. Muir would have to chat about forest preservation, but later. It was time to go. Roosevelt swallowed one last cup of coffee, strong and hot, just the way he liked it.

His horse snorted and danced sideways along the trail. The President looked back. No one seemed to be following him! Had he truly escaped the ever-watchful eyes of his Secret Service men?

Hours later, the two men arrived at Glacier Point, with its **spectacular** views. Swirling wind tried to take the President's hat as Roosevelt and Muir inched out onto Overhanging Rock at the tip of Glacier Point.

Yosemite Valley lay three thousand feet directly below them. The Merced River, a curving ribbon of gray-blue, flowed through the green valley floor. Rock walls, interspersed with waterfalls, ringed the valley. Muir pointed out Upper and Lower Yosemite Falls, with mist rising from below, and the **sheer** face of Half Dome. The rugged-looking high-mountain country stretched beyond.

For a change, Roosevelt was speechless.

Suddenly, reporters appeared, interrupting with questions and calls of "Mr. President. Mr. President." The wind picked up their words and blew them away. The President's jaws snapped shut. Where had they come from?

Once again, people and cameras surrounded him. The President was angry—very angry. He marched to his horse. "Boys, keep them away from me," Roosevelt barked at the Secret Service, glad for once that they were lurking nearby.

How could he rough it with a crowd around him?

At sunset, Roosevelt and Muir picked a new camping spot. The President grabbed an ax and insisted on starting the fire. Sweat flew from his forehead as he chopped firewood. Before long, a sizzling-hot campfire glowed in the dark. And once again, Roosevelt took the fry pan from Charlie.

While the President chewed his way through a platter of steak and fried potatoes, Muir spoke of the need to provide "government protection...around every wild grove and forest on the mountains." He urged Roosevelt to set aside land, including the Mariposa Grove of Big Trees and the state-run Yosemite Valley, which they would visit the next day.

The President had never met anyone who talked as much, or as fast, about the importance of nature. In fact, Muir seemed to live on words, not food! As Roosevelt listened, he heard a noise in the trees above him. Was it a dreaded Secret Service man, guarding him in a tree? He listened again. Then he chuckled. In his notebook, the President wrote "owl."

Four to five inches of snow covered them by morning!

"This is bullier yet! I wouldn't miss this for anything," the President shouted, shaking snow from his blankets. He shaved by the light of a roaring campfire, then trimmed and waxed his moustache.

That morning, they followed a narrow trail that hugged the vertical granite walls. It was late afternoon when the small, dust-coated group rode into Yosemite Village, a cluster of tents and wooden buildings.

A waiting crowd cheered loudly and pressed forward, hoping to shake the President's hand. He dismounted.

"[Mr. Muir and I] slept in a snowstorm last night. This has been the grandest day of my life! One I shall long remember! Just think of where I was last night. Up there"—and with a sweep of his hand, he pointed to Glacier Point—"amid the pines and silver firs...and without a tent."

The President waved his hat. "Now, Mr. Muir and I will pitch camp near Bridalveil Fall!" He mounted his horse. It reared suddenly, legs pawing the air. Charlie stepped forward to push back the throng.

Tails swishing, the pack animals stood at the edge of the campsite. The air turned chilly after the sun set. Suddenly, a mule brayed. Twigs snapped. Suspecting that they had been followed, Charlie disappeared into the dark. He told hundreds of waiting admirers in a nearby meadow to leave because the President was very tired. "They went—some of them even on tiptoe, so as not to annoy their President," he later told Roosevelt.

As the moon came up, the President took off his shoes and rolled up his pant legs. Wading in the icy-cold stream, Roosevelt hollered to John Muir. He was "as happy as a boy out of school."

Then the two men lay on their mattresses of ferns and fir branches, still talking about the waste of natural resources. For once, the President mostly listened. He respected the mountaineer's advice on the importance of preserving land around the entire country.

Above them, El Capitan glowed in the nighttime light. The Merced River flowed softly; Bridalveil Fall thundered. And it was growing late. The President was tired. "Good night, boys!" he said. He burrowed under his blankets and fell asleep. For the third night in a row, he snored.

Too soon, though, sunlight streamed into the valley. The President's horse-drawn stagecoach brought his official party.

"It was bully," the President said, pumping John Muir's hand. "I've had the time of my life!"

Roosevelt climbed into his stagecoach and leaned over. "Good-bye, John. Come and see me in Washington."

Then he motioned John to come closer. "Be patient. Congress may sleep through my long-winded speeches, but I promise to wake them up."

What a magical place, Roosevelt thought, gazing around one last time. He was glad he had come to Yosemite. He felt more alive than ever, thanks to his bully-good camping trip with John Muir. Once back in Washington, Roosevelt would be able to do "some forest good," as the old **naturalist** would say.

Roosevelt peered in every direction as his stagecoach circled the valley. He wanted to savor his memories of Half Dome, of sunlight washing over glacial rocks, Yosemite Falls roaring, of deer grazing, and the lingering smell of a Yosemite campfire. Then he waved one final good-bye.

Moments later, the President was gone in a cloud of dust.

> **STOP AND CHECK**
>
> Reread How do John Muir's ideas affect the President? Use the strategy Reread to help you.

About the
AUTHOR *and*
ILLUSTRATOR

Ginger Wadsworth's childhood adventures helped her develop a deep love of the West and nature. Growing up, Ginger spent summers working on a ranch in Idaho, where she went horseback riding, rafting, hiking, and fishing. She has written several biographies about people who worked to protect the environment, such as John Muir and Rachel Carson. She doesn't make up any of the dialogue in her biographies. Instead, she spends about two years gathering the subject's words from his or her diaries, letters, and published works.

Karen Dugan created her first masterpiece at the age of two on a white bedspread with a tube of red lipstick. Today, she has turned her talents to illustrating children's books. Karen's greatest joy is books. She says, "I get goose bumps walking into a bookstore or library."

Author's Purpose
Why do you think Ginger Wadsworth uses real quotes as dialogue in her writing? What did you learn about the President from the things he said?

Respond to the Text

Summarize

Use important details from *Camping with the President* to summarize what you learned about President Roosevelt's trip to Yosemite. Information from your Cause and Effect Chart may help you.

Cause ➡ Effect
➡
➡
➡
➡

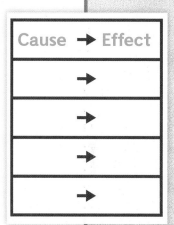

Write

Think about what President Roosevelt said and did while at Yosemite. How does the author show how Roosevelt changes because of his experience? Use these sentence frames to organize your text evidence.

> The author tells about Roosevelt's trip by . . .
> The dialogue and illustrations help me to . . .
> This helps me understand that Roosevelt . . .

Make Connections

Talk about how the camping trip changed the President's view of nature. ESSENTIAL QUESTION

How can experiencing nature tell you more than hearing or reading about it? TEXT TO WORLD

Compare Texts

Read about how an experience changed the way Theodore Roosevelt thought about birds.

A Walk with Teddy

Not long after Theodore Roosevelt's camping trip to Yosemite, he took another trip to explore the outdoors. This time he went to England.

Theodore Roosevelt, or "Teddy" as he was often called, had always been interested in birds of England. But he had only read about them in books. Roosevelt decided to take a walk in the countryside with a naturalist. He wanted to see the birds in person. While on his walk, one type of bird impressed him. He wrote of this encounter in his autobiography.

Theodore Roosevelt was known for his love of the outdoors.

We left London on the morning of June 9... Getting off the train at Basingstoke, we drove to the pretty, smiling valley of the Itchen. Here we tramped for three or four hours, then again drove, this time to the edge of the New Forest, where we first took tea at an inn, and then tramped through the forest to an inn on its other side, at Brockenhurst. At the conclusion of our walk my companion made a list of the birds we had seen...

The bird that most impressed me on my walk was the blackbird. I had already heard nightingales in abundance near Lake Como... but I had never heard either the blackbird, the song thrush, or the blackcap warbler; and while I knew that all three were good singers, I did not know what really beautiful singers they were. Blackbirds were very abundant, and they played a prominent part in the chorus which we heard throughout the day... In its habits and manners the blackbird strikingly resembles our American robin... It hops everywhere over the lawns, just as our robin does... Its song has a general resemblance to that of our robin, but many of the notes are far more musical, more like those of our wood thrush... I certainly do not think that the blackbird has received full justice in the books. I knew that he was a singer, but I really had no idea how fine a singer he was.

A Man of Action

Roosevelt realized that seeing and hearing these birds in the wild gave him more information than any book. He could see the birds in action. He could hear their calls to each other. His experience revealed much about the birds of the country.

Roosevelt continued to travel throughout his life. He took every opportunity to study animals in the wild. But his travels also showed him that habitats needed to be protected. In his years as president, Roosevelt worked to preserve land. He established 150 national forests, 4 national parks, and 51 bird reservations. These sites continue to protect the nation's wildlife.

Roosevelt declared Crater Lake a national park. This lake is the deepest lake in the United States. It has a depth of 1,943 feet.

As president, Roosevelt established Pelican Island National Wildlife Refuge. This was the first area set aside by the federal government to protect wildlife.

Make Connections

Talk about how Roosevelt's experience in England changed the way he thought about birds. **ESSENTIAL QUESTION**

How was Roosevelt's trip to England like another experience with nature you've read about? How was each experience different? **TEXT TO TEXT**

The Boy Who Invented TV

by Kathleen Krull
illustrated by Greg Couch

Essential Question
How does technology lead to creative ideas?

Read about how Philo Farnsworth came up with an invention that would change the world.

Go Digital!

The Story of Philo Farnsworth

Life Before Philo

Imagine what it was like growing up on a farm in the American West of 1906. With electricity rare out in the country, chores took up most of your day. No refrigerators, no cars, few phones, hardly any indoor bathrooms. Long distances separated you from friends and relations. Meeting up with others took some effort—you rode a horse or walked. There were trains, but riding or even seeing one was a big deal.

Getting news was another challenge. What government leaders were doing in Washington, the latest in the arts and sciences, whether sports teams were winning or losing, new information of any kind—it trickled in haphazardly by mail. Not many people had books, and libraries were few and far between.

It was all a bit lonely.

What about fun? Movies—no. Radio—no (it was only on military ships). There was music, if you played your own instruments. There were no malls to go hang out at. When you had enough money saved up to buy a bicycle or roller skates, you ordered from the "wish book"—the Sears, Roebuck mail-order catalog.

And there was no television. That's right. **NO TV.**

In 1906, inside a log cabin on a farm in Utah, a boy was born who would change things. His name was Philo Taylor Farnsworth.

No sooner did Philo Farnsworth learn to talk than he asked a question. Then another, and another. His parents answered as best they could.

Noticing Philo's interest in anything mechanical, his father took the three-year-old boy to see a train at a station. At first Philo was afraid this huge, noisy thing might be a monster. But the nice engineer invited the boy up into the cab with him, explaining a bit about how steam-powered trains worked.

That night Philo sat at the kitchen table and drew detailed pictures of what went on inside the motor of a train.

Two new machines **captivated** Philo as he grew up. One was a hand-cranked telephone, purchased by a neighbor. Holding the phone one day, hearing the voice of his beloved aunt, six-year-old Philo got goose bumps. After all, she lived a long ways away!

Another neighbor brought a hand-cranked phonograph to a dance. Music swirling out of a machine—it was almost impossible to believe.

"These things seemed like magic to me," Philo said later. Besides being incredibly clever, the inventions brought people together in whole new ways.

Philo's father shared his wonder. On clear summer nights, as they lay in the grass and gazed at the stars, his father told him about Alexander Graham Bell and the telephone, Thomas Edison and the phonograph. Inventors—these became Philo's heroes.

Away on a temporary job, his father appointed Philo, the oldest of five children, the "man" in the family. Philo was eight. His many chores included feeding the pigs, milking and grazing the cow, fetching wood for the stove. He did get his own pony—Tippy.

It was also a sort of reward to skip school for a while. Bullies there teased him about his unusual name. Shy and serious, Philo didn't fight back.

He found it far more appealing to practice reading with his grandmother's Sears, Roebuck catalog. It had toys...as well as cameras, alarm clocks, and machines that used a new, invisible source of power. Electricity, it was called.

In his spare time, Philo raised lambs and sold them. When he had enough money saved up, he visited his grandmother to pick a bicycle out of her catalog.

But somehow, she talked him into ordering a violin instead. Philo did love the sound of music, its orderly rhythms. And even at age ten, he dreamed of fame. Maybe he could find it by creating music like what he heard on the neighbor's phonograph.

Soon he was performing in dance bands, making five dollars every Friday night.

Playing the violin was one more thing for the bullies to tease him about. Then one day Philo fought back, and the teasing ended.

Trying for a better life, the Farnsworths moved from Utah to an Idaho farm with fields of beets and potatoes. Eleven-year-old Philo drove one of their covered wagons, carrying a crate of piglets, a cage of hens, his violin, and their new prize possession—a phonograph.

Arriving in the Snake River Valley, he noticed something up in the air—power lines. Their new home was wired for electricity! A generator ran the lights and water heater, the hay stacker and grain elevator, and other farm equipment.

And up in the attic was another welcome surprise. A shelf of old popular-science magazines, with thrilling articles about magnetism, electricity, and those new "magic boxes"—radios. Philo promptly **claimed** this as his bedroom. His chores began before dawn, but he trained himself to wake an hour early so he could switch on the light and read in bed. Any spare money he had went to buy more magazines.

That's when he saw the word "television" for the first time. It meant a machine that was something like a radio, only it sent pictures instead of sounds.

It didn't actually exist yet, but scientists were racing to invent one.

The electric generator broke down a lot, and repairs were costly. Each time the repairman came, Philo bombarded him with questions.

STOP AND CHECK

Ask and Answer Questions How did Philo's life change after the Farnsworths moved to Idaho? Find details in the text to support your answer.

After yet another breakdown, Philo set out to fix the machine himself. He took it apart, cleaned it, put it back together, and pressed the "on" button. It worked.

Philo's father was enormously proud of him. From then on, he was the Farnsworths' electrical engineer.

Philo tinkered with broken motors, reels of wire, old tools. He devised gadgets to hook up to the generator—anything to make his chores easier, like installing lights in the barn.

His least favorite thing was washing clothes— hours of standing while pushing and pulling the lever that swished the water around the washtub. So he attached a motor with pulleys to the lever to make it churn on its own, leaving him extra time to read.

When he was thirteen, Philo entered a contest sponsored by *Science and Invention* magazine. Using what he'd learned about magnets, he pictured an ignition lock that would make the new Model T Fords harder to steal.

When he won the contest, Philo spent the prize money on his first pair of proper long pants. Wearing boyish short pants at the Friday dances was just plain embarrassing.

Philo went on investigating television. An article called "Pictures that Fly Through the Air" stimulated him. Scientists were having no luck—so far their ideas resulted in crude mechanical **devices** that used whirling disks and mirrors.

Philo doubted any disk could whirl fast enough to work. Much better to do the job electronically. To harness electrons, those mysterious, invisible particles that traveled at the speed of light...

Pictures that Fly Through the Air

Radio Receiver

Radio Transmitter

Amplifier

Photocell

Mask

Mask

Reproducing Disk

You Looking in

Televised Subject

Scanning Disk

To Generator

A. The Transmitter

Receiver

Though it may seem far-fetched, scientists trying for years

practical application new ways of splitting pictures into electrons

One bright, sunny day, fourteen-year-old Philo plowed the potato fields. It was the best chore for thinking—out in the open country by himself. Back and forth, back and forth...the plow created rows of overturned earth. He looked behind him at the lines he was carving— perfectly parallel.

Then he almost fell off the plow seat. All his thoughts fused together. Instead of seeing rows of dirt, he saw a way to create television: breaking down images into parallel lines of light, capturing them and transmitting them as electrons, then reassembling them for a viewer. If it was done quickly enough, people's eyes could be tricked into seeing a complete picture instead of lines. "Capturing light in a bottle" was how he thought of it—using electricity, not a machine with moving parts inside.

Philo's grin was wide. He told the idea to his father, who tried to understand but couldn't keep up with his son.

In the autumn Philo started high school, riding horseback four miles each way.

Mr. Tolman, the senior chemistry teacher, noticed that this freshman devoured books the way other students ate popcorn. He started tutoring Philo, coming in early and leaving late.

One day Mr. Tolman passed by a study hall and heard loud talking. Philo's latest hero was Albert Einstein, with his controversial new theory of relativity. Now Philo stood at the front of the room, **enthusiastically** explaining it to his classmates, step by step.

Usually Philo spoke little, with a halting voice. But when he could share his knowledge of science, he was a different boy.

Philo had been aching to discuss the idea he'd gotten in the potato field with someone who might understand. One day he finally told Mr. Tolman. All over the blackboard, he drew diagrams of his television.

His teacher was boggled. Philo ripped a page out of the notebook he always kept in his shirt pocket. He scribbled a diagram of an all-electric camera, the kind of converter he **envisioned**. An Image Dissector, he called it.

Mr. Tolman pointed out that it would take a lot of money to build such a thing. The only way he could think of helping was to encourage Philo to go on to college.

But Philo was forced to quit college at eighteen, after his father died. By then the family had moved back to Utah, to the town of Provo, and Philo supported them by working at all sorts of jobs in nearby Salt Lake City.

STOP AND CHECK

Ask and Answer Questions Why did Mr. Tolman want Philo to go to college? Go back to the text to find the answer.

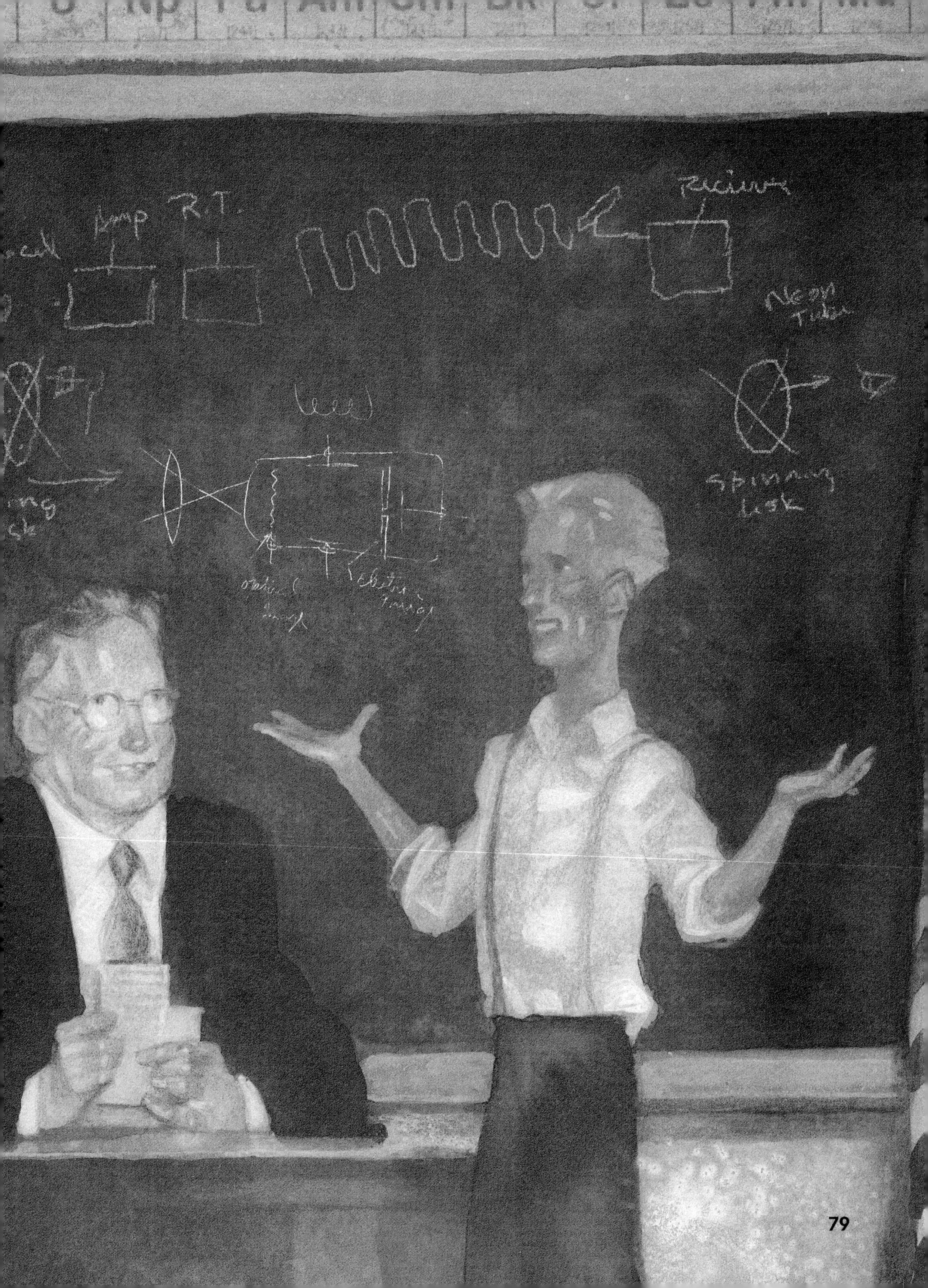
R.T.
Neon Tube

His favorite one was repairing radios. Though commercial radio broadcasts had started four years earlier, Philo couldn't believe, in 1924, how many people still hadn't heard one. On weekends he organized "radio parties" so his friends could gather around one of the bulky wooden cabinets and listen to the new stations.

Pem Gardner, the girl next door, was interested in radio—and also in Philo.

Wasn't it funny, Philo remarked to Pem, how they liked to watch the radio even though there was nothing to see? Radio was such a fine way to bring folks together. And television, he sensed, would be even better.

Thanks to his obsession with television, Philo had already lost one girlfriend, who called him too much of a dreamer. But Pem cheered him on. Now what he needed was money. He grew a mustache to look older, bought a new blue suit, and started to call himself Phil.

He met two California businessmen, and over dinner one night, he took them through a step-by-step explanation of his Image Dissector: a camera tube that would dissect an image into a stream of electrons, converting them into pulses of electrical current. A receiver would capture the current, then convert it back into points of light—the original image.

As he talked, he got more and more **passionate**. After scanning images line by line, just like rows in a potato field, this machine would beam them into homes. That was the best thing about television, he said—it would let families and whole communities share the same stories. By making people less ignorant of one another, he went on, it would teach and inspire. Maybe even lead to world peace.

The two businessmen exchanged looks, then agreed to put up $6,000 so Philo could build the first model. They gave him a year to make it work.

Philo hit upon a way to work twenty-four hours a day: he set himself problems to solve while sleeping.

He filed for several government **patents** that would protect his ideas for the next seventeen years. It was important to him to keep control, to get credit.

On their wedding night, he turned to Pem. "I have to tell you, there is another woman in my life—and her name is Television."

Pem helped out. Their first lab was their dining room table in Hollywood. Pem learned to use a precision welder to make tube elements—everything had to be built from scratch. When they needed a break, they went to one of the new talking movies.

Finally they got the lights, wires, and tubes to work in unison. But at the first demonstration, Philo forgot one item. He failed to take the power surge into account. The entire Image Dissector exploded. Pem, who took notes about everything, labeled this experiment, "Bang! Pop! Sizzle!"

STOP AND CHECK

Reread How was Philo able to build the Image Dissector? Rereading may help you.

Still, Philo was able to find new investors, who gave him another year.

At his new lab in San Francisco, Philo met the deadline. In 1927, a small group of people watched as the first image in history flickered on a TV.

He said, "That's it, folks. We've done it—there you have electronic television."

That first image was not fancy. It was a straight line, blurry and bluish. Later he was able to show a dollar sign, and then the motion of cigarette smoke.

The first person to be televised was his true love, Pem, who didn't know she was on camera and had her eyes closed.

The following year, in front of a crowd of reporters, twenty-two-year-old Philo Farnsworth announced the invention of television.

That night he was behind the wheel of a borrowed car. He and Pem were heading home after catching a movie with another couple. They stopped to buy the *San Francisco Chronicle* from a newsboy. And there was a photo of Philo holding his invention. The article praised a "young genius" for creating a "revolutionary light machine."

Pem and his friends read it aloud, bouncing up and down, yelling. Philo was silent, but a big smile crossed his face.

He was a real inventor, like his heroes—someone who connected people, a shaper of the world to come. Thanks to him, the future would include **TV.**

About the Author and Illustrator

Kathleen Krull lost her part-time job at the library at the age of fifteen for reading when she should have been working. Luckily, she didn't lose her love of books. Some of her books, such as *I Hear America Singing*, have been inspired by her background playing the organ and piano. Others, such as *The Boy Who Invented TV*, have stemmed from her natural curiosity about people. She says that the best thing about writing is that it gives her the chance to explore music, history, politics, and people, and help young people discover them, too.

Greg Couch has illustrated several children's books, including *Sun Dance, Water Dance* and *The Cello of Mr. O*. He also worked on the movie *Ice Age*. To create his illustrations, Greg uses a mix of colored pencils and acrylic wash. For *The Boy Who Invented TV*, he also drew from old magazines.

Author's Purpose

Why do you think Kathleen Krull wrote *The Boy Who Invented TV*? Use details from the text to support your answer.

Respond to the Text

Summarize

Use details from *The Boy Who Invented TV* to summarize the important events in Philo Farnsworth's life that led to the invention of television. Information from your Sequence Chart may help you.

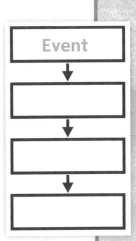

Event

Write

How does the author help you understand how passionate Philo was about his dream of inventing television? Use these sentence frames to organize your text evidence.

> Kathleen Krull begins the story of Philo by . . .
> She focuses on his . . .
> This helps me understand that Philo invented television to . . .

Make Connections

Talk about how technology helped Philo come up with his idea for the television. **ESSENTIAL QUESTION**

Identify a machine or invention in the story that you know about. How is the machine or invention different today? **TEXT TO WORLD**

Genre • Realistic Fiction

Compare Texts
Read about how one girl comes up with a
creative use of technology to solve a problem.

TIME TO Invent

Monday 8:05AM

"Lydia! I thought you were up already, but you've slept through your alarm!" Lydia opened her eyes to find her mom standing over her bed. In the background, she heard a faint beeping.

Rubbing her eyes, Lydia sat up and read the time on her alarm clock: 8:05. "Sorry, Mom," she said, leaping out of bed and quickly throwing on her clothes.

"I know this was the first time trying to get up on your own," her mom said, "but I don't want you to be late for school."

"The alarm was just on too low," Lydia told her, trying to hide her disappointment that her plan hadn't worked. She had finally convinced her mom to let her try to get up on her own. After all, she was in the fifth grade. But now, Lydia realized she would have to prove she could.

Lydia had to rush through breakfast to make the bus. As she headed out the door, she called to her mom, "I promise I'll get up on time tomorrow!" But as she boarded the bus, she wondered if she would.

Illustrator: Christina Rodriguez

Monday `8:00`PM

That night, after much pleading from Lydia, her mom agreed to let her have another try. Not wanting to take any chances that she'd sleep through the alarm, she turned the volume on the alarm up—way up. It didn't seem like the most soothing way to wake up, but Lydia was pretty sure it would do the trick.

Tuesday `7:50`AM

The next morning, a piercing beeping echoed through her room, jolting her awake. While Lydia fumbled with the off button on the alarm, her mother came running into the room with her hands over her ears. "What is that awful noise?" her mother cried. Lydia hit the alarm off.

"Well, at least I am up on time," she mumbled with embarrassment.

Her mother gave her an exasperated look. "And so is the whole neighborhood!"

Although Lydia made it to the bus on time that day, she knew her mother would never stand for that every morning. If she was going to convince her mom, she would have to think of a better way to get herself up.

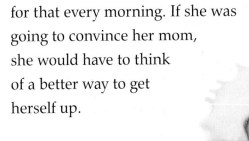

When Lydia got home from school that day, her mother asked Lydia to help her find her old cell phone. "I got a new one this afternoon. I want to give you my old one, but I can't find it anywhere." Her mother dialed her old number while Lydia searched the house. In the kitchen, she heard a muffled rattle coming from a drawer. Lydia opened the drawer, and there, shaking among the pens and pads of paper, was her mother's cell phone.

Suddenly, Lydia had a **breakthrough**. "Mom, I found it," she said, answering the phone. "And will you give me one more chance to wake myself up tomorrow?"

That afternoon, Lydia figured out how to set the phone alarm to vibrate. Then she went to the kitchen and looked through the recycling bin. She found a metal coffee can and matching lid, washed them out, and took them upstairs. She set the phone alarm to vibrate, put the phone in the coffee can, and covered it with the lid. She counted the seconds until the alarm went off: 3-2-1. Suddenly, the can rattled and shook as the phone vibrated against it. She listened and **envisioned** herself waking up to the noise. The sound was much louder than it had been in the drawer, she thought, but not so loud that it could be heard by anyone else. More important, she asked herself, was it loud enough to get her up in the morning? There was only one way to find out.

Tuesday [8:30 PM]

Before bed that night, Lydia set her phone alarm for 7:50 A.M. and put the phone in the metal can. As she covered it with the lid, she thought, why hasn't anyone thought of this before? It's so simple! Then a doubting thought crept into her head. What if it didn't work? She had tested it, but she hadn't been asleep. She hoped it would not fail. She stayed up wondering if it would work. Finally, she drifted off to sleep.

Wednesday [7:50 AM]

The next morning, a rattle awakened her. She waited to see if the noise disturbed her mother, but the house was silent.

Over breakfast, Lydia showed her mother her invention. The can rattled on the table. "What a clever idea! I've never seen anything like it!" Her mother exclaimed. "Not only have you proved you can get up on your own, but you've become an inventor as well!" Lydia beamed with pride.

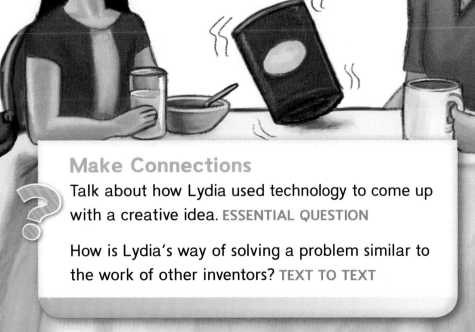

Make Connections

Talk about how Lydia used technology to come up with a creative idea. ESSENTIAL QUESTION

How is Lydia's way of solving a problem similar to the work of other inventors? TEXT TO TEXT

The Future of Transportation

Essential Question

What are the positive and negative effects of new technology?

Read about how new technology is changing transportation.

Go Digital!

Autos Advance
Cars will keep us moving into the future.

Cars are the best way for individuals to travel. They are far more comfortable than crowded trains or buses. Cars can take us wherever we want to go, whenever we want to go, and without waiting for other passengers.

Going Green

Of course, public transportation has its good points. It uses less fuel per person than a car. But over the years cars have become more fuel-efficient. To **cite** government **data**, in 1975, cars averaged 13.1 miles per gallon. In 2009, average miles per gallon had risen to 21.1. Some new types of cars also pollute less. Electric cars run on batteries that emit no carbon dioxide. These cool cars also use less energy to get to a destination than regular cars.

Automatic Autos

Some engineers have tried to **advance** plans to make driving even easier! They are testing cars that start, steer, and stop without human drivers. The cars have radar, laser scanners, and video cameras. These devices keep the car on the road, avoid other cars, and stay within the speed limit. A computer is able to **access** information from sensors in the car and make an instant **analysis** of the situation.

What is the **reasoning** behind building these automatic cars? Safety is a major goal. About 20 percent of serious car crashes are caused by people who use cell phones, eat and drink, or read maps while driving. Incidents like these caused by human error would not occur with a driverless car: Its computer cannot be distracted!

Some people fear these kinds of cars will cause more accidents. In fact, the opposite is true. So far, driverless cars have an almost perfect safety record.

There's no doubt that driverless cars and energy-efficient cars will offer improved transportation down the road.

Electric cars run on batteries. Cars are plugged in to recharge.

STOP AND CHECK

Reread According to this author, how has technology improved cars?

T-Pool/STOCK4B/Getty Images

The Rail Way
Public transportation is the way to go.

Where would we be without public transportation? We probably would be still stuck in a car in traffic! Trains, buses, and subways are the best ways to travel. Public transportation uses less energy and is better for the environment. It is an inexpensive and comfortable alternative to car travel.

Less Oil

According to government data, 70 percent of the oil consumed in the U.S. is used for transportation. Personal vehicles use more than 60 percent of that total and planes use 9 percent. Buses and trains consume only about 3 percent. About 4.2 billion gallons of oil are saved each year thanks to the people who take public transportation. Even more energy could be saved if more people traded in their car keys for a bus or train ticket.

Commuters can skip traffic jams by taking the train.

Less Pollution

Pollution is also a factor to consider. About 35 percent of carbon emissions come from passenger cars, while only 2 percent come from trains. The use of public transportation over personal vehicles avoids releasing 745,000 metric tons of carbon monoxide—a toxic gas—into the air each year.

Speed Thrills!

One latest improvement in public transportation technology is the high-speed train. These trains run mostly in Europe and Asia. They can travel at speeds of 150 miles per hour or more. High-speed trains would be perfect for travel between major American cities.

A few **drawbacks** could derail high-speed trains in the United States. Opponents cite their cost. It would take billions of dollars to build the high-speed system. Safety is also a concern. Accidents involving fast trains would be terrible. Yet, high-speed trains in other countries show great safety records.

High-speed trains also run on electricity, which would reduce pollution. According to one analysis, a fast-rail system in the U.S. would result in 29 million fewer car trips each year.

Anyone with vision knows this: High-speed trains and more advancements in public transportation would keep U.S. transportation on the right track.

In Japan, high-speed trains link distant cities.

Respond to the Text

1. Use important details from the selection to summarize. SUMMARIZE

2. Think about how the authors present their positions on transportation technology. How do they support their arguments? WRITE

3. Which advancement in transportation technology do you think has made the biggest difference in people's lives? Give reasons that support your answer. TEXT TO WORLD

kokoroimages.com/Flickr/Getty Images

93

Compare Texts

Read about how data can support improvements in transportation.

GETTING FROM HERE TO THERE

Passengers are not the only ones moving along these days. Transportation technology is moving along, too. Cars and trains are changing at a rapid pace. These advances may offer more ways of getting around in the future.

The Ways People Commute

While transportation researchers may count train passengers or the number of cars passing a toll, a survey is another way experts collect data. A government survey analysis showed most people get to work by personal vehicle. Some people interpret this to mean it is the preferred way to travel. Improving public transportation could change that.

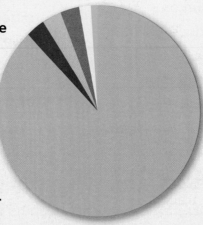

☐ Car, truck, or van	88%
◼ Bus	3%
◼ Walked	3%
☐ Worked from home	3%
☐ Railroad or subway	2%
☐ Other	1%

Source: U.S. Census Bureau, 2000 Summary File 3.

Improving energy efficiency in cars is one way technology has changed transportation. Engineers have offered a **counterpoint** to fuel-saving train transportation. They have created electric and hybrid cars. Electric cars are powered entirely by batteries. Hybrid cars are powered by both gas and batteries. These cars have better fuel economy, or use less gas per mile, than conventional cars.

Reducing Train Travel Time

(Trains from Chicago to St. Louis)

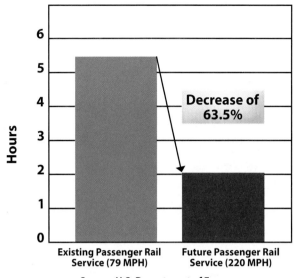

Source: U.S. Department of Energy

Fuel Economy in Cars

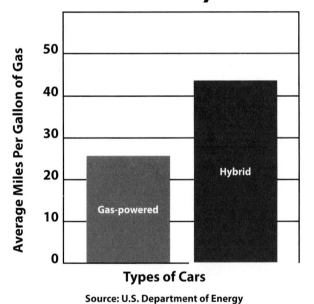

Source: U.S. Department of Energy

Trains are more energy-efficient per passenger. However, train travel times still leave room for improvement. High-speed train systems could be the solution. Increasing train speed from 79 to 220 miles per hour, for example, could greatly reduce travel time between cities in the U.S.

Whether by car or train, future transportation will likely offer faster and more efficient ways to travel.

Make Connections

How can data show the effects of changes in transportation technology? ESSENTIAL QUESTION

How are facts presented differently in this text than in other texts about transportation? What is the purpose of each text? TEXT TO TEXT

WHO WROTE THE U.S. CONSTITUTION?

by Candice Ransom

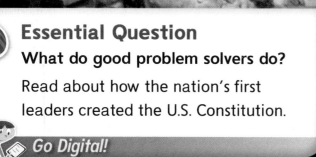

Essential Question

What do good problem solvers do?

Read about how the nation's first leaders created the U.S. Constitution.

Go Digital!

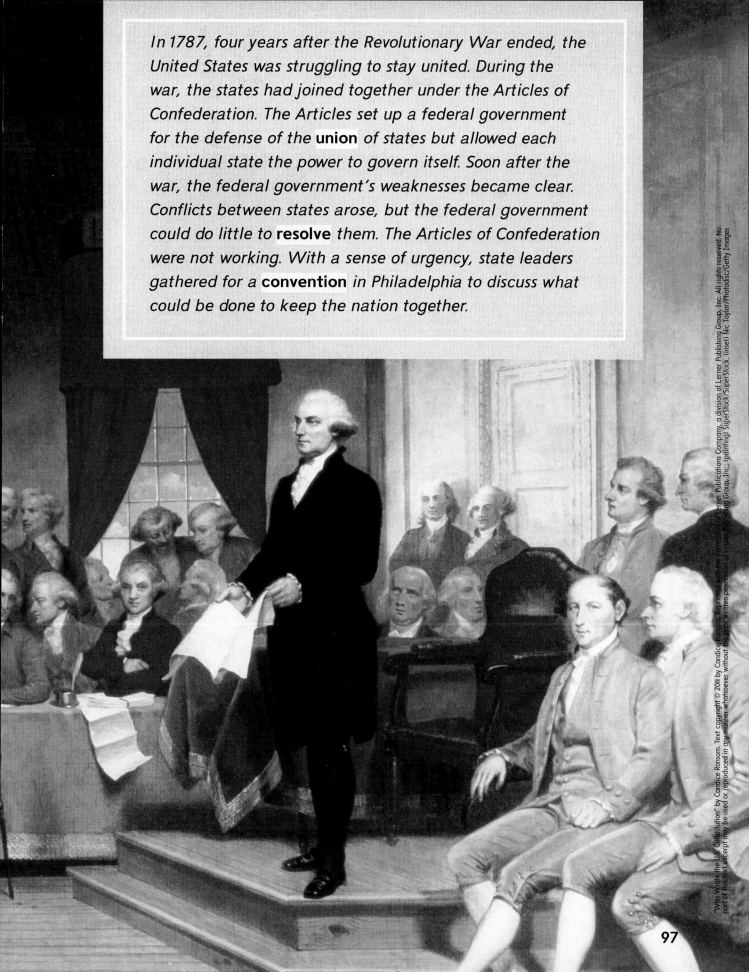

In 1787, four years after the Revolutionary War ended, the United States was struggling to stay united. During the war, the states had joined together under the Articles of Confederation. The Articles set up a federal government for the defense of the **union** of states but allowed each individual state the power to govern itself. Soon after the war, the federal government's weaknesses became clear. Conflicts between states arose, but the federal government could do little to **resolve** them. The Articles of Confederation were not working. With a sense of urgency, state leaders gathered for a **convention** in Philadelphia to discuss what could be done to keep the nation together.

A NEW PLAN

Virginia governor Edmund Randolph spoke first on Tuesday, May 29, 1787. Randolph brought up the problems with the Articles of Confederation. Many states argued over borders shared with other states. People had trouble conducting business across state lines. State governments had no money. Some states printed money. But the money was not backed up by gold or silver. Much of it was worthless.

Randolph spoke about another serious problem—taxes. The cost of the Revolutionary War left the United States in debt. The government owed money to wealthy U.S. citizens and to foreign countries such as France and the Netherlands. To raise money to pay the debt, the U.S. government asked each state to tax its residents.

Not every state agreed to do so. But states such as Virginia and Massachusetts taxed their citizens. Taxes had to be paid in cash. And that was a problem for many people. Ordinary working people did not use much cash. They lived off what they owned and grew—their land, houses, tools, livestock, and crops. If they needed something—a new tool or a pair of boots—they traded for it. But they could not trade with the state to pay their taxes.

The **situation** was especially bad for farmers. States began taking to court farmers who could not pay their taxes and other debts. The courts took away farmers' land and livestock. Some farmers were even thrown in prison.

During the summer of 1786, hundreds of angry Massachusetts farmers formed a rebel force. One of the leaders was Daniel Shays, a Revolutionary War hero, politician, and farmer. From August 1786 to January 1787, the rebels stormed courthouses in Northhampton, Worcester, and other Massachusetts towns.

They forced the courts to close. Shays's Rebellion shocked the country.

With all these problems before them, what could the convention delegates do?

Why Was Shays's Rebellion Important?

In October 1786, the Confederation Congress decided to use federal troops to stop the rebels. But Congress could not convince state governments to help pay for the soldiers. Massachusetts leaders had to raise the money themselves. In January 1787, Shays and his rebels attacked an armory (a building used to store weapons) in Springfield, Massachusetts. Troops stopped the raid, and many rebels were arrested.

In the spring of 1787, Massachusetts passed laws to help farmers in debt. The rebellion began to fade. But for many people, Shays's Rebellion showed how weak the federal government was. For them, it proved that the Articles of Confederation were failing.

Randolph presented a plan written by James Madison and other Virginia delegates. The Virginia Plan created a stronger federal government—one that could protect the American people.

Randolph explained that the plan created a national legislature. The legislature had two branches. Members of the first branch (the House of **Representatives**) would be elected by the people. House members would choose delegates to the second branch (the Senate). Together, the House and Senate would elect the U.S. president and federal judges.

Randolph spoke for more than three hours. At last, he sat down. The first real meeting of the convention had left the delegates with much to think about.

The next day, May 30, forty-one delegates began going over the Virginia Plan point by point. The Articles of Confederation had set up the Confederation Congress as the federal government. But the articles also protected each state's freedom and independence. Under the Virginia Plan, the federal government could overrule state governments. Delegates realized that the Virginia Plan did not correct the Articles. It ignored them altogether.

This idea stopped several delegates in their tracks. They thought they were at the convention to revise and strengthen the Articles of Confederation. They did *not* expect a new plan that threw out the Articles. Did they dare change the entire system of government?

Edmund Randolph

STOP AND CHECK

Reread How would the Virginia Plan change the government? Use the strategy Reread to help you.

SEPARATION OF POWERS

On May 31, 1787, convention delegates voted to create a stronger national government. They decided that it should consist of three parts: the legislative, the executive, and the judicial. The legislative part, called Congress, would make the laws. The president would be the head of the executive part. He would carry out the laws. The national court system was the judicial part. It would decide the meaning of the laws and if they were being obeyed. With three parts, or branches, power would be shared. No one branch would have more control of the federal government than the other two.

Discussion swung to the one-vote-for-one-state system described in the Articles of Confederation. In 1787 a state's importance was measured by the number of its citizens. For example, Georgia had a lot of land. But it was still considered small because of its low population. The three biggest states—Virginia, Pennsylvania, and Massachusetts—held nearly half the nation's population. But under the articles, each state had only one vote, no matter its size or population. Tiny Rhode Island's voice in Congress carried as much weight as mighty Massachusetts. This is called equal representation.

The Virginia Plan changed that. Under the plan, the House of Representatives would be elected by the people. And the number of representatives would be based on a state's population. The number of members in the Senate would also depend on population. This is known as proportional (an amount determined by size) representation.

Immediately, the convention broke into two camps: big states versus small states. The small states fought against the Virginia Plan. With proportional representation, they felt they would not have as strong a voice in the federal government.

The states had other differences beyond size. Southerners grew tobacco, sugar, and rice on large farms called plantations. Many people in the middle of the country—Pennsylvania, New Jersey, Delaware, and New York—were merchants. They ran businesses and stores. People in Massachusetts and Connecticut were shipbuilders and fishers.

Slavery was another big issue dividing the states. Southern plantation owners used African slaves to work the plantations. Slaves were treated as property. Slavery was against the law in most northern states. Some northerners wanted to make slavery illegal in every state. But southern states fiercely defended their right to own slaves.

At the 1787 convention, slavery became part of the **debate** over proportional representation. Should slaves be counted as part of a state's population? Thousands of slaves lived in states such as Georgia and South Carolina. Counting slaves would give southern states more representatives in the federal government. Northern delegates felt this was unfair. Southern states did not treat slaves like people in any other case. Why should they be allowed to use the slave population to gain more representation?

Day after day, the delegates chewed over parts of the representation issue. The room grew hot. The hours grew long.

The Virginians had taken control of the convention. Their delegates were good writers and speakers. But Virginia was not the entire nation. The small states needed to be heard.

William Paterson, a New Jersey lawyer, presented the New Jersey Plan. It was the small states' answer to the Virginia Plan.

Under the New Jersey Plan, Congress would have only one house. It would not have a House of Representatives and a Senate. The federal government would not have a president. And there would be no federal courts except the Supreme Court.

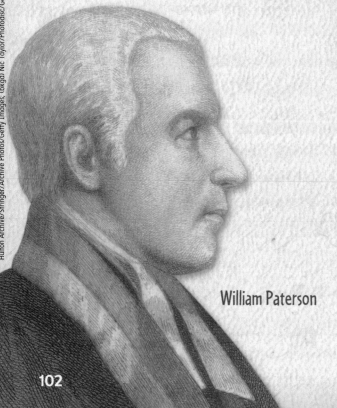

William Paterson

The New Jersey Plan proposed that all states—no matter how big or small—would have the same number of representatives. Most important, Paterson's plan did not create a new constitution. The plan was designed to become additional amendments, or formal changes, to the Articles of Confederation.

On June 19, James Madison jumped to his feet to speak first. He wanted to convince the delegates to vote for the Virginia Plan. He argued against the New Jersey Plan point by point. When he was finished, the delegates voted.

Seven states chose the Virginia Plan. Three states voted for the New Jersey Plan. (Maryland was divided and did not cast a vote). The big states had won. For the next several days, members argued. Two houses in Congress or one? The same issues were brought up but never solved. Tempers flared. The small states felt the big states were pushing them around again.

James Madison

James Madison

James Madison was a key player at the convention even before the meeting began. He had read about the governments of modern and ancient civilizations. From his studies, he came up with two theories. The first was that a national government should come from the people and not the states. The second was that powers should be divided so no one person or group controlled the government.

While waiting for the rest of the members to arrive, the Virginia delegates met each morning at Mrs. House's boardinghouse. Using James Madison's theories, the group hammered out the Virginia Plan.

STOP AND CHECK

Reread Why did state differences lead to a debate about state representation? Reread to check your understanding.

THE GREAT COMPROMISE

July 2, 1787, was a Monday. By the time the delegates met in the morning, the East Room was already hot. Once again, delegates voted on whether states should have equal representation in the Senate. Five states said yes, five said no, and Georgia was divided. A tie. Everyone was discouraged.

Benjamin Franklin understood that each state had to give up something in order for everyone to gain. He suggested a compromise. The delegates could choose parts from the Virginia and New Jersey plans that would please both the big and small states.

The delegates took off the next two days for Independence Day. On July 4, bells rang and guns fired salutes. People celebrated the country's freedom from British rule. Few knew that the entire convention was on the brink of failure.

When the members met again on July 5, they took up the same argument.

A Good Compromiser

Benjamin Franklin urged delegates to settle convention issues by compromise. He often hosted dinner parties to make the delegates feel more at home in Philadelphia. The parties also gave the delegates a chance to get to know one another better. That made it easier for delegates to discuss and decide issues at the convention.

These life-size bronze statues of convention delegates are at the National Constitution Center in Philadelphia. Benjamin Franklin is shown seated, holding a cane.

Then Connecticut's Roger Sherman came up with a solution. He pointed out that the big states had already won proportional representation in the lower house. He proposed that each state, no matter what size, would send two delegates to the upper house.

The members debated Sherman's **proposal** for eleven days.

On July 16, they voted again. The Connecticut Compromise passed, five votes to four. This vote, also known as the Great Compromise, became a turning point in the convention. Delegates from big states and small realized that they needed to think about the greater good of the nation. Almost as a sign that the right decision had been made, Philadelphia's heat wave broke.

What About Slavery?

Should slaves be counted as part of a southern state's population? To solve that debate, northern and southern delegates reached another compromise. They agreed that a slave would count as three-fifths of a free person. In other words, for every five slaves living in a state, three were counted for the purpose of proportional representation and taxes. This became known as the Three-Fifths Compromise, or the Three-Fifths Clause.

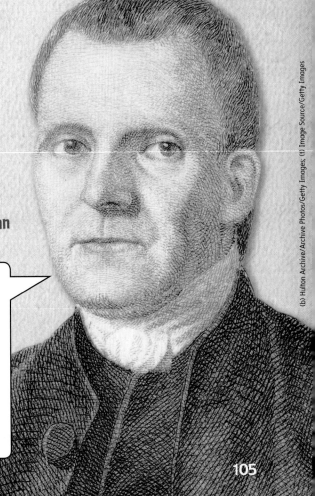

Roger Sherman

"In the second branch or Senate, each state should have one vote and no more... As the states would remain possessed of certain individual rights, each state ought to be able to protect itself."

–Connecticut delegate Roger Sherman

Convention members voted over and over. They sometimes voted again on issues they had already settled. Through it all, George Washington sat in the high-backed chair and listened. Most members believed that Washington would be the perfect first president. He had already proved to be a strong leader. And people liked him. But who would be president after Washington? The delegates knew they had to be careful about the way future presidents would be elected.

On July 26, the convention took a ten-day break. Delegates who lived close by went home. Others headed for cooler air in the mountains. Washington visited Valley Forge, a rural area northwest of Philadelphia. During the Revolutionary War, Washington and his troops had camped at Valley Forge. Freezing and hungry, they spent the winter of 1777 and 1778 in tiny log huts. The old camp was in ruins when Washington visited it that July.

Washington (*right*) and an army officer walk past troops at Valley Forge during the winter of 1777 and 1778. This image is a print made of a painting by Howard Pyle (1853-1911).

This document *(right)* is the first draft, or version, of the U.S. Constitution.

Not everyone went on vacation. Five delegates remained in Philadelphia. John Rutledge, Nathaniel Gorham, Oliver Ellsworth, Edmund Randolph, and James Wilson made up the Committee of Detail. They had the important job of copying down the resolutions that had been decided so far. It was hard work. But they finished a rough outline of a document. The document was a new plan for the government—a constitution. The draft was printed and ready to be handed out when the convention met again.

OF AND FOR THE PEOPLE

On Monday, August 6, delegates received their copies of the Constitution—seven freshly inked pages. Starting the next day and all through hot, steamy August, they debated every sentence.

The Constitution had twenty-three articles. Each article was divided into sections. The delegates needed to speed up the process of discussing and voting on all the articles. To achieve this, many items were given to **committees** to settle.

The Committee of Postponed Parts had the most issues to work out. It had to decide where the new government would be located and how Congress would charge taxes. But the executive branch was its most pressing problem.

The Committee of Postponed Parts decided the president of the United States would serve a term of four years and could be reelected. He must be a U.S. citizen and at least thirty-five years old.

The committee added the office of vice president. The vice president would lead the Senate and take over if the president died or had to leave office. The members made sure the president and Congress had the power to get things done. But each branch would not have too much power over the other.

A huge question remained. How would the country choose the president? Most delegates felt the president should be selected by Congress or state legislatures.

Back in June, James Wilson said the people should pick the president. No one had liked that idea. But members of the committee changed their minds. They agreed that Wilson's plan was a good one after all.

Wilson's plan included what came to be called the electoral college. The country would be divided into areas, or districts. People from each district would choose an elector. Those electors would decide who would be president.

The Committee of Style revised the final draft of the Constitution. Gouverneur Morris wrote the preamble with its stirring words: *"We, the People of the United States..."* The U.S. Constitution became a document of and for the people.

STOP AND CHECK

Ask and Answer Questions
Why did delegates ask committees to settle problems?

The final version was presented to the convention on September 12. George Mason felt that there should be a Bill of Rights—a list of important rights guaranteed to citizens. Elbridge Gerry agreed, but the other members did not. They believed people's rights were already protected by state constitutions.

On Monday, September 17, forty-two delegates were present. William Jackson, the convention secretary, read aloud the final version of the Constitution. Benjamin Franklin gave a speech to James Wilson to read for him.

Franklin did not like parts of the Constitution. But even with its faults, he doubted anyone could create a better system of government. He urged each man present to sign the Constitution.

George Washington signed first. Then state by state, thirty-nine delegates signed their names. Secretary Jackson witnessed their signatures. Three men refused to sign. Edmund Randolph, George Mason, and Elbridge Gerry would not sign without a Bill of Rights.

When the Constitution was signed, Franklin pointed to the half sun carved on the back of Washington's chair. He said he never could tell if the sun was rising or setting. But now he knew that it was a rising sun.

That evening the delegates held a farewell dinner at the City Tavern. They had come to Philadelphia with different ideas and interests. During the summer, they learned to work together. The result was the U.S. Constitution.

"We ought to attend to the rights of every class of the people."

–Virginia delegate George Mason, arguing that the House of Representatives should be elected by the people

George Mason

This is a copy of the U.S. Constitution. The original U.S. Constitution is kept in the National Archives Building in Washington, D.C.

CANDICE RANSOM

grew up in Virginia. In fact, her ancestors settled there even before the American Revolution. So her interest in our nation's founders isn't surprising. Today, Candice lives in the city of Fredericksburg, Virginia, a place where Thomas Jefferson and George Washington once lived.

Candice is the author of more than 100 books, from board books to chapter books. She has won many awards, and her work has been translated into about a dozen different languages.

In addition to writing, Candice teaches children's literature at a university. She helps her students learn all about writing children's books. She also visits schools to discuss some of her favorite subjects, including writing and American history.

AUTHOR'S PURPOSE

In this selection, the author includes portraits, short biographies, and even quotes from delegates. Why do you think the author includes this information?

Respond to the Text

Summarize

Use the most important details from *Who Wrote the U.S. Constitution?* to summarize how state delegates solved problems. Details from your Problem and Solution Chart may help you.

Problem	Solution

Write

How does the author help you understand that the decisions the delegates made affected not only them but all Americans? Use these sentence frames to organize your text evidence.

Candice Ransom uses text features to . . .

She creates suspense by . . .

This helps me see that the delegates . . .

Make Connections

Talk about how the delegates solved problems to create the U.S. Constitution. ESSENTIAL QUESTION

Describe the steps the delegates took to reach a final plan for the new government. How does taking a vote help a group reach the best solution? TEXT TO WORLD

Genre • Expository Text

Compare Texts
Read how people solved the problem of preserving two national treasures.

Parchment and Ink

The Declaration of Independence and the United States Constitution express our nation's most enduring ideas. However, both are also 200-year-old physical objects. Written in ink on parchment, they are fragile. Fire, water, sunlight, air—these can damage documents. So it's amazing that we still can read the original Declaration and Constitution. It has taken the efforts of many people to preserve these treasures.

The Declaration was approved in July 1776. Soon afterward, Congress assigned someone to handwrite it in ink in clear letters. It was written with a quill pen, a pen made from the tip of a feather, on a sheet of parchment, a thin, strong material made from animal skin. This document was then signed by most members of Congress.

The Declaration was official and beautiful. It traveled with Congress from Philadelphia to Baltimore and back. At different times, it was housed in Pennsylvania and New Jersey. It was later moved to the nation's new capital in Washington, D.C. The document was moved a lot during the American Revolution in order to protect it.

During the War of 1812, the British invaded Washington, D.C. The Declaration was moved to Virginia for protection.

Faded but not Forgotten

By the early 1800s, the document probably looked a little ragged. A set of exact copies had been printed directly from the original which may have caused the ink to fade. It also had continued to move from one location to another.

Then in 1841 Daniel Webster, the Secretary of State, decided that the Declaration be kept in the newly built United States Patent Office. There it was displayed in an ordinary frame near a window. Observers noticed the Declaration was fading. They didn't realize though that sunshine, changing temperature, and humidity were damaging the document.

As the nation neared its 100th birthday in 1876, new interest in the document grew. By that time technology allowed it to be better protected. At the centennial celebrations in Philadelphia it was displayed in a fireproof safe. The Declaration hung for all to see behind heavy glass doors.

On public display, people began to **debate** what to do about the document's faded state. Congress appointed a committee to find a way to preserve it for future generations. The committee made a **proposal** to restore the Declaration by adding new ink. But no one followed through on that idea. Then, in 1894, the Declaration was locked away in a steel case. Indeed, it was protected, but it wasn't displayed again for 30 years.

The Declaration was written down using a quill pen and a type of ink made of iron. Today we know that iron in the ink can damage parchment over time.

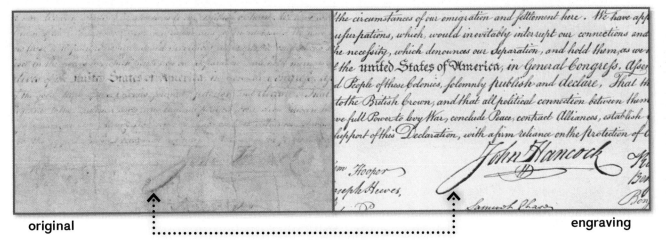

original   engraving

Comparing the signature of John Hancock on the Declaration to an engraving made during the 1820s reveals how much the document has faded.

In the Librarian's Care

The Constitution was not damaged as much as the Declaration of Independence. It traveled with the Declaration through 1814. Then the Constitution remained in the care of the State Department until 1921. That year, both documents were given to the Library of Congress.

The Librarian of Congress treasured them. He wanted people to be able to see these important documents but also wanted to make sure they were protected. He decided to place the documents in what he called a "shrine" or sacred space, surrounded by marble. The documents were framed but protected from natural light by double panes of glass. A special coating was added to the glass to further exclude light. A guard was posted to watch over both documents.

During World War II, the Declaration and Constitution were moved to Fort Knox for protection. Afterward, both documents were placed in new cases. The cases were filled with helium gas. The helium displaced oxygen, which can eat away at parchment.

A Process for Preservation

In 1951, the Declaration and the Constitution were sealed in cases filled with helium gas. Later, these cases were carefully opened (left). The documents were studied before being placed in new cases. Experts took samples of the ink (right) to learn how to better protect it.

The Declaration of Independence and the Constitution, called the Charters of Freedom, are on display at the National Archives.

A New Home

In 1952, the documents found a new home in the National Archives. This special library holds the federal government's important historical records. Staff at the National Archives set up a computerized system to monitor both documents' condition every second. In 1995, experts saw that there were tiny crystals in the cases that could damage the documents. Using the latest technology, new cases were built. This time, argon gas replaced the helium. At night, the cases are kept in a secure vault.

These treasures are currently displayed for all to see at the National Archives in Washington, D.C. The National Archives has also made these documents viewable on their Web site. Thanks to the efforts of many people over many years, you now can look at and read the originals, word for word.

Make Connections

Talk about how the Librarian of Congress and others solved the problems of preserving the nation's documents. **ESSENTIAL QUESTION**

How were the actions of people in this selection similar to the actions of other problem solvers you've read about? **TEXT TO TEXT**

2003 Dennis Brack/Black Star/Newscom

Essential Question

What can you do to get the information you need?

Read about how a girl on a quest gets the information she needs.

Go Digital!

118

WHERE THE MOUNTAIN MEETS THE MOON

by Grace Lin

In this tale set in long ago China, the young Minli seeks the Old Man of the Moon. This mysterious person has the power to read from the Book of Fortune which tells each person's **destiny**. Because he can answer any question, Minli hopes that he will be able to tell her how to change the fortunes of her poor family.

As she sets out to find him, Minli meets a series of characters who provide clues to guide her. One character, a dragon who long ago escaped from the terrible ruler Magistrate Tiger, decides to join Minli. Together they travel to the City of Bright Moonlight, where they try to figure out a puzzling clue. Minli must find the guardian of the city and ask for a "borrowed line" to bring to the Old Man of the Moon. Though Minli guesses that the guardian must be the king of the city, what could the "borrowed line" be? She must find out!

While the dragon hides outside the city gates, Minli sneaks into the king's palace in the Inner City. When she finds the king, she asks him for the "borrowed line." Hearing this odd request reminds the king of a certain page that was said to have been "borrowed" from the Book of Fortune. The king reveals that his ancestor, Magistrate Tiger, had overtaken the city long ago and that it was the Magistrate who had angrily ripped this page from the book.

"He tore a page out of the Book of Fortune?" Minli said.

"Yes," the king said, "but he, himself, was never able to read it, so it remained useless to him just as the Old Man of the Moon had said it would be."

"Come," the king said as he walked out of the pavilion onto the bridge under the moon. As Minli followed, he reached inside the breast of his shirt, slowly took out a gold-threaded pouch, and said, "This is the ripped page. It has been passed down from generation to generation, studied by the kings of the City of Bright Moonlight. None of us has ever understood what the Old Man of the Moon meant when he said it was borrowed."

Minli watched, fascinated, as the king took from the gold pouch a delicate, folded piece of paper. Paler than even the white jade tofu she had eaten for dinner, the paper seemed to have a light of its own, dimming the gold threads of the pouch that held it.

"It was my great-great-grandfather," the king said, unfolding the paper, "who realized that the words on it can only be seen in the bright moonlight. He renamed the city the City of Bright Moonlight as a reminder for the kings that followed him."

Minli looked at the paper as if in a daze. In the moonlight, the page glowed. A single line of faint words, as if written with shadows, was scrawled upon the page in a language Minli had never seen.

"So, I think this paper, which the Old Man of the Moon said he borrowed," the king said, "this written line torn from the Book of Fortune is 'the borrowed line' you seek."

"Of course," Minli said, and excitement bubbled inside of her, "it must be!" But her excitement popped as she looked at the carefully preserved page and remembered how the king had had it on his person, carefully and preciously kept in the pouch around his neck. It seemed impossible that he would give her such a cherished treasure.

"It was only after much study that my great-great-grandfather was able to decipher the words," the king said. "And this is when he realized that the words changed according to the situation at the time. From then on, whenever a King of the City of Bright Moonlight has had a problem, he **consults** the paper."

"And it tells you what to do?" Minli asked.

"Yes." The king gave a wry smile. "Though not the way you think. Sometimes the line on the page is more mysterious than the problem."

And with that, the king looked down at the line. As he read, a startled expression came across his face.

"What does it say?" Minli asked.

"It says," the king said slowly, *"You only lose what you cling to."*

The king's words seemed to hang in the air. All was silent except for the soft rustling of the page in the gentle breeze. Minli, unable to speak, watched it flutter as if it were waving at her.

"So, it seems your request," the king said, "deserves **consideration**. The line tells me as much. Let me think."

Minli looked at the king, quiet but puzzled.

STOP AND CHECK

Make Predictions Why does the king think the page is the "borrowed line"? What will he do with it? Look for details about the king to make a Prediction.

"For generations, my family has prized this paper; we have honored it for its spiritual power and authority. It has been passed on and studied and cherished and revered. It has been valued above gold or jade," the king said slowly. "But what is it really?"

Minli shook her head, **unsure** if she should respond.

"It is, actually," the king said, "simply proof of my ancestor's rudeness, his unprincipled anger and ruthless greed. Yet we've disregarded that—instead we guard and protect this written line so dearly that the rulers of the City of Bright Moonlight carry it at all times, not daring to let it out of their possession."

The moon seemed to tremble as ripples spread over its reflection caught in the water. The king continued, again, speaking more to himself than to Minli.

"We have clung to it, always afraid of losing it," the king said. "But if I choose to release it, there is no loss."

Minli felt her breath freeze in her chest. She knew the king's mind was in a delicate balance. If he refused to give her the line now, she knew she would never get it.

"And perhaps it was never meant for us to cling to. No matter whom the paper originally belonged to, this is a page from the Book of Fortune—a book that no one owns," the king said. "So, perhaps, it is time for the paper to return to the book."

A wind skimmed the water, and Minli could see her anxious face as pale and as white as the moon reflected in it.

"You only lose what you cling to," the king repeated to himself. He glanced again at the paper and then looked at Minli. A serene expression settled on his face and then he quietly smiled and said, "So, by choosing to give you the line, I do not lose it."

And, with those words, he placed the paper in Minli's trembling hands.

STOP AND CHECK

Confirm or Revise Predictions Why does the king give the page to Minli? Use the strategy Confirm or Revise Predictions to help you.

Outside the city, Dragon waited. Even after Minli had disappeared, the dragon still watched from the trees. He had felt odd when she had passed the old stone lions and the door had closed behind her. He realized that he had never had a friend before, and what a nice feeling it was to have one.

And perhaps that was why the second night, when the sky darkened and the moon rose, Dragon crept out from the shadows of the trees and approached the closed, sleeping city. While he wouldn't admit it, Dragon thought just standing by the walled city might make him feel just a bit less lonely.

The silver moon cast a frosted glow upon the rough stone wall and guardian lion statues. Dragon stared at them as he approached the gate. Their stocky, heavily built bodies seemed to weigh down the stone platforms they sat upon; and the darkness of the night made their stiff, curly manes look like rows of carved blossoms. One lion held a round ball underneath his forearm; the other held down a lion cub that seemed to be grinning at him. In fact, all the lions seemed to be grinning at him as if he were a secret joke they were watching.

"Am I so funny?" Dragon asked them as he passed.

"YES!" burst out the small lion cub, wriggling free of his mother's paw. "You're very funny!"

As Dragon jumped back in surprise, the lion cub laughed out loud, obviously highly amused at the dragon's shock. But with his laugh, both adult lions shook themselves from their platforms.

"Xiao Mao!" the mother lion scolded. "Don't laugh at the lost dragon. Besides, you know the rules. No moving in the **presence** of others."

"But it's a dragon," the cub said, "not a people. He doesn't count for the rules, does he? Besides, he is funny! Big dragon trying to tiptoe like a mouse!"

"Xiao Mao," the deep, male voice of the other lion boomed in the air. The cub gave a halfhearted look of shame and was immediately quiet and still.

By this time, Dragon had found his voice.

"You're alive, then," he said.

"Of course we are," the male lion said, scrutinizing the dragon with interested eyes. "Everything's alive—the ground you're walking on, the bark of those trees. We were always alive, even before we were lions and were just raw stone. However, carving us did give us a bit more personality."

"You're a fairly young dragon, aren't you?" the female lion said kindly. "You seem only a hundred or a hundred and fifty years old. Don't worry, you'll learn soon enough."

"A hundred!" the lion cub said. "I'm much older than you. I'm eight hundred and sixty-eight!"

"And you still have not attained wisdom," the father lion told him. "Don't tease the young one."

"Well, what are you doing here?" the cub asked, not unkindly. "Dragons don't usually come down to the earth much. Are you lost?"

Though unusual, the lions weren't unfriendly, so Dragon settled down and told them the whole story—being born, living in the forest, meeting Minli, and now their travels to find the borrowed line and the Old Man of the Moon. The lions didn't interrupt once, though the cub did snicker from time to time.

"You belonged to Magistrate Tiger?" the cub said when Dragon had finished. "That means you're the terrible dragon! You're the one that destroyed the magistrate's palace. What a lot of trouble you caused!"

Dragon looked at the older lions questioningly.

"About one hundred years ago," the female lion said, "the magistrate fled his home village. A dragon had destroyed his palace and his people had cast him out, saying he was bad luck. He came here, intending to make his home with his son and to live off his son's wealth and power as the King of the City of Bright Moonlight. There were bad times here for the city, as the magistrate and the officials he brought with him were corrupt and greedy. We were very concerned."

"You?" the dragon asked. "Why would it concern you?"

"Why would it concern us? It is completely our concern!" the male lion said. "We are the Guardians of the City. It's our responsibility to watch and keep the city turning. To see it begin to crack alarmed us to no end." And the lion held out the round ball he held in his hand and showed Dragon an old, deep fracture that was slowly being filled with the dust of the earth.

"What did you do?" Dragon asked.

A String of Destiny

We were afraid the city would break. As the times became more turbulent with secret meetings and violent outbursts, we watched the crack in our world widen. It was only a matter of time, we thought, before it would tear into two.

One night, as we despaired, we saw a figure walking in the moonlight. Bent and old, he glowed like a lit lantern. When we saw he was carrying a large book and a small sack, we knew instantly it was the Old Man of the Moon and called him over.

"Please help us," we begged him, "we need to keep the city together."

The Old Man of the Moon looked at us, our outstretched cracking globe, and our pleading faces. Without a word, he sat down before us and opened his book, leafing through the pages and stroking his beard.

After several minutes of consulting his book, he opened his sack and handed us a red thread.

"You are to hold this until it is needed," the Old Man told us, and then slapped his book shut and walked away, ignoring our words of thanks.

We knew the Old Man of the Moon had given us a string of destiny, one of the very strings he used to bind people together. It was a marvelous gift. While he left us no instructions, we guessed that we were to use it to tie around the city if it looked as if it were to split.

After that, night after night, we watched our sphere, ready to use the string at the first signs of breakage. Unsure of its power or abilities, we dared not use it for anything but the direst of **circumstances**.

But the crack did not grow. Unexpectedly, the king renounced his father. He exiled him and his officials from the city and harmony returned. Slowly, the fracture has filled with the powder of earth and stone. And I have held the string, unused.

And as the male lion finished, he lifted his paw, to **reveal** a flattened line of red thread.

"The borrowed line!" Dragon said. "That's it! Minli said she needed to get the borrowed line from the Guardian of the City! You're the guardian and that's the borrowed line we need!"

"I suppose it is," the lion said, looking at the string. "So, perhaps I have been holding it all this time so I could give it to you."

And the lion dropped the string into the dragon's outstretched hand.

STOP AND CHECK

Reread Why does Dragon think the red thread is the "borrowed line"? Reread to find details that support your answer.

The next morning, Minli woke up alone under a heavy, rich blanket. Even though she was on the floor of the garden pagoda, she had slept comfortably, and as she sat up she realized that was probably due to the silk pillows she had been lying on. The soft sunlight cast leaf shadows across her face and the wind made gentle ripples in the moss-colored lake in front of her. The Imperial Garden was just as beautiful in the day as it was by night.

On one side of her lay a small table with a small pot of tea, a bowl of rice porridge, and tea-stained eggs. "Breakfast," Minli thought to herself, but before she reached for it she saw that a yellow brocade traveling bag lay on the other side of her. Inside the bag, Minli found her humble blanket, rabbit rice bowl (with needle and bamboo piece), chopsticks, a generous supply of cakes, and her hollow gourd full of fresh water. On the very top lay the gold threaded pouch that held the ripped page of fortune. Minli took the pouch and held it with two hands.

Well, I have the borrowed line, Minli thought. *At least I hope it is.*

So after a quick breakfast, Minli quietly left the pavilion. Part of her was tempted to explore the mosaic walkways through the jewel-colored leaves, but she knew being discovered by one of the king's counselors would be disastrous. Also, she knew Dragon was patiently waiting outside the city. So, using the king's secret door, Minli carefully left the garden and walls of the Inner City.

And when she was out of the garden, Minli realized it was very early morning. The Outer City was still sleeping; the stands were bare and the umbrellas were closed. Quickly, Minli scurried to the gate. With great effort she was able to get through—she had to use a metal pole she'd found on the ground to lift the lock and lever one of the doors open. Even then, she was only able to get it open a crack and had to squeeze.

As she fell through the gate, gasping for air, she was shocked to see Dragon lying in front of the stone lions, sleeping.

It took a couple of prods before Dragon woke, and his loud morning yawns almost put Minli in a panic, but they were able to get back to the hiding shelter of the forest before anyone saw them.

"What were you doing by the city?" Minli asked. "You were supposed to stay hidden!"

"I was getting the borrowed line," Dragon said.

"What do you mean?" Minli said. "I have the borrowed line."

And in a rush, the two of them told each other about their night adventures. Dragon stared at the ripped page from the book and Minli looked at the red cord in Dragon's hand.

"So which is the real borrowed line?" Dragon asked Minli.

"I guess that is another question we'll have to ask the Old Man of the Moon," Minli said.

ABOUT THE AUTHOR AND ILLUSTRATOR

Grace Lin grew up in upstate New York where she dreamed of becoming a champion ice skater. Instead, she wound up as an award-winning children's book author and illustrator.

Some of Grace's inspiration to write *Where the Mountain Meets the Moon* came from her travels to China and Taiwan. She saw the landscapes and buildings and experienced the cultures in person. Most of Grace's books are about Asian-American experiences. She likes to write about the subject because, she says, "A book makes all cultures universal."

Grace writes and illustrates chapter books and picture books. Her work includes *Dim Sum for Everyone!, Ling and Ting,* and *The Year of the Dog.* Grace loves using bright colors and graphic patterns to illustrate her stories. She chooses a pattern that will tie to the idea of the book and add texture to her illustrations. Grace won a Newbery Honor award for *Where the Mountain Meets the Moon.*

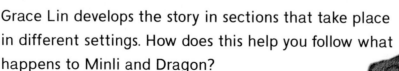

Author's Purpose

Grace Lin develops the story in sections that take place in different settings. How does this help you follow what happens to Minli and Dragon?

Respond to the Text

Summarize

Summarize how Minli gets the information she needs in *Where the Mountain Meets the Moon*. Details from your Events Chart may help you.

Event	→	Outcome
	→	
	→	
	→	
	→	

Write

How does Grace Lin show that the king and the male lion both give up something important to them? Use these sentence frames to organize your text evidence.

Grace Lin uses figurative language to . . .
She helps me understand . . .
This helps me see that the king and the male lion . . .

Make Connections

Talk about what Minli and Dragon do to get the information they need to continue their journey. **ESSENTIAL QUESTION**

Tell what the male lion revealed to Dragon in his story, "A String of Destiny." Why is it important to listen to others' stories?
TEXT TO WORLD

Genre • Fairy Tale

Compare Texts
Read about how a queen gets the information she needs.

THE PRINCESS AND THE PEA

by Hans Christian Andersen
retold by XineAnn

There was once a Prince, a lonely prince. He traveled around the world to find someone like himself, a proper princess to share his life. But this he knew: She must be a *real* princess.

In his travels, he found many princesses. Each claimed to be a real princess. Each had the proper pedigree and credentials, but there always seemed to be something wrong. At last, the prince returned home in despair; he wanted a princess so badly and he now feared that his **expectations** might never be met. The Old King and Queen welcomed him home.

Another summer passed and the leaves were falling from the trees when, one evening, a terrible storm blew in from the sea. As the prince sat by the fire reading, lightning drew closer and closer and thunder rattled the windows until it seemed sure they'd break.

Hours into the night, the storm raged. At midnight, a calm fell as suddenly as the storm itself had arrived. An eerie knock was heard at the town gate. It was a gentle but insistent knock. The townspeople and courtiers rubbed their eyes and wondered who could have been out in such a storm. The Old King himself sent his advisor to the town gate.

There stood a princess, but she was in a terrible state. Rain poured from her hair and her clothes. It overflowed her shoes and ran out the heels. She claimed she was a princess, and the advisor all but laughed aloud. Still, she swore she was a real princess.

"We'll see soon enough if that is true," whispered the Old Queen softly to herself, being careful not to **reveal** her plan. The princess was given a warm dinner and some dry clothes while the Old Queen set off to prepare a sleeping chamber for the princess. First, she stripped all the bed clothes. Then, she placed a single pea in the center of the bedstead. Next, she called for twenty mattresses and piled them, one on top of the other, on the pea. Finally, twenty feather beds were added on top of the mattresses. The princess's sleeping arrangements were made.

In the morning, the Old King and Queen met the princess when she arose. If possible, she looked worse than when she had arrived! They asked how she had slept. "Oh, terribly!" exclaimed the princess. "I scarcely closed my eyes all night. Who knows what was in that bed! It seemed as if I were lying upon some hard pebble; my whole body is black and blue this morning. It is truly terrible!" And the princess started crying.

The Old Queen saw at once that she must be a real princess. Only a real princess could have felt the pea through twenty mattresses and twenty feather beds.

So the prince asked her to be his wife, sure that he had found a real princess. The prince once again traveled the world, this time with the princess, and they were happy. And the pea? It was put into a museum, where it may still be found, if no one has stolen it.

Now this is a true story.

Make Connections

Talk about how the Old Queen gets the information she needs about the princess. ESSENTIAL QUESTION

How are the Old Queen's actions different from the way another fairy tale character gets information? How does a plan help each character? TEXT TO TEXT

The Boy Who Drew Birds

by Jacqueline Davies
illustrated by Melissa Sweet

Essential Question

How do we investigate questions about nature?

Read about how John James Audubon investigated a question about birds.

Go Digital!

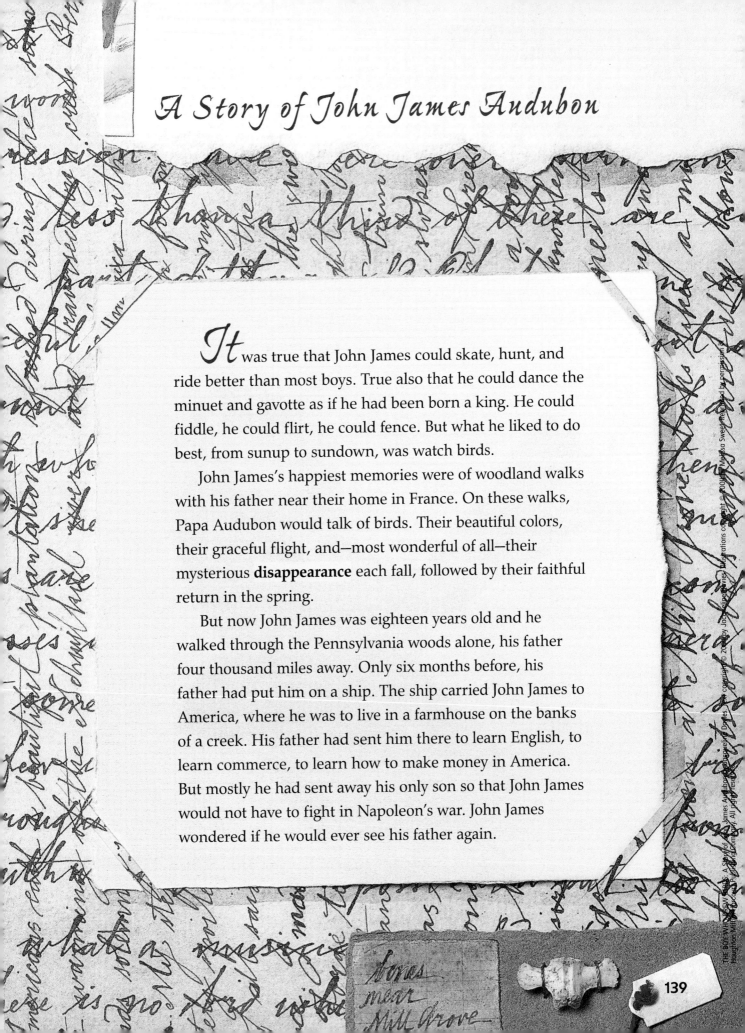

A Story of John James Audubon

It was true that John James could skate, hunt, and ride better than most boys. True also that he could dance the minuet and gavotte as if he had been born a king. He could fiddle, he could flirt, he could fence. But what he liked to do best, from sunup to sundown, was watch birds.

John James's happiest memories were of woodland walks with his father near their home in France. On these walks, Papa Audubon would talk of birds. Their beautiful colors, their graceful flight, and—most wonderful of all—their mysterious **disappearance** each fall, followed by their faithful return in the spring.

But now John James was eighteen years old and he walked through the Pennsylvania woods alone, his father four thousand miles away. Only six months before, his father had put him on a ship. The ship carried John James to America, where he was to live in a farmhouse on the banks of a creek. His father had sent him there to learn English, to learn commerce, to learn how to make money in America. But mostly he had sent away his only son so that John James would not have to fight in Napoleon's war. John James wondered if he would ever see his father again.

It was April in Pennsylvania, and slashes of snow still lay in deep hollows. John James splashed across the icy creek. He scrambled up the bank and approached the limestone cave, wondering what he would find today. Just the empty nest of a pewee bird, as he had found the last five days? Or would there be—

Ffh, Ffh, Ffh! A **flurry** of wings greeted John James. The pewee flycatchers had returned!

The female bird flew out of the cave like an arrow shot from a bow. The male bird, larger and darker, beat his wings above John James's head and snapped his beak. *Clack, clack, clack!*

John James ran out of the cave and crouched next to the creek. He watched as the birds dipped and soared, snapping up mayflies in flight. *Are these the same pewees who built the nest last year?* he wondered. *Where did they spend the winter? Will they return next spring?*

STOP AND CHECK

Reread Why did John James visit the cave? Use the strategy Reread to check your understanding.

141

John James ran home through the woods. "*Madame Thomas! Madame Thomas!*" he shouted, bursting into the farmhouse kitchen. "*Il y a des oiseaux!*" In his excitement, his words tumbled out in French.

Mrs. Thomas was the housekeeper Papa Audubon had hired to take care of Mill Grove, his American farmhouse. She pointed her long wooden spoon at John James's muddy shoes. He quickly took them off and placed them by the fire to dry.

"Birds," he said. "I see birds. Two. In cave. Beautiful!"

Mrs. Thomas frowned. She was fond of this **energetic** French boy. And yet she had to admit that he was something. Birds! Always birds! From the moment he woke up in the morning to the moment he closed his eyes at night, he thought only of birds. It was strange for a boy his age.

"Master Audubon," she scolded, "thou wouldst do well to do work by tending the farm more and chasing after birds less."

But John James, halfway up the staircase, pretended not to hear. He climbed straight to his attic room—his *musée*, he called it. Every shelf, every tabletop, every spare inch of floor, was covered with nests and eggs and tree branches and pebbles and lichen and feathers and stuffed birds: redwings and grackles, kingfishers and woodpeckers. The walls were covered with pencil and crayon drawings of birds, all signed "JJA." Every year on his birthday, John James took down these drawings—a year's worth of work—and burned them in the fireplace. He hoped some day he would make drawings worth keeping.

John James went to his bookcase and took down the natural history books, gifts from his father. *Where do small birds go in the winter? Do the same birds come back to the same nests each spring?* The scientists who wrote these books did not agree; each one gave a different answer.

Two thousand years before, the Greek philosopher Aristotle had given his answers to these questions. Aristotle said that every fall great flocks of cranes flew south and returned in the spring. But he believed that small birds did not **migrate**. Small birds, wrote Aristotle, hibernated under water or in hollow logs all winter.

Many scientists of the day still agreed with Aristotle. Small birds, they said, gathered themselves in a great ball, clinging beak to beak, wing to wing, and foot to foot, and lay under water all winter, frozen-like. Fishermen even told stories of catching such tangles of birds in their nets.

John James had never, *ever* found a tangled ball of birds under water. And he did not believe everything the scientists said. Why, some of them believed that birds **transformed** from one kind into another each winter! And one scientist claimed that birds traveled to the moon each fall and returned in the spring. He said the trip took sixty days!

Hermit Thrush *Pewee - 2 May 10* *American Robin · May 6* *Scarlet Tanager June †* *May 5*

Common Crow *Red-Winged Blackbird* *Junco May 1* *Mockingbird*

143

John James had never spent much time inside a classroom, and he had failed every exam he had taken in school. But he considered himself a naturalist. He studied birds in nature to learn their habits and **behaviors**.

I will bring my books to the cave, John James decided. *And my pencils and paper. I will even bring my flute. I will study my cave birds every day. I will draw them just as they are.* And because he was a boy who loved the out-of-doors more than the in, that is just what he did.

In a week, the birds were used to him. They ignored him as if he were an old stump. They carried bits of moist mud as he drew with his pencils. They brought in tufts of green moss as he read his French fables. They gathered stray goose feathers from the banks of the creek as he played songs on his flute.

Soon the dried brown nest had become a soft green bed. And John James had learned to imitate the throaty call of the birds: *Fee-bee! Fee-bee!*

feebee re bliebt fee bee ve

Spring slipped into summer. Summer sighed and became fall. John James watched as two broods of nestlings hatched. He watched as the young birds flew for the first time. He began to feel a part of this small family.

When the days grew shorter and the autumn air began to bite, John James knew the birds would leave soon. But would they come back? He had to know! The question was terribly important to the boy so far from his family.

In bed that night, he formed a plan.

The next day, when the mother and father birds were away from the nest, John James picked up one of the baby birds. He had read of medieval kings who tied bands on the legs of their prize falcons so that a lost falcon could be returned. Why not band a wild bird to find out where it goes? It had never been done, but John James could try.

He pulled a string from his pocket and tied it loosely around the baby bird's leg. The bird pecked it off. The next day, he tied another string to the bird's leg. Again the bird pecked it off. Finally, John James walked five miles to the nearest village and bought some thread woven of fine strands of silver. This thread was soft and strong. He tied a piece of it loosely to one leg of each baby bird.

A week later, the birds were gone.

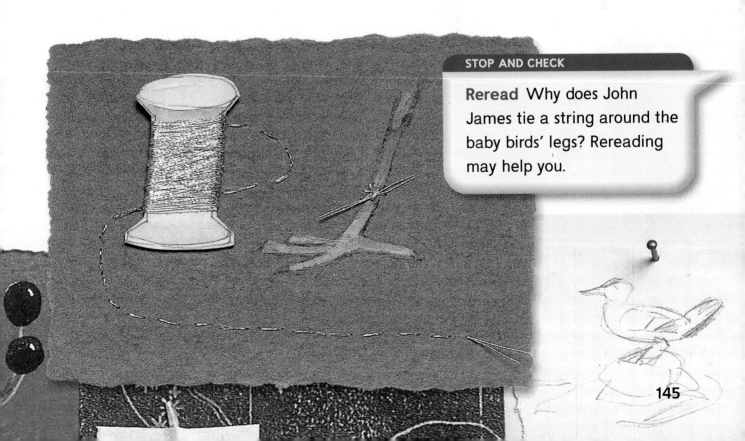

STOP AND CHECK

Reread Why does John James tie a string around the baby birds' legs? Rereading may help you.

All winter, John James worked in his *musée*, painting the pencil sketches he had made in the cave. He hoped that on his next birthday he would have one or two pictures worth saving from the fire.

The creek was frozen now, and each time John James skated past the empty cave, he thought of the two-thousand-year-old question: *Where do small birds go, and do they return to the same nest in the spring?*

The days grew longer. The ice on the creek cracked and melted.

One morning, John James heard a bird call, *Fee-bee! Fee-bee!*

He ran to the cave. He ducked his head and stepped inside.

The female bird did *not* fly out of the cave like an arrow shot from a bow. The male bird did *not* beat his wings above John James's head and snap his beak. Instead, they ignored John James as if he were an old stump. Watching the birds fly in and out of the cave, John James knew that his friends had returned.

But where were last year's babies, now grown? Had they returned, too? He began to search the woods and orchard nearby, listening for their call.

STOP AND CHECK

Ask and Answer Questions How did John James know that his friends had returned? Go back to the text to find the answer.

Out in the meadow, inside a hay shed, he found two birds building a nest. One wore a silver thread around its leg.

Up the creek, under a bridge, he found two more nesting birds. And one wore a silver thread around its leg.

John James wanted to shout, "Yes! The same birds return to the same nest! And their children nest nearby." But who would have heard him? *I will write to my father*, he decided. *I will tell him what I have learned in America. And when I am older, I will find a way to tell the whole world.*

He ran back to his house to gather his pencils, paper, and flute.

As he ran, he called, "*Fee-bee! Fee-bee!*"

more precious than diamonds

Nest
mud, moss, fine grasses
under bridges
old sheds
cliffs, on horizontal
or verticle supports
Size: 2½ inches
inside depth 1¾"

About John James Audubon

Banding a bird—that is, tying a marker around a bird's leg to track its movement—was an innovative idea in Audubon's time. In fact, in 1804 John James became the first person in North America to band a bird. His simple experiment helped prove a complex **theory**: Many birds return to the same nest each year, and their offspring nest nearby. This behavior is called *homing*. The rest of the world learned of Audubon's experiment when he wrote about it in his book *Ornithological Biography*. Later, in the twentieth century, scientists used bird banding to prove that small birds migrate.

The young John James grew to be the greatest painter of birds of all time. He was the first to paint life-size images of birds and the first to show birds hunting, preening, fighting, and flying. His revolutionary paintings pleased two audiences: scientists, who were drawn to their accuracy, and ordinary people, who simply enjoyed the beauty of his birds.

Audubon made hundreds of sketches of his cave birds; none survived. He painted this watercolor of the Pewee Flycatcher (now called Eastern Phoebe) in Louisiana around 1825. (Collection of The New-York Historical Society)

About the Author and Illustrator

Jacqueline Davies likes to sit and watch the world, especially from the front steps of her house in Massachusetts. She likes to look for and listen to birds, but she also likes to study people. She wonders about each person's story. Like John James Audubon, she pays close attention to the world around her and takes many notes. Then she draws on these experiences to write her award-winning books.

Melissa Sweet knows how important it is to study places and people. For that reason, she often visits locations that she will draw or paint for a book.

When Melissa begins her illustrations, she first makes quick sketches on tracing paper. Then she posts her drawings to a wall in her studio. This helps her see how the drawings fit together as a book. Later, she adds more details and splashes of color.

Author's Purpose

In this biography, the author includes sketches of birds. Why do you think she does this?

150

Respond to the Text

Summarize

Use the events in your Sequence Chart to help you summarize how John James investigated birds in *The Boy Who Drew Birds*.

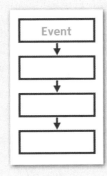

Write

How does the author effectively paint a picture of who John James was and how it helped him become an innovative researcher? Use these sentence frames to organize your text evidence.

Jacqueline Davies uses text features to . . .
She describes . . .
This helps me understand that John James . . .

Make Connections

Talk about how John James investigated a question he had about birds. **ESSENTIAL QUESTION**

Describe some tools John James used to study birds. What are some ways people might study birds today? **TEXT TO WORLD**

Genre • Myth

Compare Texts

Read about how Daedalus and Icarus investigated bird flight.

DAEDALUS and ICARUS

retold by Eric A. Kimmel
illustrated by Pep Montserrat

Daedalus, the world's greatest inventor, was invited to the island of Crete by King Minos to design the king's palace and a labyrinth, an underground maze. When the labyrinth was completed, the king rewarded Daedalus with a palace and his daughter's hand in marriage.

After many years, Daedalus's wife died and Daedalus wished to return with his son Icarus to his home city of Athens. Upon hearing Daedalus's request, the king refused, as he did not want Daedalus to work for anyone else. Instead, the king threatened to lock Daedalus and Icarus in the labyrinth should they attempt to leave.

Though Daedalus was scared, he still pondered an escape. As he gazed out at the heavily guarded shore, he noticed a flock of sea gulls. He made an **observation** that flight allowed the birds to easily leave the island. He had a **theory** that if he learned how birds fly, he could use this knowledge to escape.

For the next several months he studied the birds. He watched as they flew around the island. He discovered how warm air rising from the sea carried them higher. He examined birds to learn how feathers, bones, and muscles came together to form a wing. Daedalus began scratching designs on a wax tablet. He and Icarus walked along the seashore, collecting feathers.

Minos soon learned what they were doing. He ordered that Daedalus and Icarus be brought to him.

"What are you up to?" he asked. "Tell me the truth or I'll put you both back in the labyrinth."

"I'm going to build a pair of wings for Icarus and myself," Daedalus answered. "We're going to learn how to fly."

How Minos laughed! "What a foolish idea! People can't fly! Flying is for birds!"

"People can do anything if they think long and hard about it," Daedalus replied.

Minos dismissed them. "Go ahead! Make all the wings you like. You'll never escape from Crete that way."

Daedalus only smiled. He bowed and went back to his work room.

Daedalus made two pairs of wings. The frames were wood and wire, covered with wax. Daedalus stuck the feathers into the wax when it was soft. The wax would hold them in place when it hardened.

Daedalus and Icarus chose a day when a strong breeze blew from the mountains to the ocean. They carried their wings up to the roof and strapped them on.

"Hold out your arms," Daedalus told his son. "Pretend you are a bird. Let the air carry you. Don't tire yourself out by flapping too much."

Icarus felt so excited that he barely heard Daedalus's last warning: "Remember to not fly near the sun. The wax on your wings will melt. The feathers will come loose. You will fall into the sea."

"I'm ready, Father," said Icarus. "May I go first?"

"Go ahead," said Daedalus. "Lead the way. I will follow."

Icarus stepped onto the balcony. He climbed on top of the wall and leaped into space. Daedalus gasped as he saw his son falling. But then his wings caught the air. Up, up, flew Icarus. Daedalus watched him soar higher and higher, until he was a dot in the sky.

Now came Daedalus's turn. He leaped from the balcony. The air lifted him up. He tried his wings. They carried him perfectly.

The gulls flew by to have a look. "What is this strange new bird?" they seemed to call to each other. Daedalus looked up. He saw Icarus flying toward the roof of the sky. "Where is that boy going?" he muttered. "He is much too high. He must not go near the sun." Daedalus raised his voice. "Icarus! Come back!"

But Icarus was too far away to hear. He flew even higher into the clear, blue sky. Looking down, he saw the mighty ocean. It seemed no more than a puddle. The great city of Cnossos looked like an anthill. Icarus turned his eyes upward. *I want to fly higher*, he told himself. *I want to see what the gods see!*

He did not notice how close he was coming to the sun. He did not see the wax of his wings beginning to melt.

"Come back, Icarus!" Daedalus shouted one last time. A feather floated down past his face. Then another. And another.

"Icarus!" Daedalus screamed as his son toppled out of the sky.

"Father! Help me!" Icarus cried as he tumbled down, down, down.

It was too late. Hovering in the air, Daedalus could only watch helplessly as his son plunged into the sea.

Daedalus flew down. He pulled Icarus's broken body from the waves. He carried him to a nearby island. There he buried his son on the highest peak. The island is still called Icaria, in honor of Icarus, the boy who soared with the birds.

Make Connections

How do Daedalus and Icarus investigate a question about nature? ESSENTIAL QUESTION

How is Daedalus's study of birds similar to another study of nature in a story or text you've read? What was the purpose of each investigation? TEXT TO TEXT

Genre • Folktale

Blancaflor

by Alma Flor Ada
Illustrated by Beatriz Vidal

Essential Question

When has a plan helped you accomplish a task?

Read about how Blancaflor's plan helps a prince.

Go Digital!

A young prince had gone riding very early in the morning, before the sunrise. Now, tired and sad, he sat under the branches of a large oak tree. He was thinking about his father, the king, who lay in the castle, sick with an illness no one knew how to cure.

Physicians had been called in from all the neighboring kingdoms, wizards had been consulted, and the queen had prepared with her own hands all the herbal medicines suggested. But nothing seemed to help the king, who grew weaker and weaker with each passing day.

The young prince had been sitting under the tree for a while, lost in thought, when he was surprised by a deep voice that seemed to come from the branches of the oak tree: "What would you be willing to give for your father's health?" The prince looked around, but could see no one.

"I would give anything and everything for my father's health," he responded, trying to disguise the fear in his voice.

"Then, in three years' time, you shall bring yourself to me, to the Three Silver Towers, in the Land of No Return. Do I have your promise?" the deep voice bellowed as every leaf of the oak tree quivered.

"Yes," agreed the young man. "I, Prince Alfonso, do solemnly promise that I will do as you ask, if my father is indeed cured."

"Three years from today...," said the voice so loudly that all of the leaves fell, cascading down upon the startled prince. Shaking them off his shoulders, he jumped on his horse and back to the palace and to his father's room.

"Son!" His mother greeted him with a smile, the first he had seen on her loving face in many days. "Look at your father! He seems so much better." And, indeed, the sleeping king seemed to have regained all his color, and his sleep was sound and placid.

The king was completely healthy again in no time. But now the queen worried about her son. He seemed delighted, as was everyone, to see the kind king recover. And yet, once in a while, the queen **detected** a profound sadness in her son's eyes.

The king was determined that Prince Alfonso should marry. His prolonged illness had left him with a renewed urgency for life. "I want to see you start a family. I want to get to know my grandchildren."

Even though the prince insisted that he was not ready for marriage, the king ordered portraits of every marriageable princess brought in from all the neighboring kingdoms. When they all failed to interest the prince, the king organized banquets, dances, and outings to have the prince meet every noble girl he could possibly invite. But while the king managed to create a great deal of work for the seamstresses and coiffeurs of the kingdom, and while many young people had a wonderful time at the events, he could not get the prince to change his mind.

As time passed, the prince's behavior became stranger and stranger. He spent most of his time outside of the castle, riding his horse. During the evening he wrote poems and composed sweet, sad music on his lute. Finally, one morning, exactly one month before three years had gone by from the day on which he had heard the mysterious voice, he set out on his journey.

He left behind a stack of poems that talked about his love for his mother, his **gratitude** toward his father, and his joy in everyone and everything. He also left a letter for his parents, asking forgiveness for causing them sorrow, but **assuring** them that he was leaving only because he needed to honor a promise.

The king could not understand the disappearance of his son. He was ready to send his knights and guards to comb the world until they found him. But the queen requested that he honor his son's wishes, just as his son was honoring his promise. Inside her mother's heart she sensed a connection between her husband's healing and her son's departure.

Young Prince Alfonso rode for many days, eating sparingly of the food he had taken with him. Several times he asked shepherds he met along the way for directions to the Land of No Return. They always pointed in the same direction, toward the setting sun. And when they wondered, "Why should anyone want to go there?" the prince would respond, "To honor my word."

On the seventh day of his journey the prince saw a white dove who seemed to signal him to follow her. And so he did. But after many hours of following the dove, he found himself facing a deep ravine. He stopped, puzzled, knowing well that he could not cross the gorge on horseback or on foot. Then a majestic eagle appeared in front of him and looked piercingly into his eyes.

"Might you carry me to the other side?" he asked the eagle.

"Only if you give me your chain," the eagle responded.

Young Alfonso took off the heavy gold chain that bore the eagle emblem of his kingdom and hung it around the eagle's neck.

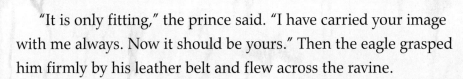

"It is only fitting," the prince said. "I have carried your image with me always. Now it should be yours." Then the eagle grasped him firmly by his leather belt and flew across the ravine.

The eagle released the young prince on the other side, where the land was deserted and barren. Basalt and obsidian rocks burned hot under the fierce sun. Far in the distance, high above the steep walls, three towers of silver glittered.

Alfonso had just taken a few steps toward the towers when he was stopped by a thundering voice: "Who dares step on my land?"

"I am here to honor my promise," the young prince answered.

"That is as it should be," the voice replied. "And to reward you, I will give you an opportunity to win your life back. If you fulfill the three tasks that I ask of you, you will stay here and marry one of my three daughters. But if you do not complete the tasks, you will be food for my hounds."

Alfonso took a deep breath. Squaring his shoulders and steadying his voice he asked, "What would you like me to do?"

"Take this sack of wheat. Walk up to the valley, plant it, harvest it, and mill it. With the flour, bake some bread and bring it to me tomorrow by eleven o'clock in the morning." To Alfonso's great surprise a small sack of wheat appeared before his eyes.

The young man lifted the sack and began to walk up the path among the rocks. What else could he do? His head hung low and his shoulders drooped because he knew there was no way he could fulfill his task. But he had not walked far when a young girl appeared in front of him.

STOP AND CHECK

Make Predictions How will Alfonso accomplish the task? Use the strategy Make Predictions.

"What's wrong?" she asked him. "Why are you so sad?"

"I have been asked to do an impossible task. And my life depends on it."

"My father must be up to one of his tricks," she responded. "But do not worry. I will help you. Take this stick and poke the earth with it. Keep walking on a straight line and poke as you walk. I will drop the seeds and all will be well."

That afternoon, after all the wheat had been planted, they watched the sunset together. The young girl said, "My name is Blancaflor. And if you trust me, we will save your life. Now I have to go; otherwise they will miss me at dinner."

After she left, Alfonso went to sleep, resting his back against a large boulder. In the morning the valley was covered with ripe wheat, its golden spikes shining under the early sun.

Alfonso was still rubbing his eyes when Blancaflor appeared.

"It's time to harvest the grain, mill it, and bake bread with the flour," she said. And as she spoke the wheat flew out of its stalks and formed a golden mountain. A mill and an outdoor oven appeared next to the mountain of wheat.

"Keep fetching wood for the oven," Blancaflor told Alfonso. And while he did, the mill ground the wheat, and loaf upon loaf of bread dough appeared ready to be baked. When the smell of the recently baked bread filled the valley, Blancaflor disappeared. "It's better that my father doesn't find me here when he comes for his bread," she told Alfonso before leaving.

Soon a thundering voice was heard: "Either you are a wizard or you have met Blancaflor."

Alfonso kept silent.

"Well, you still have two more tasks!" shouted the voice. "Better get started. Plant these grapevines and have the wine ready for me by eleven o'clock tomorrow morning." And while the loaves of bread moved through the air as if carried by giant hands, Alfonso found one hundred grapevine saplings at his feet.

It was not long before Blancaflor appeared again. And just as the pair had grown the wheat the **previous** day, now they planted the saplings. That evening, as they watched the sunset, Alfonso told Blancaflor about his mother and father and the promise he had made. And once again she asked him to trust her.

The next morning the valley was covered by fully grown grapevines loaded with ripe bunches of grapes. And it took only a few words from Blancaflor for the grapes to be harvested and crushed and for the wine to be stored in huge oak casks.

Just before eleven, after Blancaflor had already departed, the thundering voice was heard again: "Either you are a mighty wizard or you have been talking to Blancaflor."

Alfonso remained silent. But he shivered when he heard the voice laugh.

"Well, let's see how you do with your last task. You need to bring back the ring my great-great-grandmother lost in the ocean. And if you do not have it here by eleven o'clock tomorrow, you will be food for my hounds."

When Blancaflor returned, there were tears in Alfonso's eyes. "I'm not afraid to die. But I hate to break my mother's heart. This task will be impossible," he told her.

"No, it won't be. But you will need to trust me even more," she replied.

Blancaflor led Alfonso to a set of high cliffs next to the ocean. There the prince spotted the eagle who had carried him across the gorge.

"The eagle will take us to the middle of the ocean, and then you must let go of me and let me fall in," Blancaflor instructed.

"But I will not be able to do that," he argued.

"Yes, you will. You must," insisted Blancaflor.

When they were high above the ocean, Blancaflor asked the prince to let her go. But at the last minute he held on desperately to her hand. As her fingers slipped from his, he heard a crack. Her little finger hung broken.

Alfonso felt his heart stop as he saw Blancaflor disappear under the water. His eyes filled with tears as the eagle flapped her wings. Before he knew it, he was standing in the meadow, next to the boulder against which he had slept the last two nights. There, on top of the boulder, was an extraordinary ring in the shape of a dragon with two emeralds for eyes.

He had not admired the ring for very long before he heard the thundering voice. "So you found the ring. Either you are the king of all wizards or you have been helped by Blancaflor."

Alfonso remained silent.

The voice continued, "Follow the path to the castle. Tonight you will meet my three daughters and choose one for your wife!"

When Alfonso reached the Three Silver Towers, the gates were open. He entered, and in the main banquet hall there were three white doves.

"Choose one, right now!" the voice echoed against the thick walls.

Alfonso studied the three doves. They looked identical. But he noticed that one had what looked like a broken wing. He remembered Blancaflor's little finger, hanging twisted from her hand.

"I choose this one," he said, and walked toward the dove with the broken wing. Suddenly Blancaflor stood in front of him surrounded by her sisters, who looked just like her. No one would have been able to tell them apart. But when Alfonso observed Blancaflor's hand, he could see that one of her little fingers had been bandaged.

"Take your wife," ordered the voice. "And let's all go to sleep now. We will celebrate the wedding tomorrow."

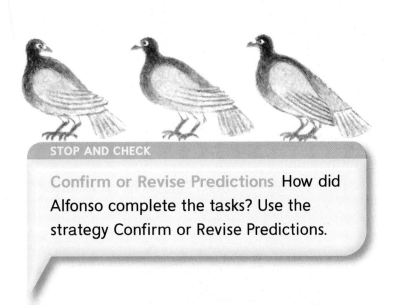

STOP AND CHECK

Confirm or Revise Predictions How did Alfonso complete the tasks? Use the strategy Confirm or Revise Predictions.

165

Blancaflor guided Alfonso to her bedroom. Once inside, she closed the door and whispered to him, "They will kill us tonight. We must escape." She arranged the covers on the bed to look as if they were both sleeping. She blew on the glass of water next to her bed and led Alfonso outside.

"I will stay here on guard in case my father comes in **pursuit**. You go to the stables to fetch a horse. And bring it here. But mind you, there are two horses there. One is young and strong. His name is Viento, which means 'wind.' The other one is old and thin. His name is Pensamiento, which means 'thought.' Make sure you do not take Viento. Take Pensamiento."

But when Alfonso got to the stable and saw the two horses, he thought, *That old skinny horse will never be able to carry us both.* And he proceeded to saddle Viento.

While Alfonso was getting the horse, Blancaflor's father was at his daughter's door. He called softly, to see if she was asleep, "Blancaflor?"

And the breath she had left on the water answered, "Yes, Father? Do you need me?"

After a few minutes he called again, "Blancaflor?"

And the breath repeated faintly, "Yes, Father?"

But when he called again, a third time, the breath only let out a sigh. He stormed into the room and quickly realized that neither Blancaflor nor the prince was there. And so he set out after them.

Blancaflor was dismayed when Alfonso came to fetch her riding
Viento, but seeing that her father was **emerging** from the castle,
she jumped on the horse behind the prince and urged him to go on.

They had galloped across the valley for only a few minutes when
they heard Pensamiento, carrying her father, catching up with them.

"If only we had taken Pensamiento instead of Viento," said
Blancaflor, "my father would never have been able to keep up with
us." Then she took the comb that held her hair and threw it on the
road behind them.

The comb turned into a chain of steep mountains that blocked the way and allowed them to gain a little distance. But very soon they heard the sound of Pensamiento's hooves approaching again.

Blancaflor took the gold pin that held her shawl and threw it on the road behind them.

The gold pin turned into a desert of very hot sand, and that allowed them to gain a little distance. But soon they heard Pensamiento's hooves again.

"If only we had taken Pensamiento instead of Viento," said Blancaflor. And she took her blue silk shawl and threw it on the road behind them.

The blue silk shawl turned into a large sea with high waves covered with foam.

Then Alfonso urged Viento, "Take on all my good thoughts—the thoughts of my mother's love, the thoughts of my father's kindness, my thoughts of love for Blancaflor. You can take these thoughts, Viento. Let them lighten your step."

Spurred by Alfonso's thoughts, Viento became as fast as Pensamiento. Before they knew it, the prince and Blancaflor were at the doors of Alfonso's own castle, being greeted by his kind father and his loving mother, who held them both in one embrace.

They were still holding one another when a terrible gust of wind began ripping the leaves off the trees, and they could see a black tornado approaching. Alfonso gathered all his courage and shouted into the wind, "My word has been honored! How about yours?"

The wind blew even more wildly for a moment, but then it subsided, and they heard in the dying wind a deep voice that sounded as though it came from far away, "You have proven to be wise, my daughter. Now...be happy!"

And this is the story of Blancaflor. It began with threads of silver and ended with threads of gold, all woven for you in the story I told.

STOP AND CHECK

Reread **How do Blancaflor and Alfonso escape? Rereading may help you.**

About the Author and Illustrator

Alma Flor Ada knew that she would be a writer by the time she was in fourth grade. "Most of my stories I told aloud before I ever wrote them down," she says. "And it was other people listening and other people being interested that gave me a motivation to write them."

Alma Flor Ada grew up in Cuba, but she has also lived in Spain and Peru. Today she makes her home in San Francisco, California. For Alma, knowing two languages—English and Spanish—has made her world richer. She believes that all children should be given the chance to learn two or more languages.

Beatriz Vidal grew up in Argentina, but later traveled to New York. There, she met an artist who inspired her to begin a career as an artist, so she began to study painting and design. Soon, her work was shown in magazines and later books and exhibitions. Beatriz has won awards for her colorful work and has taught others to enrich children's books through illustration.

Author's Purpose

In the story, the author gives the horses names that are Spanish words: Viento and Pensamiento. Blancaflor tells Prince Alfonso to take Pensamiento, meaning "thought." What message is the author trying to send?

Respond to the Text

Summarize

Use the most important events in *Blancaflor* to summarize how Blancaflor helps Alfonso accomplish his tasks. Details from your Theme Chart may help you.

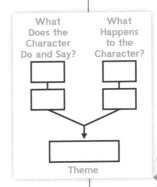

Write

Think about how the author uses figurative language. How does the tone and mood change from the beginning of the folktale to the end? Use these sentence frames to help organize your text evidence.

The author sets the tone by . . .
She uses figurative language to show . . .
The mood changes because . . .

Make Connections

Talk about how Blancaflor and Alfonso follow a plan to accomplish the tasks. **ESSENTIAL QUESTION**

In the story, Blancaflor has a plan in mind to accomplish each task. What is the purpose of making a plan? **TEXT TO WORLD**

Compare Texts
Read about how a recipe can help you accomplish a task.

From Tale to Table

Whether it's a princess turning into a dove or a frog turning into a prince, many folktales and fairy tales include a magical transformation of one thing into another. Though it seems like an impossible task that only a magician could do, transformations can in fact happen in real life—even in your own kitchen!

Philip Nealey/Digital Vision/GettyImages

A Wise Plan

Through the process of cooking and baking, individual ingredients can be transformed into something delicious. Did you know that the bread in the sandwich you had for lunch was probably made with only six basic ingredients: flour, water, oil, yeast, salt, and sugar? It may seem impossible, but by combining and heating these ingredients you can create something different: bread. It's not magic, but it does require a plan.

When you bake bread, or anything else, that plan is a *recipe*. A recipe includes a list of ingredients with amounts of each and steps to follow. The following recipe provides the guidance you need for making a loaf of bread. By combining, stirring, kneading, and shaping, you can change the separate ingredients into a mixture that has a different look and feel than each of the individual ingredients. After baking, this mixture will also have a different form, color, texture, and—of course—taste!

Recipe for Basic Bread

Ingredients:

1 cup warm water

1/4 cup sugar

2 teaspoons active dry yeast

1 teaspoon salt

3 cups all-purpose flour

2 tablespoons vegetable oil

1. In a bowl, combine the warm water and two teaspoons of sugar. Make sure the water is not hot. Sprinkle the yeast on top of the solution. Set the bowl aside. Then wait five minutes.
2. Stir the solution in the bowl. Then add the salt, oil, and the rest of the sugar.
3. Put flour in another bowl. Slowly pour in the solution and stir until the mixture comes together. Shape the dough with your hands to make it round.
4. Knead the dough on a floured surface for eight minutes. Then place it in a covered, greased bowl. Put it somewhere warm for an hour to rise. The dough should double in size.
5. Take out the dough and punch it down. Shape the dough into a loaf.
6. Place the loaf in a greased bread pan. Then cover the loaf. Wait for about an hour.
7. Remove the cover and bake the dough in the oven at 375 degrees Fahrenheit for 25-30 minutes. Check that the crust is golden brown.
8. Remove the pan from the oven. Let the pan cool.

Too Hot, Too Cold, and Just Right

A recipe has usually been tried and tested previously, so it is important to follow the steps carefully to get the same result. Slight changes in temperature can affect the **outcome**. For example, in step 1, the water should be warm, not hot. Why? Though it's hard to tell by looking at it, yeast is a living organism. At the right temperature, it gives off gases that create bubbles in the dough. This is what makes the dough rise. If you use hot water in the recipe, you can kill the yeast. If you use cold water, the yeast may create very little or no gas. Without the gas that the yeast produces, the dough will not rise.

First combine ingredients (top left). Next, shape the dough (top right). After kneading, let the dough rise (left). Ingredients must be at the right temperature and combined in the right order to make a dough that will rise.

Kneading is a process of folding and pressing the dough. This step affects the consistency of the baked bread.

When the Clock Strikes . . .

Timing is an important detail in any recipe. Step 4 tells you to knead the dough for eight minutes. What would happen if you left out that step? Or, what if you only kneaded the dough for a minute or two? Kneading breaks up the large gas bubbles in the dough. So you could end up with large holes in your baked bread. That would not be a good result!

The temperature of the oven and the baking time in step 7 are important, too. If you bake the bread for more than thirty minutes, you might burn it. If you bake it for too short a time, it will be soft and doughy. But if you time it correctly, the bread will turn out just right!

It doesn't take wishes, luck, or a magician in the kitchen to bake up something special. With a little planning you, too, can amaze your friends and family with your powers of transformation.

Make Connections

 How can a recipe help you accomplish a task?
ESSENTIAL QUESTION

In what ways is a recipe like another plan you've read about? In what ways is a recipe different? TEXT TO TEXT

(bkgd) Dave King/Dorling Kindersley/Getty Images; (b) Brand X Pictures/Brand X Pictures/Getty Images

Stage Fright

I wanted the role.
The Prince.

The Prince.

I got it.
Knew it.
I was totally convinced.

I memorized each line.
Learned them by heart.
I studied and studied
my perfect Prince-part.

But—
when I took center stage
   I stammered
    stuttered
    hemmed
    hawed
    suddenly shuddered.

Essential Question

What motivates you to accomplish a goal?

Read about how ambitious people can accomplish their goals.

 Go Digital!

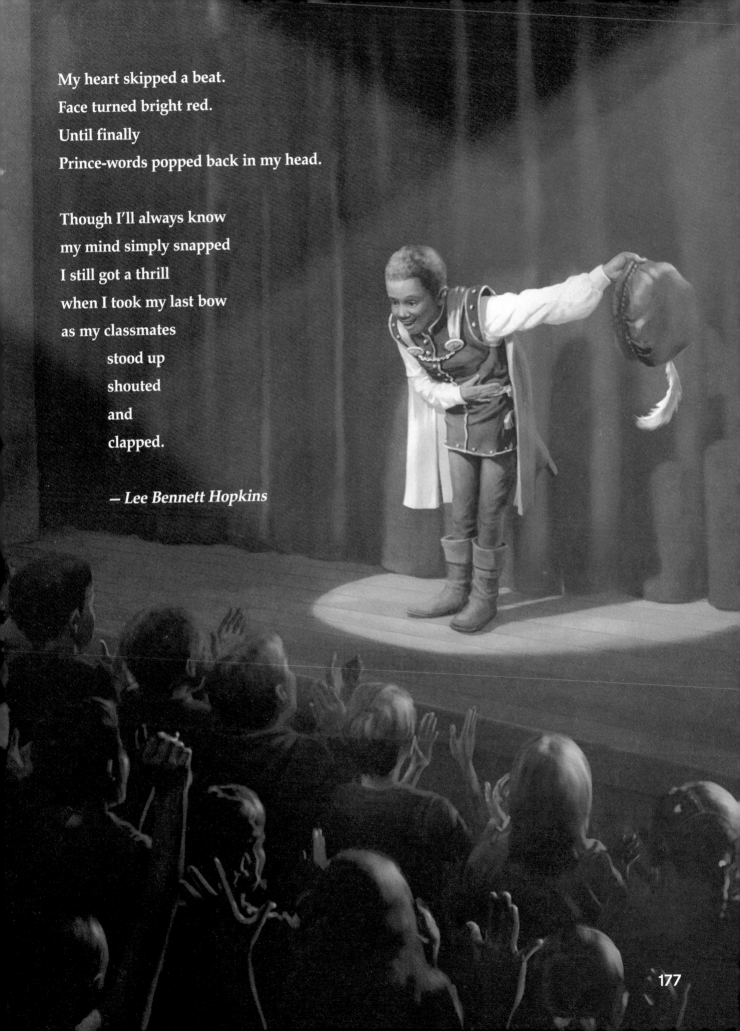

My heart skipped a beat.
Face turned bright red.
Until finally
Prince-words popped back in my head.

Though I'll always know
my mind simply snapped
I still got a thrill
when I took my last bow
as my classmates
   stood up
   shouted
   and
   clapped.

— *Lee Bennett Hopkins*

Catching Quiet

It's hard to catch quiet
In the city.
You have to be quick.
It isn't around long.
You might find it
after the roar of a truck,
before a jet flies by.
You might find it
after the horns stop honking,
before the sirens start.
You might find it
after the ice cream man's bell,
before your friends call you
to play.
But when you find it,
stick it in your heart fast.
Keep it there.
It's a bit of the sky.

— *Marci Ridlon*

Respond to the Text

Summarize

Use important details from "Stage Fright" to summarize the poem. Information from your Theme Chart may help you.

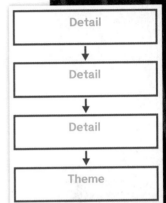

Write

Think about the way both poems are organized. How do techniques like line arrangement and repetition help convey each poem's theme? Use these sentence frames to help organize your text evidence.

In "Stage Fright" the poet uses . . .
In "Catching Quiet" the poet . . .
Both techniques help me to . . .

Make Connections

Tell what motivates the speaker of each poem. How does each speaker express satisfaction in accomplishing a goal? ESSENTIAL QUESTION

What other benefits come from accomplishing a goal? TEXT TO WORLD

Compare Texts

Read how an ambitious player accomplishes a goal.

FOUL SHOT

With two 60's stuck on the scoreboard
And two seconds hanging on the clock,
The solemn boy in the center of eyes,
Squeezed by silence,
Seeks out the line with his feet,
Soothes his hands along his uniform,
Gently drums the ball against the floor
Then measures the waiting net,
Raises the ball on his right hand,
Balances it with his left,
Calms it with fingertips,
Breathes,
Crouches,
Waits,
And then through a stretching of stillness,
Nudges it upward.

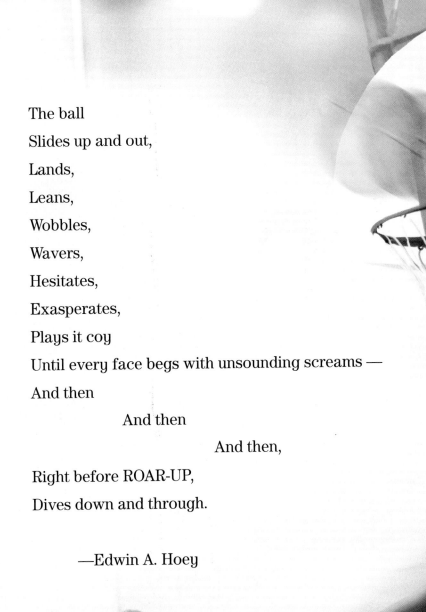

The ball
Slides up and out,
Lands,
Leans,
Wobbles,
Wavers,
Hesitates,
Exasperates,
Plays it coy
Until every face begs with unsounding screams —
And then
     And then
         And then,
Right before ROAR-UP,
Dives down and through.

— Edwin A. Hoey

Make Connections

What motivates the player to accomplish his goal? How does he accomplish it? ESSENTIAL QUESTION

Think of another poem in which a speaker accomplishes a goal. How is the player's approach in this poem different? TEXT TO TEXT

"They Don't Mean It!" by Lensey Namioka, copyright 2004, from FIRST CROSSING: STORIES ABOUT TEEN IMMIGRANTS, edited by Donald R. Gallo. Reprinted by permission of Lensey Namioka. All rights are reserved by the Author.

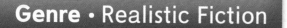

They Don't Mean It!

by Lensey Namioka

illustrated by John Carrozza

Essential Question

What can learning about different cultures teach us?

Read about how two friends learn about each other's culture.

Go Digital!

Our family moved here from China two years ago, and we thought we were pretty well adjusted to American ways. So my parents decided to give a party on Chinese New Year and invite some of our American friends.

When we first came to the United States, we had a hard time getting used to the different customs, but we gradually learned how things were done. We learned American table manners, for instance. We stopped slurping when we ate soup or ramen noodles. (At least we didn't slurp when we were with other Americans. When we ate by ourselves at home, we still sneaked in a juicy slurp every now and then.)

Mother stopped **complimenting** people here on how old and fat they looked. She learned that Americans thought being old was pitiful, and that being slender was beautiful.

Father's English pronunciation was improving. He used to have trouble with the consonant *r*, so instead of "left" and "right," he would say "reft" and "light." Since he's a professional musician, making a correct sound is important to him, and he practiced until he mastered his *r*. Now he can tell me to pass him the krispies crisply.

I worked harder than anybody at doing the right thing, and I even kept a little notebook with a list of English expressions (one of my favorites was "It's raining cats and dogs"). I even adopted an American name: Mary. I knew my friends in school would have a hard time with my Chinese name, Yingmei, so now I'm Mary Yang.

I really believed that our family had adjusted completely. We had even joined in celebrating American holidays, such as Independence Day, Labor Day, Thanksgiving, Easter, Christmas, and New Year—Western New Year, that is. My parents decided to show our American friends what Chinese New Year was like.

Chinese New Year, which falls in late January or early February, is sometimes called the Lunar New Year because it's based on the phases of the moon. It doesn't always fall on the same day in the solar calendar, but depends on when the first new moon occurs after the winter solstice, or the shortest day of the year. Anyway, in China it's also called the Spring Festival, because by that time you're pretty tired of winter and you're looking forward eagerly to spring.

In China we celebrate the New Year by setting off firecrackers, and we were delighted when we learned that firecrackers were also set off here in Seattle's Chinatown at New Year.

But eating special foods is the most important part of the celebration. So a week before the party, we helped Mother to shop and cook the special New Year dishes. We had to serve fish, since the Chinese word for fish is *yu*, which sounds the same as the word for "surplus." It's good to have a surplus of money and other valuables.

Mother admitted that living in America for two years had made her soft, and she no longer felt like killing a fish with her own hands. These days, she bought dead fish, but she always apologized when she served it to our Chinese guests. When we first came to America, Mother used to keep live fish in the bathtub because that way she knew the fish would be fresh when it came time to cook it. Even for the New Year party, she bought a dead fish, but at least she went to a special store in Chinatown where they had live fish and killed it for you on the spot.

For our New Year dinner we also had to have noodles. We normally eat noodles on birthdays, because the long strands stand for a long life. Why noodles on New Year, then? Because in the old days, instead of having your own special birthday, everybody's birthday was on New Year's Day, no matter what day you were actually born on.

The New Year dish that involves the most work is the ten-vegetable salad. Mother tells us that each of the ten vegetables is supposed to promote health, and eating it on New Year makes you healthy for the whole year. I can understand why some of the vegetables are healthy—things like carrots, bean sprouts, and cabbage, which have lots of vitamins. But the salad also includes things like dried mushrooms and a kind of lichen. When I asked Mother why they were supposed to be healthy, she thought a bit and then admitted that she always included those ingredients because *her* mother and grandmother always included them.

So we got to work. We had to soak the dried ingredients. We had to wash the fresh vegetables and slice them up into thin strips. In addition to all the cooking, we vacuumed every room thoroughly, since we wanted to start the New Year with a really clean house. Mother said that we had to do the cleaning before New Year, because doing it on the day itself was bad luck. It was believed that you'd sweep out good fortune together with the dirt.

With all the cooking and the cleaning, I was exhausted by the time our guests arrived at our house for the New Year party.

STOP AND CHECK

Summarize How does the Yang family adjust to American ways and keep Chinese customs? Use the strategy Summarize to help you.

The first of our guests to arrive were the Engs, a Chinese-American family. Paul Eng, their son, was in Eldest Brother's class. Paul and Second Sister were beginning to be interested in each other, although we pretended we didn't notice. I was glad that Second Sister had finally thrown away her Chinese cloth shoes. They had developed big holes, and we could see her toes wiggling around inside. Tonight she was wearing a new pair of sneakers she'd bought with her baby-sitting money.

The O'Mearas arrived next. Kim O'Meara was my best friend in school, and we'd been at each other's house lots of times. The last to arrive were the Conners. My youngest brother's best friend was Matthew Conner, who was a really good violinist and took lessons from my father.

"Happy New Year, Sprout!" Matthew said to Fourth Brother. "Sprout" was my brother's nickname, because for school

lunch he used to eat sandwiches filled with stir-fried bean sprouts. Now he eats peanut butter and jelly sandwiches just like his friends, but the nickname stuck.

Because we had too many people to seat around the dining table, we served dinner buffet style, and the guests helped themselves to the food. When they saw all the dishes arranged on the dining table, they exclaimed at how beautiful everything looked.

"Oh, no, it's really plain, simple food," said Mother. "I've only added a few small things for the New Year."

The guests paid no attention to her and began to help themselves. Mrs. Conner wanted to know how Mother had cooked the fish. Mrs. Eng said that she also cooked fish and served noodles on New Year, but she didn't do the ten-vegetable salad. Maybe it wasn't served in the part of China where her family originally came from.

Nobody had complaints about the food, from the way they devoured it and came back for seconds. The kids even ate up the salad. Kim O'Meara laughed when she saw her brother Jason taking a second helping. "Hey, Jason, I thought you hate vegetables!"

Jason's mouth was full, so he just mumbled an answer.

Mrs. O'Meara looked at me and smiled. "I bet you and your mom put a lot of work into making that salad, Mary. Doesn't it hurt to see it disappear in a matter of minutes?"

It *was* a lot of work to make the ten-vegetable salad. I got a blister on my finger from slicing all those celery and carrot sticks. "I'm glad to see how much you people like it," I said. "You'll all be very healthy this coming year!"

Looking at the platters of food getting emptied, I began to worry. "We'd better do something about dessert!" I whispered to Mother. At this rate, our guests would still be hungry after the main courses were finished.

"But I never make dessert!" Mother whispered back. Dessert isn't something Chinese normally eat at the end of a dinner.

So I ran into the kitchen, found a carton of almond cookies, and hurriedly dumped them on a platter. When I put the platter on the dining table, the cookies disappeared before I could say *abracadabra* (*abracadabra* was one of the words in my little notebook).

Since it was a weekday night, people didn't stay long after the last cookie crumb was eaten. There was a congestion at the front door as the guests thanked us for inviting them and showing them what a real Chinese New Year dinner was like.

"The fish was delicious!" Mrs. Eng said to Father. "I'll have to get the recipe from your wife one of these days. She's a wonderful cook, isn't she?"

"Oh, no, she's not a good cook at all," said Father. "You're just being polite."

I heard a little gasp from my friend Kim. She stared wide-eyed at Father.

"What's the matter, Kim?" I asked.

Instead of answering, Kim turned to look at Mrs. O'Meara, who was saying to my mother, "I *loved* your ten-vegetable salad. Even the kids loved it, and they don't usually eat their vegetables. You and the girls must have spent *hours* doing all that fine dicing and slicing!"

"The girls did the cutting, and I'm sorry they did such a terrible job," said Mother. "I'm embarrassed at how thick those pieces of celery were!"

I heard another little gasp from Kim, who was now staring at Mother. But I didn't get a chance to ask her what the problem was. The O'Mearas were going out the front door, and the rest of the guests followed.

"How come your father and your mother were so nasty last night?" asked Kim when we were walking to the school bus stop the next morning.

"What do you mean?" I asked. I didn't remember Father or Mother acting nasty.

"It was when Mrs. Eng was telling your dad what a good cook your mom is," replied Kim.

That's right. Mrs. Eng did say something about Mother being a good cook. "So what's bothering you?" I asked.

Kim stopped dead. "Didn't you hear your dad?" she demanded. "He said that your mom wasn't a good cook at all, and that Mrs. Eng was just being polite!"

I still didn't understand why Kim was bothered. "So what? People are always saying things like that."

But Kim wasn't finished. "And then when my mom said how hard you worked to cut up the vegetables, your mom said she was embarrassed by what a terrible job you did in slicing!"

I had to laugh. "She doesn't mean it! It's just the way she talks."

When the school bus arrived and we got on, Kim began again. "Then why do your parents keep saying these bad things

if they don't mean it? I'd be really hurt if my mom said I did a terrible job—after I worked so hard, too."

What Kim said made me thoughtful. I suddenly realized that whenever people said good things about us, my parents always **contradicted** them and said how bad we really were. We kids knew perfectly well that our parents didn't mean it, so our feelings weren't hurt in the least. It was just the way Chinese parents were supposed to talk.

Finally I said to Kim, "I think that if my parents agreed with the compliments, then that would be the same as bragging. It's good manners to contradict people when they compliment your children."

"It's bragging only if you say good things about *yourself*," protested Kim. "It's different when your parents are talking about *you*."

I shook my head. "We Chinese feel it's the same thing. Boasting about our children, or husband, or wife, is the same as boasting about ourselves. People even think it's bad luck."

It was Kim's turn to be thoughtful. "So that's why your parents never said what good musicians you were. That would be bragging, right?"

Music is the most important thing in our family. My elder brother plays the violin, my second sister plays the viola, and I play the cello. We all practice very hard, and I know Father thinks we are all doing well—only he has never said so to other people.

"The funny thing is," continued Kim, "your kid brother is the only one in your family who isn't a good musician. But I've never heard your parents say anything about how badly he plays."

I thought over what Kim said about Fourth Brother. He is the only one in our family who is no good at all with music. But we don't talk about his terrible ear. Finally I said, "It's like this: We're not hurt when we hear our parents say bad things about us, since we know they're only doing it because it's good manners. We know perfectly well that they don't mean it. But if they say my younger brother has a terrible ear, they'd really be telling the truth. So they don't say anything, because that would hurt his feelings."

Kim rolled her eyes. "Boy, this is confusing! Your parents can't tell the truth about your playing because it would be bragging. And they can't say anything about your brother's playing because that would be telling the truth."

I grinned. "Right! You got it!"

I think Kim understood what I was driving at. She didn't make a face when she heard my mother saying that the cookies Second Sister baked for the PTA bake sale were terrible.

After our Spring Festival party, the days became longer, and cherry trees burst into bloom. The baseball season began, and Fourth Brother's team played an opening game against another school. My brother might have a terrible ear for music, but he was turning out to be a really good baseball player.

In the seventh inning Fourth Brother hit a home run, something he had wanted to do for a long time but had never managed before. All his teammates crowded around to **congratulate** him. "You did it, Sprout! You did it!" shouted Matthew Conner, his best friend.

Mr. Conner turned to Father. "I bet you're proud of the boy!"

"He was just lucky when he hit that home run," said Father.

Overhearing the exchange, Kim turned to me and smiled. "I see what you mean," she whispered.

STOP AND CHECK

Summarize What have Kim and Mary learned since the New Year's party? Summarizing the events may help you.

That Easter, the O'Mearas invited our family for dinner. I knew that Easter was a solemn religious holiday, but what I noticed most was that the stores were full of stuffed rabbits and fuzzy baby chicks. Chocolate eggs were everywhere.

For the dinner, Mrs. O'Meara cooked a huge ham. She had also made roast potatoes, vegetables, salad, and the biggest chocolate cake I had ever seen. I had eaten a lot at Thanksgiving dinners, but this time I stuffed myself until I was bursting. The rest of my family did pretty well, too. We all loved ham.

As Mrs. O'Meara started cutting up the cake for dessert, Mother said, "I'm not sure if I can eat one more bite. That was the best ham I've ever tasted!"

"Aw, that ham was terrible," said Kim. "I bet you could do a lot better, Mrs. Yang."

There was a stunned silence around the table. Mrs. O'Meara stared at Kim, and her face slowly turned dark red.

I heard a low growl from Mr. O'Meara. "You and I are going to have a little talk later this evening, young lady," he said to Kim.

Our family was speechless with surprise. My parents, my brothers, and sister all stared at Kim. I was the most shocked, because Kim was my best friend, and in the two years since I've known her, I'd never seen her do or say anything mean. How could she say something so cruel about her own mother?

The rest of the evening was pretty uncomfortable. Our family left early, because we could all see that Mr. and Mrs. O'Meara were waiting impatiently to have their "little talk" with Kim as soon as we were gone.

Next morning at the school bus stop, Kim wouldn't even look at me. Finally I cleared my throat. "What made you talk like that to your mother, Kim?" I asked.

Kim whirled around. She looked furious. "B-but you were the one who t-told me that saying nice things about your own family was the s-same as bragging!" she stuttered. "Last night I was just trying to act modest!"

I finally saw the light. I saw how Kim had misunderstood what I had said. "Listen, Kim," I said, "Chinese *parents* are supposed to say **critical** things about their own *children*, and husbands and wives can say bad things about each other. But *young people* must always be respectful to their *elders*."

The school bus came. "I guess I'll never understand the Chinese," sighed Kim as we sat down. At least we still sat together.

After school I went over to Kim's house and explained to Mrs. O'Meara about how the Chinese were supposed to sound modest about their own children. I told her that Kim had thought I meant children also had to sound modest about their parents. Mrs. O'Meara laughed. Although her laugh sounded a little forced, it was a good sign.

STOP AND CHECK

Reread How does Mary's view of Kim's behavior change? Reread to look for details that support your answer.

I soon forgot about Kim's **misunderstanding**, because I had other things to worry about. Our school orchestra was giving its spring concert, and the conductor asked me to play a cello solo as one of the numbers. Father said I should play a dance movement from one of Bach's unaccompanied cello suites. It was a very hard piece, and I was really scared to play it in public. But Father said we should always try to meet challenges.

I practiced like mad. On the day of the concert, I was so nervous that I was sitting on pins and needles waiting for my turn to play ("sitting on pins and needles" was another expression in my little notebook). My legs were wobbly when it came time for me to walk to the front of the stage. But as I sat down with my cello and actually started playing, I became so wrapped up in the music that I forgot to be nervous.

After the concert, my friends came up to congratulate me. It was the proudest moment of my life. "You were great, Mary, simply great!" said Kim. Her eyes were shining.

Mother's eyes were shining, too. "Yes, she *was* good," she **blurted** out. Then she covered her mouth and looked embarrassed.

Kim turned to me and winked. "That's all right, Mrs. Yang. We all know you didn't mean it!"

About the Author

Lensey Namioka, like the fictional Yangs, lives in Seattle, Washington and moved from China to the United States. Lensey was nine years old when she made the transition, and remembers what it was like to come to a new country and learn a new language. Several books and short stories she has written, such as "They Don't Mean It!", reflect her experiences.

The Yang family appears in other books by Lensey, such as *Yang the Youngest and His Terrible Ear* and *Yang the Third and Her Impossible Family*. She has also written about Japanese culture in her stories about Japanese warriors called samurai. Lensey continues to write short stories and books for readers of all ages.

Author's Purpose

Authors sometimes have more than one purpose for writing. What was entertaining about the story? What did you learn from it?

Respond to the Text

Summarize

Summarize how Mary and Kim learned about each other's culture in *They Don't Mean It!* Details from your Theme Chart may help you.

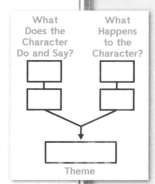

Write

How does the author show how the Yangs change as they try to find a balance between their Chinese traditions and their new American life? Use these sentence frames to help organize your text evidence:

The author uses dialogue to show . . .
The illustrations help me to see . . .
This helps me understand how the Yangs . . .

Make Connections

Talk about what Mary and Kim learned about each other's culture. ESSENTIAL QUESTION

What are some of the ways people learn about other cultures? Why is it important to know about different cultures? TEXT TO WORLD

Genre • Expository Text

Compare Texts
Read about how other cultures have influenced our way of life.

Where Did That Come From?

People from places around the world have come to live together in the United States. They have formed diverse communities and shared traditions, languages, ideas, and activities. Over time, these kinds of **cultural** exchanges have contributed to our American culture.

From Bite...

Food is one of the most common ways people have shared cultures. Dishes we think of as American have in fact come from all over the world. Hamburgers were crafted by German immigrants. Macaroni was rolled out by Italians. Apple pie was first served not in America but England.

...To Beat

People from different backgrounds have also drummed distinct sounds into the music we hear today. Hip hop and rap, for example, have been traced to West African and Caribbean storytelling. Salsa music comes from a type of Cuban music called "son," which has been linked to both Spanish and African cultures. These unique genres owe their rhythms to the drum. This instrument can be found in nearly every culture in the world.

United in Sports

Even the sports we play have come from other places. Soccer's origins have been connected with a number of countries, including Italy and China. Tennis likely came from France, but some think it may have even been played in ancient Egypt. While no one may know the exact origin of some of these sports, there is no doubt they are now considered popular American activities.

Our nation has been enriched by a diversity of cultures. Learning the origins of what makes up American culture can lead to a new **appreciation** for the people and places from which they come.

Soccer is one sport that many cultures share.

Words from Around the World

Many words used in American English have been "borrowed" from languages around the world.

- chimpanzee: **Kongo (African)**
- chipmunk: **Ojibwa (Native American)**
- bazaar, caravan: **Arabic**
- ketchup: **Chinese**
- voilà, genre: **French**
- kindergarten, dunk: **German**
- bandana, shampoo: **Hindi**
- bravo, magenta: **Italian**
- karaoke, tsunami: **Japanese**
- ranch, mosquito: **Spanish**

Make Connections

What can learning about other cultures teach us?
ESSENTIAL QUESTION

How has a character in a story been influenced by American culture? How is this similar to the way other cultures have influenced people in America?
TEXT TO TEXT

Essential Question

How can learning about nature be useful?

Read about how one boy uses what he learns about nature to create a new civilization.

Go Digital!

198

Weslandia

by Paul Fleischman

illustrated by Kevin Hawkes

"Of course he's miserable," moaned Wesley's mother. "He sticks out."

"Like a nose," snapped his father.

Listening through the heating vent, Wesley knew they were right. He was an outcast from the **civilization** around him.

He alone in his town disliked pizza and soda, alarming his mother and the school nurse. He found professional football stupid. He'd refused to shave half his head, the hairstyle worn by all the other boys, despite his father's bribe of five dollars.

Passing his neighborhood's two styles of housing—garage on the left and garage on the right—Wesley alone dreamed of more exciting forms of shelter. He had no friends, but plenty of **tormentors**.

Fleeing them was the only sport he was good at.

Each afternoon his mother asked him what he'd learned in school that day.

"That seeds are carried great distances by the wind," he answered on Wednesday.

"That each civilization has its staple food crop," he answered on Thursday.

"That school's over and I should find a good summer project," he answered on Friday.

As always, his father mumbled, "I'm sure you'll use that knowledge often."

Suddenly, Wesley's thoughts shot sparks. His eyes blazed. His father was right! He could actually *use* what he'd learned that week for a summer project that would top all others. He would grow his own food crop—and found his own civilization!

STOP AND CHECK

Summarize How did Wesley come up with the idea to found his own civilization? The strategy Summarize may help you.

The next morning he turned over a plot of ground in his yard. That night a wind blew in from the west. It raced through the trees and set his curtains snapping. Wesley lay awake, listening. His land was being planted.

Five days later the first seedlings appeared.

"You'll have mighty bedlam on your hands if you don't get those weeds out," warned his neighbor.

"Actually, that's my crop," replied Wesley. "In this type of garden there are no weeds."

Following ancient tradition, Wesley's fellow gardeners grew tomatoes, beans, Brussels sprouts, and nothing else. Wesley found it thrilling to open his land to chance, to invite the new and unknown.

The plants shot up past his knees, then his waist. They seemed to be all of the same sort. Wesley couldn't find them in any plant book.

"Are those tomatoes, beans, or Brussels sprouts?" asked Wesley's neighbor.

"None of the above," replied Wesley.

Fruit appeared, yellow at first, then blushing to magenta. Wesley picked one and sliced through the rind to the juicy purple center. He took a bite and found the taste an entrancing blend of peach, strawberry, pumpkin pie, and flavors he had no name for.

Ignoring the shelf of cereals in the kitchen, Wesley took to breakfasting on the fruit. He dried half a rind to serve as a cup, built his own squeezing device, and drank the fruit's juice throughout the day.

Pulling up a plant, he found large tubers on the roots. These he boiled, fried, or roasted on the family barbecue, seasoning them with a pinch of the plant's highly aromatic leaves.

It was hot work tending to his crop. To keep off the sun, Wesley wove himself a hat from strips of the plant's woody bark. His success with the hat inspired him to **devise** a spinning wheel and loom on which he wove a loose-fitting robe from the stalks' soft inner fibers.

Unlike jeans, which he found scratchy and heavy, the robe was comfortable, reflected the sun, and offered myriad opportunities for pockets.

His schoolmates were scornful, then curious. Grudgingly, Wesley allowed them ten minutes apiece at his mortar, crushing the plant's seeds to collect the oil.

This oil had a tangy scent and served him both as suntan lotion and mosquito repellent. He rubbed it on his face each morning and sold small amounts to his former tormentors at the price of ten dollars per bottle.

STOP AND CHECK

Summarize How does Wesley use the plants he grows? Summarize his actions to check your understanding.

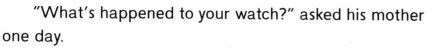

"What's happened to your watch?" asked his mother one day.

Wesley admitted that he no longer wore it. He told time by the stalk that he used as a sundial and had divided the day into eight segments—the number of petals on the plant's flowers.

He'd adopted a new counting system as well, based likewise upon the number eight. His domain, home to many such innovations, he named "Weslandia."

Uninterested in traditional sports, Wesley made up his own. These were designed for a single player and used many different parts of the plant. His spectators looked on with envy.

Realizing that more players would offer him more scope, Wesley invented other games that would include his schoolmates, games rich with strategy and **complex** scoring systems. He tried to be patient with the other players' blunders.

August was unusually hot. Wesley built himself a platform and took to sleeping in the middle of Weslandia. He passed the evenings playing a flute he'd **fashioned** from a stalk or gazing up at the sky, renaming the constellations.

STOP AND CHECK

Make Predictions How will Wesley's schoolmates treat him when they go back to school? Use the strategy Make Predictions to help you.

His parents noted Wesley's improved morale. "It's the first time in years he's looked happy," said his mother.

Wesley gave them a tour of Weslandia.

"What do you call this plant?" asked his father. Not knowing its name, Wesley had begun calling it "swist," from the sound of its leaves rustling in the breeze.

In like manner, he'd named his new fabrics, games, and foods, until he'd created an entire language.

Mixing the plant's oil with soot, Wesley made a passable ink. As the finale to his summer project, he used the ink and his own eighty-letter alphabet to record the history of his civilization's founding.

In September Wesley returned to school . . .

He had no **shortage** of friends.

About the Author and Illustrator

Paul Fleischman, like Wesley in *Weslandia*, created his own world while he was growing up in California. Paul and his friends invented their own sports and ran an underground newspaper. Paul's vivid imagination comes from his father, Sid Fleischman, who also wrote books. Often he would ask Paul to help him with the plot of a story. Words and imagination come naturally to Paul. "They were as much fun to play with as toys," he said.

Kevin Hawkes says he learned how to draw by practicing, practicing, and practicing some more. As a child he drew pictures and used modeling clay and other materials to create sculptures. Today Kevin uses his talents to bring stories like *Weslandia* to life. When he begins illustrating a book, he makes a "dummy" book first. The sketches help him create the final illustrations.

Author's Purpose

In *Weslandia*, the author describes a made-up world. How does the author help you picture this world?

Respond to the Text

Summarize

Use the events on your Theme Chart to help you summarize *Weslandia*. In your summary include details that show how Wesley used what he learned about nature.

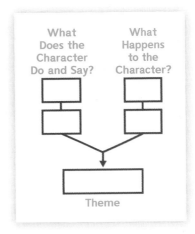

What Does the Character Do and Say?

What Happens to the Character?

Theme

Write

Think about how the author structures the events in the story. How do Wesley's creativity, imagination, and ability stay true to who he is help his family and schoolmates see him in a new light? Use these sentence frames to organize text evidence.

> The author organizes the story . . .
> He uses dialogue to . . .
> This shows me how Wesley . . .

Make Connections

Talk about how Wesley uses what he learns about nature to help him create Weslandia.
ESSENTIAL QUESTION

Tell the most interesting invention or activity Wesley created from his plants. How is this invention or activity similar to one in our world? **TEXT TO WORLD**

Compare Texts
Read about the many ways people use plants.

PLANTS WITH A PURPOSE

Most living things, including humans, depend on plants for survival. Trees and other plants provide necessities, such as oxygen, food, shelter, and medicine. However, plants can provide us with much more than these basic needs. Over time, people across the world have learned to use plants in new and innovative ways.

One Plant, Many Uses

Some **resourceful** people have found numerous ways to use a plant that grows well in their region. Bamboo, for example, is a type of plant originally from tropical parts of the world. Bamboo can grow quickly and closely together. This makes it a useful crop. People can cook and eat bamboo shoots. Yet bamboo in its raw form is a very strong building material. It is used to construct fences, bridges, and homes. People can use it to weave baskets and mats. They have even developed a process to soften bamboo to make cloth.

Corn, a plant from the western hemisphere, has a variety of uses too. Corn is a staple food crop and used to feed livestock. Additionally, it is made into fuel, plastic, and textiles.

Bamboo has a tough outer bark that can be cut into thin strips and used to weave baskets and mats.

(bkgd) FrÃ©dÃ©ric Soreau/Photononstop/Getty Images; (b) Dinodia Photos/Alamy

The rubber used to make erasers is based on a natural substance—the sap of the tropical rubber tree.

Plants Inspire Invention

Plants have also been used as models to make new materials. For example, rubber is a manufactured material that is based on a substance that comes from a tree. The rubber tree oozes a sap that can be processed to make it very durable and flexible. By studying the plant's sap, scientists figured out a way to make rubber on their own. About 70% of all rubber used today is now made by humans. But without these unique trees, we might never have created this useful material.

Replacing What We Use

We **cultivate** plants to meet many different needs. So it is important that we do not use them up or overuse the land on which they are grown. Plants that are harvested should be replaced. Crops should be rotated so that nutrients in the soil that are used up can be restored. By following these practices, we ensure the survival of living things and provide opportunities for more innovative uses.

Make Connections

How can learning about plants be useful? ESSENTIAL QUESTION

What other uses of plants have you read about? How is the use of a plant in this selection different? TEXT TO TEXT

THE STORY OF
SNOW

The Science of Winter's Wonder

by Mark Cassino with Jon Nelson

illustrations by Nora Aoyagi

Essential Question

Where can you find patterns in nature?

Read about how patterns in snow crystals form.

Go Digital!

Our story starts on a winter day,
high up in the sky,
in a cloud that is
very, very cold.

This is the story of snow.

Clouds are mostly made of air, which we can't see.
Then there is water vapor (water in the form of a
gas), which we also can't see. We do see the billions
of tiny droplets of liquid water and ice crystals that
float in the cloud. They reflect light, making the
cloud **visible**.

Snow begins with a speck.

Clouds are mostly made of air and water, but there are also bits of other things, like tiny **particles** of dirt, ash, and salt. Even living bacteria can float in the wind and end up in a cloud. A snow crystal needs one of these "specks" to start growing. These specks are all much smaller than the eye can see. But if you could see them...

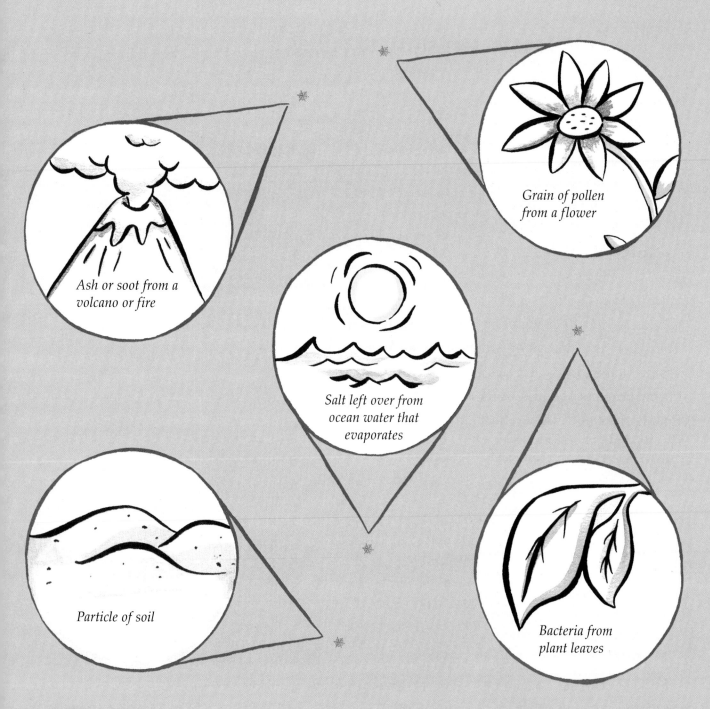

Ash or soot from a volcano or fire

Grain of pollen from a flower

Salt left over from ocean water that evaporates

Particle of soil

Bacteria from plant leaves

The speck becomes the center of a snow crystal.

When a speck gets cold enough, water vapor will stick to it. If you had a microscope that could see such small things, here is what you would see...

Water vapor sticks to the cold speck, making the speck wet.

More water vapor sticks to the wet speck, forming a water droplet.

The droplet freezes into a ball of ice.

More water vapor sticks to the ball of ice, and it grows into a hexagon-shaped ice crystal.

Water vapor continues to stick to the crystal. Faster growth on the corners causes six branches to sprout.

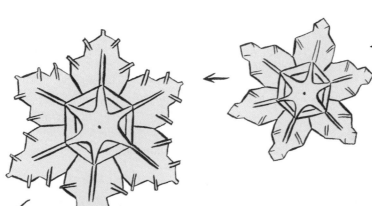

The branches keep growing, sprouting little arms of their own...

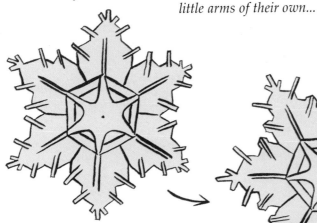

...and a beautiful snow crystal is born!

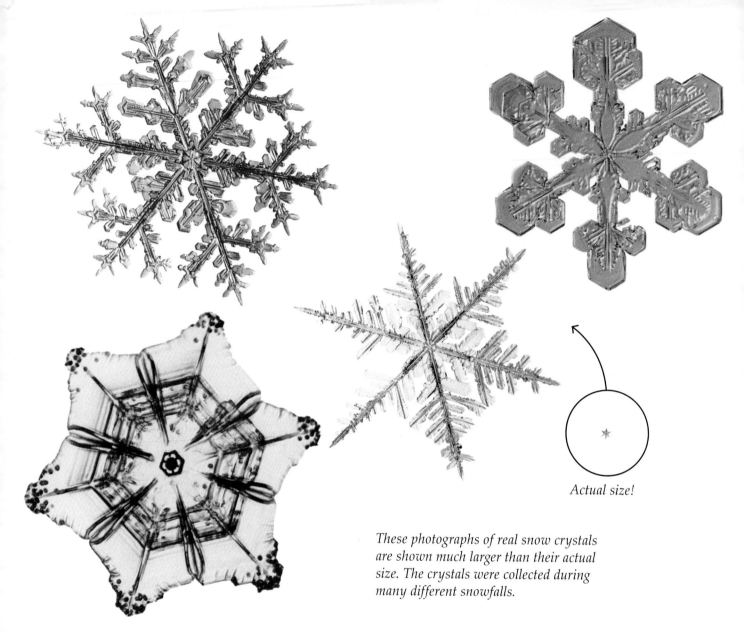

These photographs of real snow crystals are shown much larger than their actual size. The crystals were collected during many different snowfalls.

Actual size!

As the snow crystal gets bigger and heavier, it starts to fall to earth. It keeps growing as it falls through its cloud, taking on its own special shape. The shape depends on how *wet* the cloud is and how *cold* it is. A snow crystal can start to grow one way, but then grow another way when it passes through a wetter or colder part of its cloud. The crystal stops growing soon after falling below the clouds.

STOP AND CHECK

Ask and Answer Questions How does a snow crystal take shape? Go back to the text to find details that support your answer.

Snow crystals can be stars.

One common snow crystal shape is the star. Star-shaped snow crystals usually have six arms reaching out from a center point. The center point is the home of the speck that started the crystal. The six arms look alike, but they are almost never *exactly* alike.

Parts of a snow crystal can break during the fall to earth, causing the arms to look different.

Star-shaped snow crystals are called dendrites *(which means "tree-like shapes"). They form when a cloud is full of* **moisture***, and when the temperature hovers around 5 degrees Fahrenheit (-15 degrees Celsius).*

Snow crystals can be plates.

Plate crystals are thin like star crystals, but they don't have arms. The simplest kind of plate is a hexagon with six straight sides. More complicated plates have points where arms almost grew.

This is the simplest kind of plate crystal, a hexagon. Plates form when there's not enough moisture in the cloud for stars to form, and when the temperature conditions are a few degrees warmer or colder than the temperature range that stars require.

The points on this plate crystal are the beginnings of arms that were just starting to develop when the crystal fell out of its cloud and stopped growing.

Snow crystals can also be columns.

Column-shaped snow crystals are shaped like pencils. They're
not flat like stars and plates. Columns can form high in the
clouds and at very cold temperatures. They are *very* tiny, and
when they fall, they make for very slippery snow.

A column has six sides. These are the three types:

Solid column
*These are the smallest
type of column.*

Hollow column
*These are longer and
more common than
solid columns.*

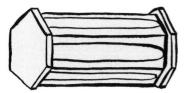

Capped column
*The caps on each end of
these columns can be plate
crystals or star crystals.*

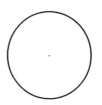

← *Actual size!*
*Column crystals are
very tiny, usually no
longer than half a
millimeter!*

Capped columns like this
one develop when a column
crystal moves into a part
of its cloud where the
temperature is right for
plates or stars to grow at
the ends. The two end caps
can grow to different sizes,
as you can see here.

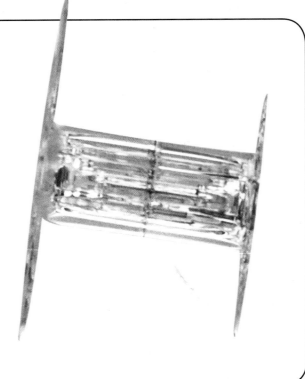

STOP AND CHECK

Ask and Answer Questions How are
hollow column crystals different from
other types of column crystals? Use the
diagrams and text to find the answer.

6 is the magic number for snow crystals.

This is because of the nature of water. Water molecules (the smallest units of water) attach themselves into groups of six, which usually leads to crystals with six arms or six sides.

A perfect star or plate snow crystal has six-fold symmetry. That means, if you divided the crystal into six pie wedges, each pie wedge would have the same shape.

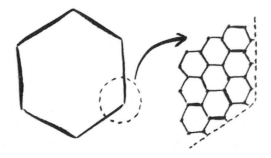

Water molecules attach to each other in six-sided rings, like six kids holding hands. When many of these hexagonal rings are joined together, a larger hexagonal crystal is formed.

So much can happen during a snow crystal's fall to earth, it is rare that one will turn out perfectly. If a droplet of water passes close to one arm of a snow crystal, that arm can start to grow faster. Before long, that one arm will be a lot longer than the others!

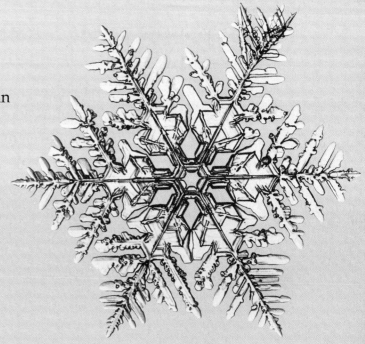

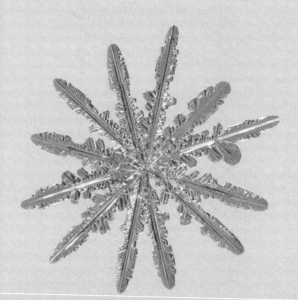

A snow crystal can be a twin!

A snow crystal can have twelve arms. This is a twin crystal, which happens when two crystals start from the original speck and form on top of each other.

A snow crystal can have bumps!

If there are enough water droplets near the crystal, some can strike the crystal and freeze on **contact**. This gives the crystal little bumps called rime.

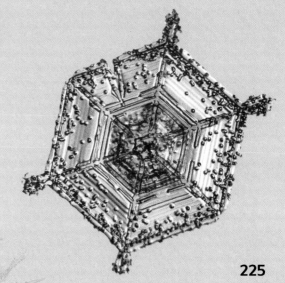

225

Many snow crystals make one snowflake.

Often, snow crystals bump into each other and get stuck together. When this happens, snowflakes form. Hundreds or even thousands of snow crystals can be found in a single snowflake.

Two snow crystals stuck together.

Snowflakes we see falling from the sky are usually clumps of snow crystals like these. Individual crystals (which are sometimes also called "snowflakes") can fall on their own, but they are much smaller and harder to see.

Snow crystals can't keep growing after they fall from the clouds. And when a crystal stops growing, it immediately starts to wither. Soon, the arms of the crystal break down and the crystal's shape becomes rounded. This means that if you want to see a snow crystal, you need to catch it in the air, or find it very soon after it lands.

*When they're not in the clouds, surrounded by the water vapor they need to grow, snow crystals quickly start to **erode**. Try catching one on your sleeve or glove to see the crystal **structure** at its best.*

STOP AND CHECK

Summarize How does a snow crystal change after it falls from a cloud? Use the strategy Summarize to help you.

Are no two snow crystals alike?

Some simple plate crystals may appear exactly alike, as seen through a high-quality microscope. When it comes to more complicated snow crystals though, odds are that no two are exactly alike. But then, no two leaves, flowers, or people are exactly alike, either! Snow crystals are like us—we're each different, but we have a lot in common.

About the Authors and Illustrator

Mark Cassino is a fine art and natural history photographer. He first became interested in snow crystals when he noticed them land on his windshield as he was driving. Before long, he was photographing individual crystals to show these tiny structures close up.

Jon Nelson is a teacher and physicist who has studied clouds and snow crystals for over 15 years. He has many opportunities to observe them because he likes exploring outdoors, including rock climbing and taking walks on icy mornings.

Nora Aoyagi loves drawing interesting creatures from well-known folk stories. Here, she uses her techniques to help illustrate the story of snow. Nora works in many different mediums, including painting, printmaking, and drawing.

Authors' Purpose Why do the authors use so many different images of snow crystals to illustrate their text?

Respond to the Text

Summarize

Use the most important details from *The Story of Snow* to summarize what you learned about patterns in snow crystals. Use details from your Main Idea and Key Details Chart.

Main Idea
Detail
Detail
Detail

Write

How does the way Mark Cassino presents information help you understand snow crystals? Use these sentence frames to organize text evidence.

> Mark Cassino organizes information by . . .
> He uses text features to . . .
> This helps me understand. . .

Make Connections

Talk about patterns you can find in snow crystals. **ESSENTIAL QUESTION**

How do photographs of snow crystals reveal patterns? What can people learn by finding patterns in nature? **TEXT TO WORLD**

(clockwise from top) realeoni/Flickr/Getty Images; Stockbroker xtra/age fotostock; Darlyne A. Murawski/National Geographic/Getty Images; Dinodia Photo RF/age fotostock; Ted Morrison/Botanica/Getty Images

Compare Texts

Read about a series of numbers that can be found in nature.

FIBONACCI'S
AMAZING FIND

What do the numbers 1, 1, 2, 3, 5, 8, 13, 21, and 34 have in common? These are the first numbers in the Fibonacci sequence, a series of numbers calculated over 800 years ago by a mathematician named Fibonacci. But that's not all they have in common. These numbers also can be found in nature. They can be found, for example, in the number of petals of flowers.

Numbers from the Fibonacci sequence can be found in the numbers of petals of many flowers.

Black-eyed Susan: 13 petals

Field Daisy: 34 petals

Buttercup: 5 petals

Iris: 3 petals

The Origin of Our Number System

Fibonacci was born in the late 12th century in the Italian town of Pisa. As a teenager, Fibonacci moved to live with his father in North Africa.

At the time, most Europeans used the abacus to do their calculations. They would write their answers in Roman numerals. In North Africa, Fibonacci learned about a different numbering system. It used Hindu-Arabic numbers such as 1, 2, 3, and 4. To share what he had learned, Fibonacci wrote a book that helped spread the use of the Hindu-Arabic numbers throughout Europe. This is the numbering system we use today.

Fibonacci is now considered one of the most important mathematicians of his era. One reason is his creation of the Fibonacci sequence.

A Pattern of Numbers

It all started with a number problem—about rabbits! Fibonacci wondered how a population of rabbits would grow if each month a pair of rabbits produced two baby rabbits. He calculated the number of pairs of rabbits there would be each month. The result was a series of numbers: 1, 1, 2, 3, 5, 8, 13, 21, and so on. He noticed that each number in the series was the sum of the two numbers that came before it (1+1=2; 1+2=3; 2+3=5; 3+5=8). He recorded this sequence in one of his books.

An abacus is a frame that has beads that slide on wires or in grooves. It was once widely used to do arithmetic.

Centuries later, people noticed these numbers in nature. Naturalists found that the growth pattern of some living things reflected Fibonacci numbers. For example, the chambered nautilus, a type of marine animal, adds a new chamber to its shell as it grows. Each additional chamber is the same shape as the previous one, but larger in size. This maintains the shell's overall shape. The diagram and directions below illustrate how this type of growth can produce a pattern that reflects the Fibonacci sequence.

On graph paper, draw a square with a side length of 1. Add another square with side length of 1 next to it. Then add a square above that has a side length equal to the sum of the side lengths of the two preceding squares (2). Add on three more squares using the same process, moving in a counterclockwise direction. Each square will have a side length that is a Fibonacci number. An arc drawn from the first square counterclockwise through the squares produces a spiral.

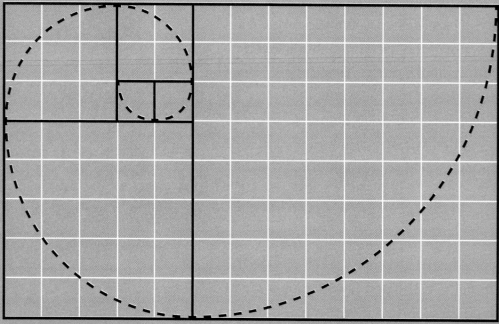

The cross-section of a chambered nautilus shell reveals a **repetition** of curves and a spiral shape.

In Curves and Clusters

The spiral appears in many natural objects from seashells to clusters of seeds in flower heads. Leaves on some trees grow in a spiral. Pinecones and pineapples show a spiral **formation**. No one knows for sure why the spiral appears so often, but it seems to allow many seeds to grow in a small area and allow sunshine to reach most of the leaves on a plant or tree.

Fibonacci's amazing find led others to discover a surprising pattern throughout the natural world. When you look around, you, too, may recognize numbers from the Fibonacci sequence.

Spirals on a pinecone

Spirals of seeds in the head of a sunflower

Fern fronds unfold in the shape of a spiral.

Make Connections

Where can you find patterns in nature that reflect the Fibonacci sequence? ESSENTIAL QUESTION

How are patterns that reflect the Fibonacci sequence different from other patterns found in nature? TEXT TO TEXT

Essential Question
What benefits come from people working as a group?

Read about how a group of people worked together to help an animal in need.

Go Digital!

Winter's Tail

How One Little Dolphin Learned to Swim Again

told by **Juliana, Isabella,** and **Craig Hatkoff**

One cold winter morning, just off the east coast of Florida, a baby female dolphin managed to get tangled up in a crab trap. In the effort to free herself, the dolphin caused the ropes securing the crab trap to the buoy to become wrapped around her tail. The more she struggled, the tighter the ropes became, quickly strangling her tail. Luckily, a nearby fisherman caught a glimpse of this unusual situation and came to set the little dolphin free. It was not clear she would survive. And even if she did survive, how would a dolphin manage without a tail? How would she swim? How would she thrive?

Life without her tail would cause many challenges, but with the help and care of a great number of **dedicated** people, a dolphin named Winter would beat the odds. In return, Winter's story would inspire and warm the hearts of people all over the world.

From WINTER'S TAIL: HOW ONE LITTLE DOLPHIN LEARNED TO SWIM AGAIN by Juliana Hatkoff et al. Scholastic Inc./Scholastic Press, map by Jim McMahon. Copyright © 2009 by Turtle Pond Publications LLC. Reprinted by permission.

A badly injured Winter in Mosquito Lagoon shortly after being freed.

December 10, 2005, was a chilly Saturday. Jim Savage was the only fisherman braving the bitter wind in Mosquito Lagoon that morning. As Jim steered his boat in the dim light, he noticed a line of crab traps rigged just beneath the water's surface. One trap seemed to be going in a direction opposite from the others. Something was pulling it against the strong wind. Jim idled his boat and steered slowly toward the trap. Even before he could see anything, he heard a harsh, rasping sound over the sound of the waves. When he searched the murky water, Jim found a baby dolphin gasping for breath. She was caught. A rope from the trap was wrapped tightly around both her mouth and tail.

The dolphin was so tangled in the rope that her small body was curled like a horseshoe, her mouth pulled close to her tail. Jim spoke to her, assuring her that he was there to help. He knew he needed to free her head first so she could raise her blowhole out of the water and breathe normally. The dolphin struggled as Jim used his fish-cleaning knife to cut the line that tied her mouth and tail together.

Several minutes later, Jim pulled off the last of the rope, and the young dolphin swam away from the boat. She kept her distance from the fisherman, but she did not leave the lagoon. After thirty minutes, Jim understood that she was too exhausted, too injured. He called Florida's Fish and Wildlife Conservation Commission. The workers there would know how to take care of a wounded dolphin.

Jim watched over the dolphin until the rescue team arrived a few hours later. As soon as they saw the cuts around the dolphin's tail, they knew they would need to move her somewhere safe so she could heal.

Even though she was injured, the dolphin was not easy to catch. But they finally corralled her. After lifting her from the lagoon, the rescue team tried to help her relax before carrying her to the transport van. They had a long drive ahead of them, all the way across Florida to the Clearwater Marine Aquarium.

Teresa, from the Hubbs-SeaWorld Research Institute, tries to keep a shivering, injured Winter warm and calm.

A small, anxious crowd awaited the dolphin's arrival at the aquarium. The group included a veterinarian, dolphin trainers, and volunteers. When the van pulled up, they were all ready to help. It had not been an easy journey. The dolphin had been out of the water for more than three hours. On top of that, the night air was cold. It was so chilly that the group decided to name the dolphin Winter.

The rescue workers carefully moved Winter to a holding tank. Abby, the head dolphin trainer, stood alongside Winter in the tank. Immediately, the veterinarian evaluated Winter's health. It was clear the little dolphin was badly injured. The vet estimated that Winter was only two or three months old. In the wild, baby dolphins drink their mother's milk until they are about two years old. Winter was so young that she would not know how to eat a fish if they offered it to her. But she needed food. The only choice was to gently insert a special feeding tube down her throat. Winter was probably still scared from her ordeal so, although the tube did not hurt, she continued to struggle.

Abby and the rest of the aquarium staff knew, however, that it was good that Winter was struggling—it showed she still had the heart and energy to try to protect herself.

It would take time for Winter to accept help from all of the many people who were making it possible for her to survive.

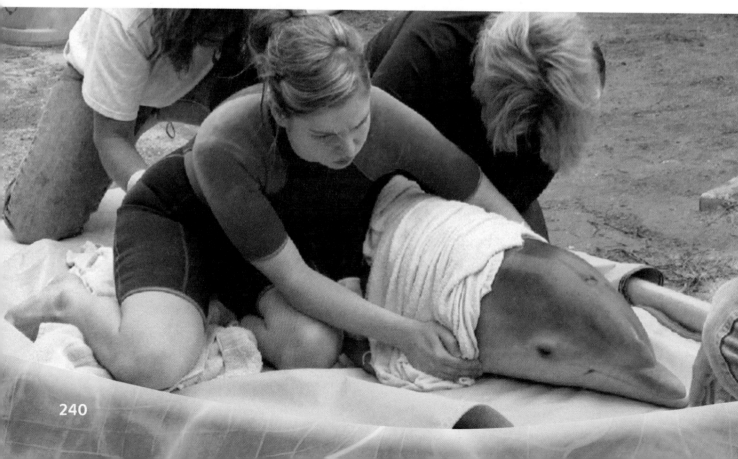

A volunteer coaxes Winter to drink from a bottle.

Clearwater Marine Aquarium

On Winter's second day at the aquarium, Abby showed her a bottle. The bottle contained a milk formula developed for zoo animals. At first, Winter did not know what the bottle was for. It took her a week to get the hang of drinking from it, and then the staff no longer needed to feed her with the tube. Each day, they weighed Winter. She started to gain weight. It was a good sign.

Winter was still very sick. The rope from the trap had been wrapped so tightly around her tail that it had stopped the blood flow. Pieces of her tail were starting to flake off, little by little.

Nonetheless, by the end of the week, Abby and the other trainers no longer felt they had to support Winter in the water. They encouraged her to swim on her own. And then, just as everyone feared, Winter lost her tail. What was left was a fleshy stump that would heal over time.

Would Winter be able to swim without her tail?

STOP AND CHECK

Ask and Answer Questions How did the aquarium trainers help Winter? Go back to the text to find the answer.

241

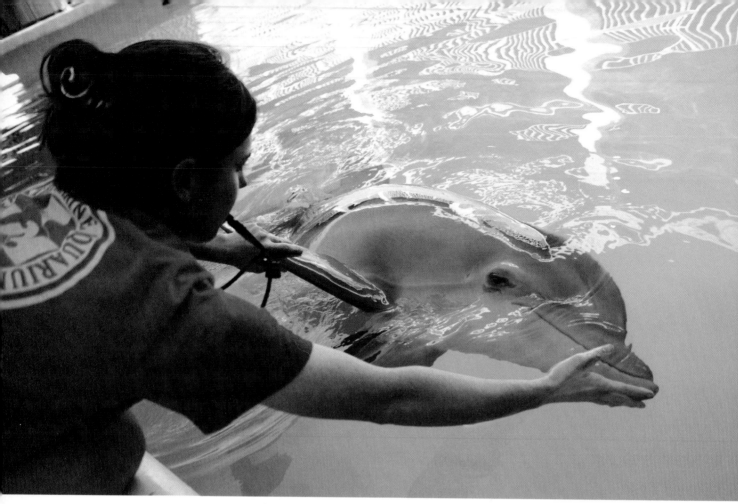

Winter and Abby enjoy their training sessions together.

Winter did start to swim on her own, but she did not swim like other dolphins. Her tail stump swished from side to side, more like the motion of a fish or a shark than the up-and-down tail action of a dolphin. Still, it was amazing! Winter had taught herself an entirely new way to swim! Her trainers were impressed, but they were also concerned that she might damage her backbone by swimming the wrong way.

Although Winter's tail had fallen off, the wound had healed. She was getting used to her new home and her handlers. Whenever someone arrived next to her pool with a bottle, she gave a cheery welcome of clicks and whistles. By the time Winter was about five months old, she began daily training sessions with her handlers. They used training **techniques** similar to those used with the aquarium's other dolphins, and she learned to listen to their signals. Winter was a quick and enthusiastic learner.

Winter had learned to trust the people who cared for her, but she had not seen another dolphin since arriving at the aquarium. Now it was time to meet a new friend. The trainers decided to introduce Winter to Panama, a female dolphin who had been rescued as well. The trainers were not sure how Winter would react to Panama—or how Panama would react to Winter. Would Panama even recognize Winter as a dolphin?

When they first brought Winter to the new tank, Panama kept her distance. Winter stayed by the edge, where she felt safest, and watched the older dolphin swim laps around the pool. But Winter got tired of waiting. If she wanted to make a friend, it was clear she would have to make it happen. Now, whenever Panama passed, Winter swam out to greet her. Panama tried to ignore Winter, but Winter was unfazed. She kept playfully approaching Panama. Finally, after three long days, Panama gave up. She stopped trying to swim away from Winter, and the two dolphins have been together ever since.

Panama lets Winter trail just behind her, the way baby dolphins follow their mothers.

Turtle Pond Publications

When Winter was about a year old, NBC's *The Today Show* broadcast a story about her on television. Now the word was out. Winter was famous. People started to come in droves to visit her at the Clearwater Marine Aquarium. The charming young dolphin also started to receive letters from her new fans, including many people who knew someone who had, or had themselves, lost or been born without a limb or had other disabilities. Everyone could relate to Winter.

Winter seemed to be able to overcome any **obstacle**. While her vets and trainers were happy that Winter was adjusting to her new life, they knew she was about to face her biggest challenge. Months of swimming from side to side had taken their toll. Abby helped Winter do special poolside exercises, but Winter's muscles were not as **flexible** and developed as they should have been. Winter needed to be able to swim like a dolphin again.

Luckily, Kevin Carroll heard about Winter on the radio and contacted the aquarium. Kevin was not only a dolphin lover, he was also a premier creator of prostheses—special devices that can help replace a body part such as an arm or a leg. Kevin believed he could help.

Winter helps others understand what it means to have a disability and how people can adapt to almost any circumstance.

(t) Turtle Pond Publications, (b) Yago Veith/Flickr/Getty Images

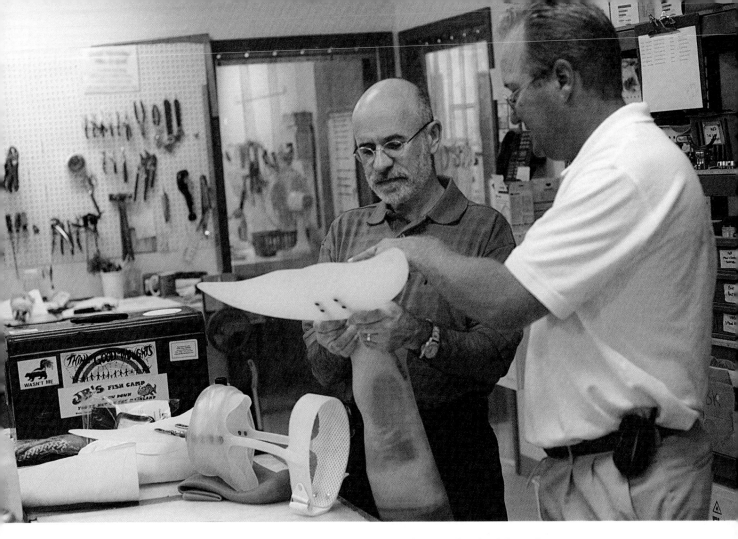

Kevin Carroll (left) and his team face many challenges in devising the perfect tail for Winter.

(t) Turtle Pond Publications

Being a dolphin, Winter was a special case. Not only would her prosthesis have to work in the water, it would also have to handle the force of each thrust of her tail. A team of experts—including Kevin Carroll, vets, dolphin trainers, and marine mammal researchers—came together to help make Winter's new tail a reality.

Everyone shared ideas about how to create the best prosthesis for Winter. It was something that had never been done before, and there were many obstacles. The first was the fit. Winter did not have a tail joint or any other place for a prosthesis to attach to her body. In addition, dolphins have especially sensitive skin. The team would need to figure out how to connect the tail without causing irritation or discomfort to Winter. The second concern was the tail's **function**. They needed a design that would **mimic** the up-and-down movement of a swimming dolphin.

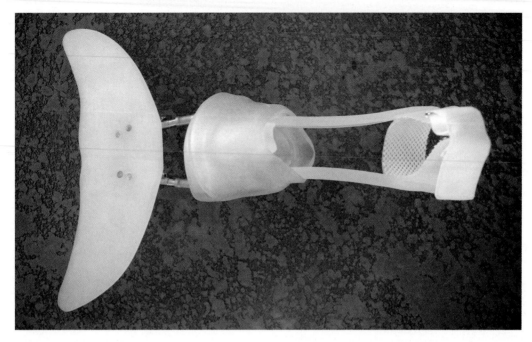

(t) Turtle Pond Publications; (b) Yago Veith/Flickr/Getty Images

Winter's special tail

Finally, there was a concern for Winter herself. How would she react to wearing the tail? Abby and the other trainers worked tirelessly, preparing Winter. First they needed to help Winter get used to the feel of wearing a prosthesis. Then they could teach her how to swim with her own prosthetic tail.

The development team quickly realized they would have to create a sleeve designed specifically to fit Winter. They made a mold of her peduncle so the new sleeve would be a perfect fit. Then Kevin Carroll went one step further. He created a special silicone gel that would be smooth against Winter's skin and would add a cushion to make the prosthesis more comfortable for Winter to wear.

It took several months and several designs for the team to develop a prosthetic sleeve and a tail that matched the natural motion of an actual dolphin tail. They ended up with a unique design. There would be two sleeves. The main silicone sleeve would fit right on Winter's peduncle. A second sleeve would fit on top of the first and would hold the tail and its brace in place.

STOP AND CHECK

Ask and Answer Questions How is Winter's prosthetic tail unique? Find details that support your answer.

Abby spent many hours training Winter how to move her body while wearing the prosthetic tail. Abby needed Winter to understand that, when she was wearing the prosthesis, it was a signal for her to swim by using her tail, not her fins, to move herself forward.

Winter seems to like her new tail. She will sometimes swim in circles, chasing it, or show off by swimming right past Panama and flicking her tail in her friend's face. Some days, she doesn't want her trainers to take it off!

Winter now wears her tail every day for a short period of time. A trainer is always close by to keep an eye on her. The goal is for Winter to eventually wear the prosthesis a few hours every day, which will be enough to keep her backbone healthy and her body flexible. Even after Winter's first brief outings with the new tail, her trainers could already see an improvement.

Turtle Pond Publications

Winter adjusts like a pro and learns to swim with her new tail.

Winter had a big party on her third birthday, complete with a cake and candles. Many people came to help her celebrate, and she seemed happy to see them all.

We cannot know what Winter is really thinking, but her trainers admit that she seems to have a special understanding with the people who visit her. The people feel a connection to her as well. From children who have prostheses, to veterans who lost a limb fighting in a war, to one little girl who didn't want to wear a hearing aid until she met Winter, people see how Winter has learned to adapt and are inspired by her story.

With the help of Kevin Carroll, Winter is also sharing her prosthetic technology. After creating the silicone gel for her sleeve, Kevin realized that the same material that made it more comfortable for Winter to wear her prosthetic tail could help people who wear prostheses, too. Kevin put the gel to the test on a veteran of the Iraq war who was having difficulty with his **artificial** legs. The silicone gel created an extra cushion that helped reduce the veteran's discomfort. It was a big breakthrough, making life a little easier for people needing prostheses.

Special guests present Winter with her birthday cake!

Winter may have lost her family, her home, and eventually her tail, but she found a new home and family at the Clearwater Marine Aquarium. She found Panama, Abby, and the vets, trainers, and volunteers who take care of her on a daily basis. With the help of all of these people, she also has a new tail. Through these changes, one thing has stayed the same: Winter's uplifting spirit and her resilience have helped her adjust and make the most of every situation.

And her story is far from over. She is still learning all of the things she can do with her special tail, and her trainers and prosthetic designers are still learning how they can help her even more. Every step of the way, they will need to be open to new ideas and be willing to try different solutions. Their shared goal is to help Winter live a long, healthy, and happy life.

As for Winter, she seems ready for any new challenge. As champion, inspiration, and friend, Winter is one little dolphin who gives people hope and shows us that anything is possible.

Turtle Pond Publications

STOP AND CHECK

Summarize How has Winter affected the lives of others? The strategy Summarize may help you.

About the Authors

Juliana, Isabella, and Craig Hatkoff

are a family of authors. Their story began when Juliana Hatkoff was nearly five years old and about to have her tonsils removed. Her father, Craig Hatkoff, suggested that they research the procedure and write about it in a notebook. Soon the Hatkoffs had their first book, *Good-Bye Tonsils!* Later, Juliana's younger sister, Isabella, read a newspaper article about a rescued baby hippo who became close friends with an old tortoise. Isabella thought the story of the hippo and the tortoise would make a good book, too. She was right!

Since then, writing books has become a team activity for this New York City family. Most of their books focus on animals that face difficult circumstances. Dad and daughters work together to do research and craft their stories. The family hopes that books like these will help others find the strength to get through tough times.

Authors' Purpose

The Hatkoffs like to write about special animals that inspire. How do the authors show that Winter is special? Give examples from the text that support this point.

Respond to the Text

Summarize

Use important events from *Winter's Tail* to summarize how groups of people worked together to help a dolphin. Information from your Main Idea and Key Details Chart may help you.

Main Idea
Detail
Detail
Detail

Write

How do the authors help you understand how many people have been inspired by Winter's story? Use these sentence frames to organize text evidence:

The authors show that the aquarium staff . . .
They tell about people who . . .
This helps me understand how Winter . . .

Make Connections

Talk about how groups of people working together helped Winter swim again. ESSENTIAL QUESTION

Trainers and experts worked together to help Winter. What other groups work to help animals? What are the benefits of people working as a group? TEXT TO WORLD

Compare Texts

Read about how a group of girls created an award-winning prosthetic device.

Helping Hands

Once upon a time, six flying monkeys sat in a big, old fir tree and plotted ways to make a little girl's life a whole lot better. "The Flying Monkeys" is the team name for a group of six Girl Scouts who joined together from different troops to enter a competition. These young inventors proposed a new prosthetic device to help people write.

Courtesy Flying Monkeys

The Flying Monkeys, from left to right: Zoe Groat, 12; Kate Murray, 13; Maria Werner Anderson, 12; Gaby Dempsey, 12; Mackenzie Grewell, 12; Courtney Pohlen, 12.

A Need Inspires

The rules of the competition asked participants to come up with new and innovative ways to help heal, repair or improve the human body. One of the group members, Kate Murray, understood the difficulties people with an injury or impairment can face. Kate was born with a left hand that was not fully formed. But that didn't stop Kate from taking part in activities. When she decided she wanted to learn how to play the violin, she and her mother worked with a team of specialists to create a device to allow her to hold a bow.

The Flying Monkeys wondered if they could create something similar for the competition. When one of their Girl Scouts coaches learned about Danielle Fairchild, a three-year-old who was born without fingers on her right hand, the Flying Monkeys found their inspiration.

Doing the Research

The Flying Monkeys focused on creating a device that would allow Danielle to write with her right hand. But because Danielle lived in Georgia and the girls lived in Iowa, they couldn't work with her directly. What they could do, however, was figure out a way to make a device that would attach a pen or pencil to Danielle's hand.

Soon enough, the girls realized that they would need to **collaborate** with experts. Their coaches helped them make contacts. They talked to people who had physical impairments as well as medical experts who created and made prosthetic devices. Old ideas were cast aside, and new ideas began to take shape. The girls made models and tested them before creating their initial prototypes, the first series of creations.

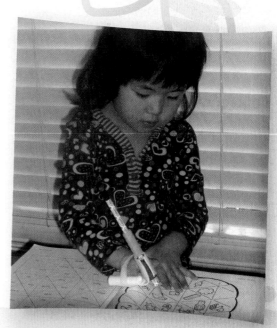

The Flying Monkeys designed a device to help Danielle Fairchild write with her right hand.

Courtesy Dale Fairchild

253

Introducing the BOB-1

Before long, the Flying Monkeys settled on a final design for their invention, which they called the BOB-1. They used a **flexible** plastic substance, a pencil grip, and hook-and-eye closures to build it. Everyone involved was impressed by how well the device would fit on Danielle's hand. What's more, it was very simple and inexpensive to make. Why hadn't anyone thought of creating a device like this before?

The Flying Monkeys created fliers, a portfolio, and even a skit to take to the competition and showcase their invention. The competition judges were impressed.

The Flying Monkeys won a regional and state-level innovation award. From there, it was on to the global round of the contest, where the BOB-1 would be judged alongside 178 other entries from 16 countries. The winning team would receive $20,000 to further develop the product.

Danielle Fairchild uses the BOB-1.

The Flying Monkeys had the chance to meet Danielle at the award ceremony in Washington, D.C.

People from around the world voted online for the project they thought was best and a panel of judges reviewed the top projects. After the **dedicated** team had spent nearly 200 hours developing the BOB-1, the Flying Monkeys were invited to attend the final awards ceremony in Washington, D.C. Their hard work paid off. They won the grand prize!

The best part of their adventure, however, came when the girls finally met Danielle Fairchild in person. Danielle showed the girls how she used the BOB-1 to draw and color with her right hand. The device was a success!

The Flying Monkeys have already revised the BOB-1. They hope to use the prize money to receive a full patent and make the device available to others who might benefit from it. Having more people test the device may even lead to further improvements. When it comes to helping others, these creative young girls aren't just monkeying around!

Make Connections

How did working with others help the girls create an invention? ESSENTIAL QUESTION

How is the Flying Monkeys' work similar to another group's work you've read about? What was the purpose of each effort? TEXT TO TEXT

Machu Picchu: Ancient City

Essential Question

How do we explain what happened in the past?

Read two different views about a past civilization.

Go Digital!

Machu Picchu sits on the side of a high ridge in the Andes Mountains of Peru.

The Royal Treatment
Machu Picchu was a royal estate.

Machu Picchu (pronounced MA-choo PEEK-choo) was a city that was part of the ancient Inca empire, a civilization which once ruled much of western South America. Machu Picchu was built during the reign of the emperor Pachacuti. It was abandoned in the early 1500s. Machu Picchu was found in 1911 by an American **historian** named Hiram Bingham. He came upon an **intact** settlement of stone structures.

Because Machu Picchu was isolated, it was extremely well **preserved**. Though Bingham was not a trained **archaeologist**, he uncovered many remains from the site. Over the years, other archaeologists have studied these objects and structures to learn about the Incas. They have tried to figure out why they built a settlement in this location. Researchers have examined artifacts, such as **fragments** of pottery and metal pins, to find clues about the activities of the people who lived there. Historians have also looked at architectural details. This can help them determine how the buildings were used.

A Reasonable Retreat

Some experts have concluded from these studies that Machu Picchu was built to be an astronomical observatory. They point out structures they believe were used to track the movements of the sun. However, other strong evidence supports a different view: The site was once a royal estate of the Inca leader.

Historians of this opinion argue that Machu Picchu was too small to be a city. The number of dwellings suggest that only about 750 people ever lived there. The settlement and its objects were also constructed with great care. Moreover, the site was a relatively short distance from the capital city of Cuzco. When it was cold there, the emperor and his family could head for a warmer environment at Machu Picchu. There, he would have hunted, relaxed, and met with noblemen.

Given this evidence, it is only reasonable to conclude that Machu Picchu was the emperor's home away from home.

> **STOP AND CHECK**
>
> **Summarize** Why does the author think that Machu Picchu was a royal estate? Summarize the most important points to help you.

Eyes on the Skies

Machu Picchu was used as an observatory.

Machu Picchu was a city built on a site more than 7,000 feet high in the Andes Mountains of Peru. This special place was built during the 1400s, the **era** of Pachacuti. He was the ruler of the ancient empire of the Incas at that time. Some archaeologists think that the city was used by Pachacuti as a retreat. But other experts argue that the structures found at Machu Picchu indicate it was an Inca observatory.

Incas and the Sun

Historians have pieced together what they know about Inca life. They have studied explorers' written accounts and **remnants** of Inca settlements. Historians know that the sun was important to the Inca religion. The Incas believed the movements of the sun in the sky affected their way of life. The Incas tracked the movements of the sun and used their observations to create calendars needed by farmers to plant their crops.

Window to the Sky

The fact that religion and agriculture were closely tied to the movements of the sun has led some experts to look at the structures at Machu Picchu in a new light. They believe the Inca probably built some of these as tools for tracking the sun, stars, and planets.

One such structure is called the Temple of the Sun. Its curved walls partially enclose a space with a carved stone in the center. This stone appears to point to the center of a window that faces east. Archaeologists have studied these features to try to **reconstruct** how it worked as an observatory. They have found that at a certain time of the year called the winter solstice, light from the rising sun in the east aligns precisely with the carved stone.

The winter solstice is the shortest day of the year, which occurs in June in South America. Historical accounts of Inca life in other settlements indicate that this date was important to the culture, especially royal families. They would hold a Festival of the Sun, during which they performed ceremonies in honor of the sun god. Similar ceremonies could have also taken place at Machu Picchu.

An Ancient Observatory

While other evidence indicates that the royal family used the site as a retreat, the royal family could have traveled here for the winter solstice. The importance of the sun to the culture and the placement and design of structures like the Temple of the Sun show that it likely was used as an observatory. Machu Picchu helped the Incas keep an eye on the sky.

The Temple of the Sun marks the winter solstice.

Respond to the Text

1. Use important details from the selection to summarize. SUMMARIZE

2. How do the authors use details to support their positions? WRITE

3. Why is it important to learn about different views of history? Which view of Machu Picchu do you agree with? Why? TEXT TO WORLD

Compare Texts

Read about how historians use technology to gather information.

Dig This Technology!

When Machu Picchu was discovered in 1911, archaeologists found most of the city covered by plants. This growth had to be cut back to see the structures. Artifacts from the site, however, were often harder to reach. At the time, researchers had to rely on a careful process of removing earth to reach artifacts.

New technology has changed that. Archaeologists can now analyze, explore, and even discover remnants of the past in other ways.

A big help to researchers of Machu Picchu today is the use of a 3-D scanner. They can use this machine to scan the site with laser beams and reconstruct the city as a digital three-dimensional picture.

The images let researchers study the city from every angle, from a distance, and from so close up you could see details of the stonework. This technology also helps researchers store information about the site. Researchers no longer have to trek up 7,000 feet above sea level to see the site in person. They can study Machu Picchu digitally.

Another tool archaeologists use is a device that looks like a lawn mower. Called "ground penetrating radar" (GPR), it uses radar to locate artifacts under the ground. Radar bounces radio waves off an object to show its location. The diagram below shows how GPR helps archaeologists find artifacts.

These cool tools make the work of uncovering objects from the past a little easier. Moreover, since digging around a site can harm the area, these technologies also help preserve historic sites. Now, archaeologists can dig into the past, without having to lift a shovel.

Make Connections

How have new tools helped historians get information about the past? ESSENTIAL QUESTION

Think of a historian's opinion about a place or artifact. How could new tools find evidence to support this point? TEXT TO TEXT

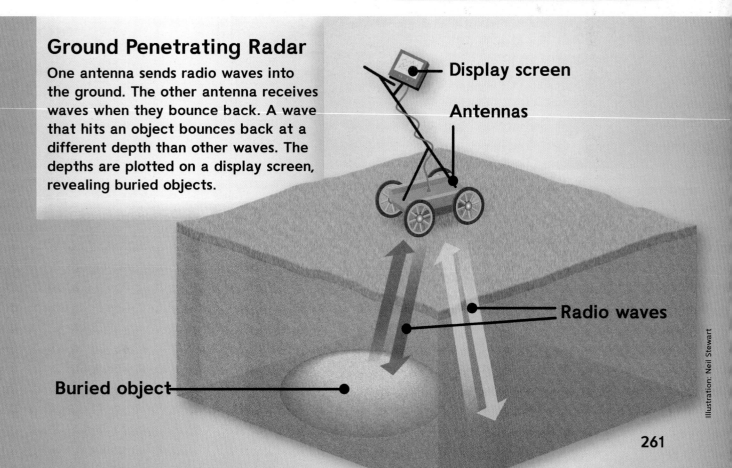

Ground Penetrating Radar

One antenna sends radio waves into the ground. The other antenna receives waves when they bounce back. A wave that hits an object bounces back at a different depth than other waves. The depths are plotted on a display screen, revealing buried objects.

Display screen

Antennas

Radio waves

Buried object

Illustration: Neil Stewart

Genre • Tall Tale

DAVY CROCKETT SAVES *the* WORLD

BY ROSALYN SCHANZER

Essential Question

What kinds of stories do we tell? Why do we tell them?

Read about how Davy Crockett's actions made him a hero in American tales.

Go Digital!

I reckon by now you've heard of Davy Crockett, the greatest woodsman who ever lived. Why, Davy could whip ten times his weight in wildcats and drink the Mississippi River dry. He combed his hair with a rake, shaved his beard with an ax, and could run so fast that, whenever he went out, the trees had to step aside to keep from getting knocked down.

Folks always crow about the **deeds** of Davy Crockett, but the biggest thing he ever did was to save the world. This here story tells exactly how he did it, and every single word is true, unless it is false.

About the time our tale begins, the world was in a heap of trouble. A way past the clouds and far beyond all the stars and planets in outer space, scientists with telescopes had discovered the biggest, baddest ball of fire and ice and brimstone ever to light up the heavens.

Its name was Halley's Comet, and it was hurling itself lickety-split straight toward America. Why, its tail alone was two million miles long. If it were to hit the earth, everyone would be blown to smithereens!

The President of the United States started getting big piles of letters telling him to stop Halley's Comet before it was too late. He made a law telling the comet it couldn't crash into the earth, but the comet paid no attention. It just kept speeding toward America and growing bigger every day.

Finally the President had an idea. He had heard of a brave man named Davy Crockett, who lived somewhere in the mountains far away. He put an advertisement in all the newspapers in America that said:

WANTED
BY THE PRESIDENT
OF THE UNITED STATES
DAVY CROCKETT
TO PULL THE TAIL OFF OF
HALLEY'S COMET

Meanwhile, Davy Crockett didn't know a thing about any comet. He had no idea that the earth was even in danger. Davy was off in the forest with his pet bear, Death Hug. He was teaching himself to dance so that he could **impress** a real purty gal named Sally Sugartree, who could dance a hole through a double oak floor. He was not reading any newspapers.

It took two whole weeks, but once Davy had learned all the latest dances, he combed his hair nice and slow with his rake, shaved his face real careful-like with his ax, and **sauntered** off toward Sally Sugartree's cabin just as easy as you please.

All this time, of course, Halley's Comet was getting closer and closer to the earth and moving faster by the minute.

Now, Sally Sugartree was not just purty, but she was right smart too. Sally read the newspaper front to back every day, and she knew all about Halley's Comet. She had also seen the advertisement from the President.

Sally climbed up a fifty-foot hickory tree and commenced to look for Davy Crockett. Before long, she spotted him a way far off in the forest. Sally grabbed up her newspaper and waved it around just as hard as she could. When Davy saw her, he grinned and started to walk a mite faster.

As soon as Davy got close enough, Sally jumped right out of that tree. Davy caught her in his arms and gave her such a hug that her tongue stuck out half a foot and her eyes popped out like a lobster's. Then she showed Davy the want ad from the President.

Davy still didn't know what Halley's Comet was, but if the President of the United States wanted to see him, he would waste no time getting to Washington. He bridled up Death Hug and set out like a high-powered hurrycane. He could dance with Sally later.

Death Hug was so fast that rocks and trees and cows and snakes and other varmints all flew out behind him.

STOP AND CHECK

Visualize How does the narrator show Davy's strength and courage? Look for descriptive phrases that help you visualize his actions.

By the time they reached the White House, Halley's Comet was getting so close that there wasn't a minute to lose.

The President told Davy to climb the highest mountain he could find right away, and to **wring** that comet's tail off before it could destroy the earth. Then the President **posed** with Davy for pictures and pretended to look calm.

Davy combed his hair with his rake, rolled up his sleeves, and ate a big plateful of pickled rattlesnake brains fried by lightning to give him energy. Then he **commenced** to climb all the way to the top of Eagle Eye Peak in the Great Smoky Mountains.

Eagle Eye Peak was so high you could see every state and river and mountain in a whole geography book.

You could also look a way far off into outer space. By the time Davy reached the top, it was night.

Halley's Comet spotted Davy Crockett right away. It took a flying leap and zoomed past all the stars and planets. Then it laughed and headed straight toward Davy like a red-hot cannonball!

Lightning and thunder shot out of its eyes! So many sparks flew out of its tail that, even though it was night, the entire countryside lit up and all the roosters set to crowin'!

That comet must have thought Davy looked mighty tender, for it licked its chops, howled louder than a hundred tornadoes, and roared toward him with its mouth wide open!

This made Davy so mad that he jumped right over its shoulders and onto its back. Then he planted his teeth around the comet's neck and hung on. Halley's Comet spun around and around like a whirlwind trying to throw Davy off, but it couldn't.

Next off, that comet tried to drown Davy by diving into the Atlantic Ocean. The water got so all-fired hot that it boiled! The whole world was covered with steam, and the sun didn't shine as bright as usual for a month.

Just in time, the ocean put out that comet's fire and melted all its ice. It washed up on an island, and before it could grow back to its original size, Davy grabbed what was left of Halley's tail, spun around seventeen times, and hurled the comet back into outer space. It was so discombobulated that the next time it ever came in this direction, it missed the earth by 39 million miles.

STOP AND CHECK

Visualize How is Davy able to get hold of the comet? Visualizing the events may help you.

That's how Davy Crockett saved the world. In fact, he did such a good job that there was a huge parade in his honor, he got to marry Sally Sugartree, and he was even elected to Congress.

Of course, that infernal fireball singed the hair right off Davy's head. A whole new crop grew back in tufts like grass and kept in such a snarl that he couldn't even comb it without breaking his rake.

That's why these days Davy Crockett always wears a coonskin cap.

STOP AND CHECK

Summarize How does Davy save the world? Use the strategy Summarize to help you.

ABOUT THE AUTHOR AND ILLUSTRATOR

ROSALYN SCHANZER loves adventure just as much as Davy Crockett. She fished for piranhas in South America, swam with sharks in Belize, kayaked with whales in Alaska, and even sailed a boat through the Bermuda Triangle. When Rosalyn wants to create a new story, she treks to a different part of the globe to seek an unusual adventure.

Before words ever hit the page, Rosalyn illustrates her books. While traveling she asks questions, snaps pictures, and researches facts that can be used for artistic inspiration. After Rosalyn illustrates her new ideas and adventures, she brings the story to life with words. It seems only fitting that Rosalyn, who has gone on such unique adventures, takes such an unusual and adventurous approach to creating books.

AUTHOR'S PURPOSE

Why do you think the author exaggerates details in this story?

Respond to the Text

Summarize

Use the most important details to summarize how Davy Crockett became a hero in *Davy Crockett Saves the World*. Your Point of View Chart may help you.

Details	Point of View

Write

Think about how the author uses literary devices. What effect do these techniques have on the story? Use these sentence frames to help organize your text evidence.

The author uses personification to . . .

The way she exaggerates events helps me to see . . .

The sensory language she uses makes the story . . .

Make Connections

Talk about ways in which the story both teaches and entertains. **ESSENTIAL QUESTION**

What person living today would be a good subject of a tall tale? Why? Give details about the person you would exaggerate in a tale. **TEXT TO WORLD**

Genre • Legend

Compare Texts

Read a Native American legend about the heroic actions of a group of animals.

HOW GRANDMOTHER SPIDER STOLE THE SUN

told by Joseph Bruchac

A legend is a story about a hero. Legends are often passed down and retold from one generation to another. As each storyteller retells a legend, he or she may use **exaggeration** *to emphasize a character's* **heroic** *actions.*

278

When the Earth was first made, there was no light. It was very hard for the animals and the people in the darkness. Finally the animals decided to do something about it.

"I have heard there is something called the Sun," said the Bear. "It is kept on the other side of the world, but the people there will not share it. Perhaps we can steal a piece of it."

All the animals agreed that it was a good idea. But who would be the one to steal the Sun?

The Fox was the first to try. He sneaked to the place where the Sun was kept. He waited until no one was looking. Then he grabbed a piece of it in his mouth and ran. But the Sun was so hot it burned his mouth and he dropped it. To this day all foxes have black mouths because that first fox burned his carrying the Sun.

The Possum tried next. In those days Possum had a very bushy tail. She crept up to the place where the Sun was kept, broke off a piece and hid it in her tail. Then she began to run, bringing the Sun back to the animals and the people. But the Sun was so hot it burned off all the hair on her tail and she lost hold of it. To this day all possums have bare tails because the Sun burned away the hair on that first possum.

Then Grandmother Spider tried. Instead of trying to hold the Sun herself, she wove a bag out of her webbing. She put the piece of the Sun into her bag and carried it back with her. Now the question was where to put the Sun.

Grandmother Spider told them, "The Sun should be up high in the sky. Then everyone will be able to see it and benefit from its light."

279

All the animals agreed, but none of them could reach up high enough. Even if they carried it to the top of the tallest tree, that would not be high enough for everyone on the Earth to see the Sun. Then they decided to have one of the birds carry the Sun up to the top of the sky. Everyone knew the Buzzard could fly the highest, so he was chosen.

Buzzard placed the Sun on top of his head, where his feathers were the thickest, for the Sun was still very hot, even inside Grandmother Spider's bag. He began to fly, up and up toward the top of the sky. As he flew the Sun grew hotter. Up and up he went, higher and higher, and the Sun grew hotter and hotter still. Now the Sun was burning through Grandmother Spider's bag, but the Buzzard still kept flying up toward the top of the sky. Up and up he went and the Sun grew hotter. Now it was burning away the feathers on top of his head, but he continued on. Now all of his feathers were gone, but he flew higher. Now it was turning the bare skin of his head all red, but he continued to fly. He flew until he reached the top of the sky, and there he placed the Sun where it would give light to everyone.

Because he carried the Sun up to the top of the sky, Buzzard was honored by all the birds and animals. Though his head is naked and ugly because he was burned carrying the Sun, he is still the highest flyer of all, and he can be seen circling the Sun to this day. And because Grandmother Spider brought the Sun in her bag of webbing, at times the Sun makes rays across the sky which are shaped like the rays in Grandmother Spider's web. It reminds everyone that we are all connected, like the strands of Grandmother Spider's web, and it reminds everyone of what Grandmother Spider did for all the animals and the people.

Make Connections

Which animals in this legend are heroic? What is the author's purpose for writing this legend? **ESSENTIAL QUESTION**

How is a hero in this legend similar to a hero in another tale you've read? How does each author show what it takes to be a hero? **TEXT TO TEXT**

A WINDOW INTO HISTORY

THE MYSTERY OF THE CELLAR WINDOW

by David Adler
illustrated by Patricia Castelao

Essential Question

What can you discover when you give things a second look?

Read about how a second look at an old house leads to a discovery.

Go Digital!

THE PLAYERS

Jean "Grandma J." Andrews, owner of the house

Celia Andrews, Jean Andrews's daughter

Jacob and Caleb, Jean Andrews's grandchildren

Daniel Cruz, a TV news reporter

Jennifer, the camerawoman

Nell, the director

Vera and Miguel, Jacob's and Caleb's friends

Patricia Cole, president of the city council

Dr. Cedric Brown, a local historian

ACT 1, SCENE 1

SETTING: The living room of an old house.

Grandma J. is showing a letter to her daughter, Celia. Jacob and Caleb enter and head toward Grandma J. and their mother. Jacob is wearing a mitt and is carrying a baseball.

CELIA ANDREWS: How can they do this?

CALEB: Who?

JACOB: Do what? What's the matter, Grandma J.?

GRANDMA J.: The city council has just sent me a letter. They want to tear down this house!

CALEB: How can they do that?

CELIA ANDREWS: *(reads from the letter)* It says here, "The city council has evaluated the area for a site to construct a playground for the city's largest elementary school."

JACOB: The school at the end of the street?

CELIA ANDREWS: *(nods and continues to read)* "The property located at 1135 East Chester Road has been identified as the best construction site for the proposed playground."

GRANDMA J.: "Best construction site"? This is my home!

CALEB: Mom, what are we going to do?

CELIA ANDREWS: I'm not sure. We'll figure something out. *(pauses)* Let me make some phone calls. *(Exits)*

ACT 1, SCENE 2

SETTING: Outside Grandma J.'s house, a few days later.

*Jacob, Caleb, Vera, and Miguel are on the steps with
Grandma J. Daniel Cruz is in front of the house with Patricia Cole.
Celia is pacing behind Nell and Jennifer. Nell holds up her hand,
counts down to air time, and points to Daniel.*

DANIEL CRUZ: I am reporting from an old house on East
Chester Road. With me is Patricia Cole, president of the city
council. Patricia, tell us your plans for this house.

PATRICIA COLE: We're building a playground for the children of
our great city.

DANIEL CRUZ: And you're tearing this house down.

PATRICIA COLE: The family will be fairly compensated and the
playground we're building will be in a central area, close to one
of our largest elementary schools.

(Daniel walks over to Celia. Jennifer and Nell follow.)

DANIEL CRUZ: This is Celia Andrews, the daughter of the
owner, Jean Andrews. Tell us, how do you feel about the
city's plans?

CELIA ANDREWS: *(looks right at the camera)* The city council may offer us money, but money isn't everything. I grew up in this house. My mother grew up here. Our family has been here for years. It's not right to tell an old woman to move out. It's not right! The city council should **reconsider** its plans.

DANIEL CRUZ: *(holds the microphone in front of Jacob)* How do you feel about the playground?

JACOB: A new playground is great but it doesn't have to be built in this **precise** spot. It could be put somewhere else and my grandma could keep her home.

CELIA ANDREWS: That's right. *(Daniel moves the microphone to Celia.)* It's an old house, but it's ours and it should be important to the town. This house has been here since 1859.

DANIEL CRUZ: *(to camera, gesturing toward the house)* It's too bad these old walls can't talk. I'm sure they would have some stories to tell. But soon the final story of this house will be written, a story that will end with a wrecking ball. This is Daniel Cruz reporting to you from East Chester Road.

NELL: That's a wrap. That was great.

GRANDMA J.: *(taps her cane)* This is not great. You have your report and I'm going to lose my house.

PATRICIA COLE: I'm sorry about your house, but this playground will benefit everyone.

> **STOP AND CHECK**
>
> **Visualize** How do Celia's actions reflect her feelings? Look for details in the stage directions to help you Visualize her actions.

285

ACT 2, SCENE 1

SETTING: The backyard of Grandma J.'s house, one week later.

Jacob, Caleb, Vera, and Miguel are playing catch with a baseball. After a catch Jacob tosses the baseball off stage.

(Sound effect: glass breaking)

JACOB: Oops! I'll get it.

MIGUEL: You broke the cellar window!

(Jacob walks off stage.)

VERA: *(to Caleb)* I hope your grandmother won't be upset about the window.

CALEB: She's already upset about the whole house. In a month, everything will be gone.

(Jacob reappears.)

JACOB: It's not there. I searched the cellar and it's not there! And something else: None of the cellar windows is broken.

CALEB: Of course a window is broken. You can look right there *(points)* and see it. The baseball's probably at the back of the cellar.

JACOB: It's easier said than done. I went downstairs and there is no baseball and no broken window.

VERA: I'm **perplexed**. Is the window broken or not?

CALEB: Up here it is.

JACOB: In the cellar it's not.

MIGUEL: Let's go to the cellar, get the baseball, and figure this out.

ACT 2, SCENE 2

SETTING: The cellar of Grandma J.'s house, moments later.

Against the wall is a bookcase. Jacob, Caleb, Vera, and Miguel are in the cellar, searching.

JACOB: I thought I broke the window, but maybe I didn't...

MIGUEL: I'll go outside and look into the window. Maybe it'll help us figure out where the ball went. *(He exits and the group continues searching another minute. Miguel calls from off stage.)* Hey! Who turned off the lights?

VERA: *(calls back)* No one! The lights are on!

(Miguel runs back.)

MIGUEL: I looked through the broken window and it is dark inside! I can see into the cellar through all of the other windows, except for that one!

CALEB: We were playing at the back of the house. That means the broken window should be back here. *(Caleb heads toward the back wall and the others follow.)*

VERA: *(looks around)* But there's no window here.

CALEB: *(inspects the bookcase)* There's something **suspicious** about this bookcase. Isn't it oddly placed? *(He looks at the base, below the bottom shelf.)* And look—don't these look like wheels? Let's see if we can move it and see what's behind it!

(Caleb and Jacob push the bookcase and expose a small door.)

JACOB: A door!

(Jacob opens the door, revealing a darkened room.)

MIGUEL: Wait here. I'll get flashlights. *(Exits)*

STOP AND CHECK

Visualize How does the broken window lead to an investigation? Visualizing the events may help you.

ACT 2, SCENE 3

SETTING: The cellar, a few days later.

*Grandma J., Celia Andrews, and the children are in the cellar.
Daniel Cruz, Nell, and Jennifer are there along with Patricia Cole
and Dr. Cedric Brown, a local historian. Dr. Brown is holding
some old newspapers and scraps of clothing. Nell holds up her
right hand, counts down to air time, and points to Daniel Cruz.*

DANIEL CRUZ: I'm in the cellar of the old house on East Chester
Road, the site of the proposed new playground. Jean Andrews
has lived here since she was a child and now she's almost
ninety. Last week her grandchildren went in search of a baseball
and were **astounded** by what they found instead. Here to tell us
about all that is history professor Dr. Cedric Brown.

CEDRIC BROWN: Well, first of all, old houses like this one have
a lot to tell us about the history of this area. An old house like
this is a window into history. *(He pauses.)* The children found a
room that had been **concealed** behind a bookcase. Inside they
found these remnants of abolitionist newspapers and scraps of
clothes made from burlap bags.

DANIEL CRUZ: But tell us, what does this mean?

CEDRIC BROWN: Well, some time ago, we found letters that
indicated that some houses in this city might have housed
enslaved people who escaped to the North around the time of
the Civil War. We had thought that these houses had burned
in a town fire long ago. Given these historical records, the age
of this house, and the contents of this hidden room, I **interpret**
this to mean that this old house was a stop on the Underground
Railroad.

DANIEL CRUZ: *(to Grandma J.)* To give credit where credit
is due, it was your **inquisitive** grandchildren that made the
discovery. Were you surprised by what they found?

GRANDMA J.: Yes. All these years I was living in a house with
such history and didn't know it!

DANIEL CRUZ: Dr. Brown, please tell us what this means to the
Andrews family and what this means to our city.

CEDRIC BROWN: This house can't be torn down, not for a playground, not for anything. It will be declared an historic monument.

DANIEL CRUZ: City council president Patricia Cole is here. *(He turns to Patricia Cole.)*

PATRICIA COLE: I am proud of the role this city played in trying to help people gain their freedom. This great monument to our past will remain, but the children will have their playground. In light of this discovery, we've decided to keep this property intact and extend the playground onto another lot near the school.

GRANDMA J.: *(taps her cane on the floor; Daniel Cruz turns to her)* The city gets its playground and I hope I'll get what I like most—visitors! I'd be happy to show the families who visit the playground a part of the city's—and my—past.

DANIEL CRUZ: *(to camera)* This is Daniel Cruz, reporting to you from East Chester Road, where a house that offered a second chance at life during a time of slavery, gets a second chance, too.

STOP AND CHECK

Reread How has Patricia Cole's view of the house changed? Rereading may help you.

ABOUT THE AUTHOR AND ILLUSTRATOR

DAVID ADLER was a math teacher in New York City for nearly a decade, but today he is the author of over two hundred books for young people. How did that happen? A clue to that mystery is in the title of his first book: *A Little At a Time*.

Over the years, David Adler has written mysteries, historical fiction stories, biographies, and even math books. Little by little, David turned many of his books into series, some with characters that readers can follow from one adventure to the next. His most famous character is Cam Jansen, a sleuth with photographic memory, who appears in more than fifty books.

PATRICIA CASTELAO also did not plan on becoming the illustrator she is today. She studied medicine when she went to college in her native Spain, but then decided to begin a career as an illustrator. Since then she has illustrated a number children's books, posters, and animations.

AUTHOR'S PURPOSE
How does David Adler create a feeling of suspense in the play?

Respond to the Text

Summarize

Summarize the events of *A Window Into History* using the most important details from the play. In your summary, include the events that led the characters to make a discovery. Details from your Point of View Chart may help you.

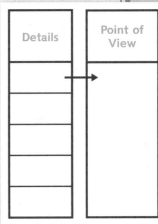

Details	Point of View

Write

Think about Daniel Cruz's role as a reporter. How does the author use his interviews to help you understand the events in the play? Use these sentence frames to help organize your text evidence.

> The author uses Daniel Cruz to . . .
> The interviews help the author to . . .
> They help me understand . . .

Make Connections

Talk about how taking a second look in the cellar led to a discovery that saved the house. **ESSENTIAL QUESTION**

What other kinds of historical discoveries have you heard about? Why do historians reexamine places and objects from the past? **TEXT TO WORLD**

Compare Texts

Read how taking a second look helps a boy solve a mystery about his pet.

A Second Chance for Chip

THE CASE OF THE CURIOUS CANINE

There's not much to be frightened of in Jubilee Falls, but you can't convince my dog Chip of that. Whenever a car backfires or the tornado warning wails, it's under the bed for Chip. Sputtering lawn mower? Under the bed. Thunder? Under the bed.

Chip's a German shepherd, mostly black with coffee-colored splotches. He is more than half my height on all fours, but he looks huge when he jumps up on me. Because his ears are perked up most of the time, he's what you might consider an **inquisitive** listener.

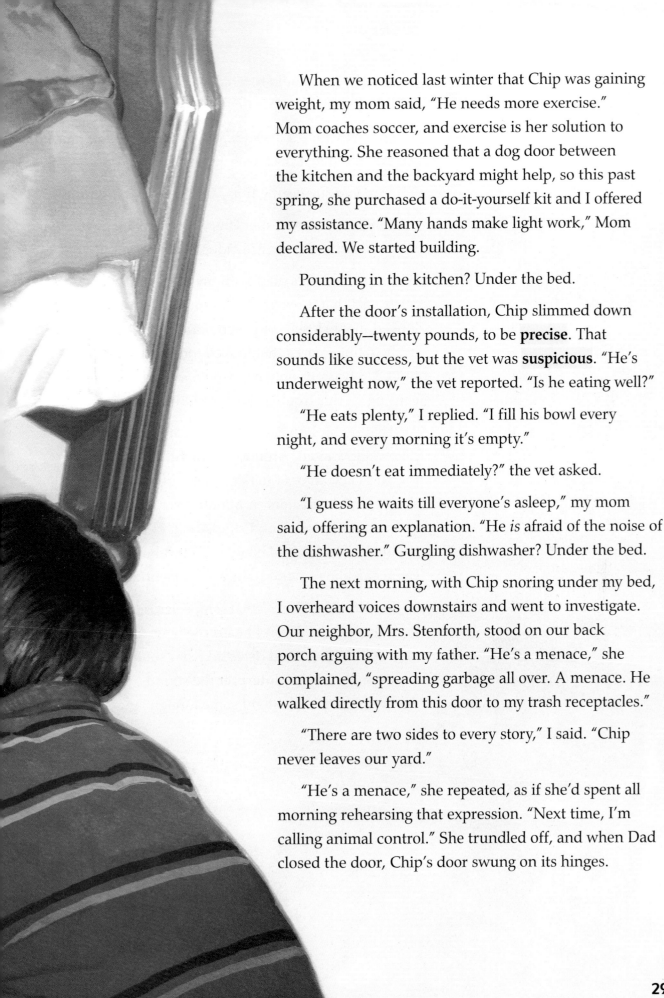

When we noticed last winter that Chip was gaining weight, my mom said, "He needs more exercise." Mom coaches soccer, and exercise is her solution to everything. She reasoned that a dog door between the kitchen and the backyard might help, so this past spring, she purchased a do-it-yourself kit and I offered my assistance. "Many hands make light work," Mom declared. We started building.

Pounding in the kitchen? Under the bed.

After the door's installation, Chip slimmed down considerably—twenty pounds, to be **precise**. That sounds like success, but the vet was **suspicious**. "He's underweight now," the vet reported. "Is he eating well?"

"He eats plenty," I replied. "I fill his bowl every night, and every morning it's empty."

"He doesn't eat immediately?" the vet asked.

"I guess he waits till everyone's asleep," my mom said, offering an explanation. "He *is* afraid of the noise of the dishwasher." Gurgling dishwasher? Under the bed.

The next morning, with Chip snoring under my bed, I overheard voices downstairs and went to investigate. Our neighbor, Mrs. Stenforth, stood on our back porch arguing with my father. "He's a menace," she complained, "spreading garbage all over. A menace. He walked directly from this door to my trash receptacles."

"There are two sides to every story," I said. "Chip never leaves our yard."

"He's a menace," she repeated, as if she'd spent all morning rehearsing that expression. "Next time, I'm calling animal control." She trundled off, and when Dad closed the door, Chip's door swung on its hinges.

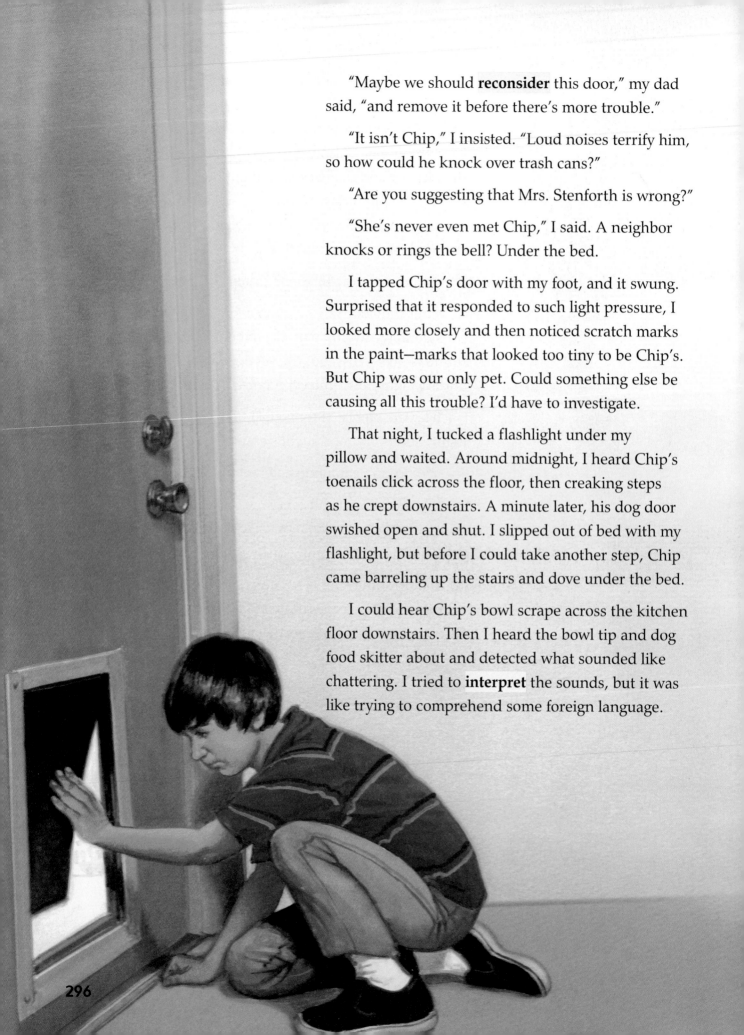

"Maybe we should **reconsider** this door," my dad said, "and remove it before there's more trouble."

"It isn't Chip," I insisted. "Loud noises terrify him, so how could he knock over trash cans?"

"Are you suggesting that Mrs. Stenforth is wrong?"

"She's never even met Chip," I said. A neighbor knocks or rings the bell? Under the bed.

I tapped Chip's door with my foot, and it swung. Surprised that it responded to such light pressure, I looked more closely and then noticed scratch marks in the paint—marks that looked too tiny to be Chip's. But Chip was our only pet. Could something else be causing all this trouble? I'd have to investigate.

That night, I tucked a flashlight under my pillow and waited. Around midnight, I heard Chip's toenails click across the floor, then creaking steps as he crept downstairs. A minute later, his dog door swished open and shut. I slipped out of bed with my flashlight, but before I could take another step, Chip came barreling up the stairs and dove under the bed.

I could hear Chip's bowl scrape across the kitchen floor downstairs. Then I heard the bowl tip and dog food skitter about and detected what sounded like chattering. I tried to **interpret** the sounds, but it was like trying to comprehend some foreign language.

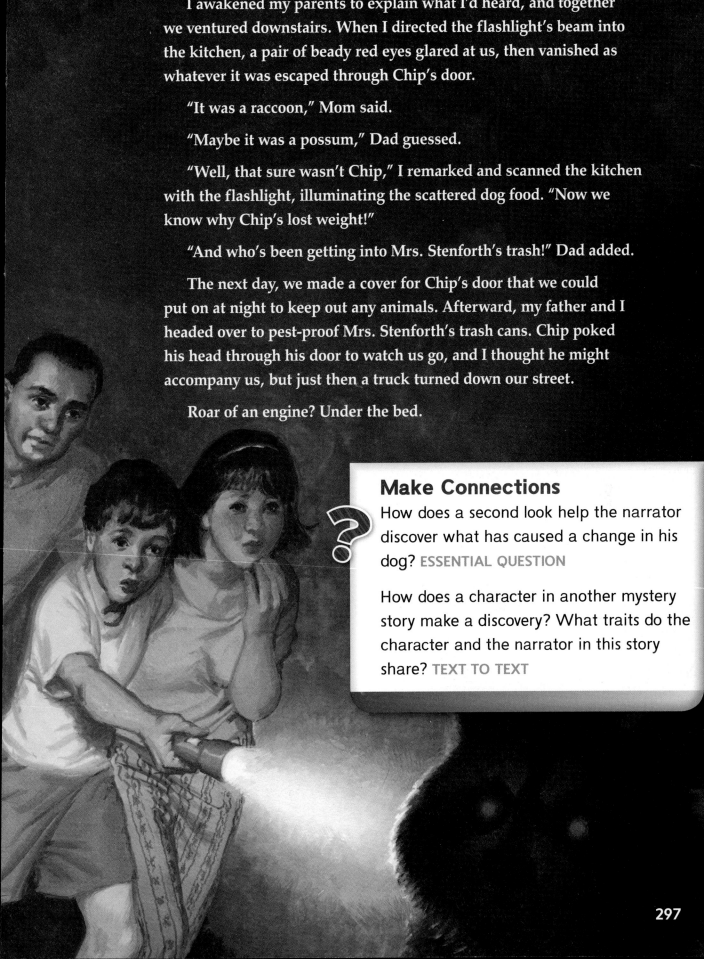

I awakened my parents to explain what I'd heard, and together we ventured downstairs. When I directed the flashlight's beam into the kitchen, a pair of beady red eyes glared at us, then vanished as whatever it was escaped through Chip's door.

"It was a raccoon," Mom said.

"Maybe it was a possum," Dad guessed.

"Well, that sure wasn't Chip," I remarked and scanned the kitchen with the flashlight, illuminating the scattered dog food. "Now we know why Chip's lost weight!"

"And who's been getting into Mrs. Stenforth's trash!" Dad added.

The next day, we made a cover for Chip's door that we could put on at night to keep out any animals. Afterward, my father and I headed over to pest-proof Mrs. Stenforth's trash cans. Chip poked his head through his door to watch us go, and I thought he might accompany us, but just then a truck turned down our street.

Roar of an engine? Under the bed.

Make Connections

How does a second look help the narrator discover what has caused a change in his dog? ESSENTIAL QUESTION

How does a character in another mystery story make a discovery? What traits do the character and the narrator in this story share? TEXT TO TEXT

Rosa

by Nikki Giovanni

illustrated by Bryan Collier

Essential Question

What can people do to bring about a positive change?

Read about how Rosa Parks took a stand to bring about change.

Go Digital!

Mrs. Parks was having a good day. Mother was getting over that touch of flu and was up this morning for breakfast at the table. Her husband, Raymond Parks, one of the best barbers in the county, had been asked to take on extra work at the air force base. And the first day of December was always special because you could just feel Christmas in the air.

Everybody knew the alterations department would soon be very, very busy. Mrs. Parks would laugh each year with the other seamstresses and say that "those elves in the North Pole have nothing on us!"

The women of Montgomery, both young and older, would come in with their fancy holiday dresses that needed adjustments or their Sunday suits and blouses that needed just a touch— a flower or some velvet trimming or something to make the ladies look festive.

Rosa Parks was the best seamstress. The needle and thread flew through her hands like the gold spinning from Rumpelstiltskin's loom. The other seamstresses would tease Rosa Parks and say she used magic. Rosa would laugh. "Not magic. Just concentration," she would say. Some days she would skip lunch to be finished on time.

This Thursday they had gotten a bit ahead of their schedule. "Why don't you go on home, Rosa," said the supervisor. "I know your mother is feeling poorly, and you might want to look in on her."

The supervisor knew Rosa would stay until the work was done, but it was only December 1. No need to push. Rosa appreciated that. Now she could get home early, and since Raymond would be working late, maybe she would surprise him with a meatloaf, his favorite.

"See you in the morning." Rosa waved good-bye and headed for the bus stop. She fiddled in her pocket for the dime so that she would not have to ask for change. When she stepped up to drop her fare in, she was smiling in **anticipation** of the nice dinner she would make. As was the evil custom, she then got off the bus and went to the back door to enter the bus from the rear.

Rosa saw that the section **reserved** for blacks was full, but she noticed the **neutral** section, the part of the bus where blacks or whites could sit, had free seats.

The left side of the aisle had two seats and on the right side a man was sitting next to the window. Rosa decided to sit next to him. She did not remember his name, but she knew his face. His son, Jimmy, came frequently to the NAACP Youth Council affairs. They exchanged pleasantries as the bus pulled away from the curb.

Rosa settled her sewing bag and her purse near her knees, trying not to crowd Jimmy's father. Men take up more space, she was thinking as she tried to squish her packages closer. The bus made several more stops, and the two seats opposite her were filled by blacks. She sat on her side of the aisle daydreaming about her good day and planning her special meal for her husband.

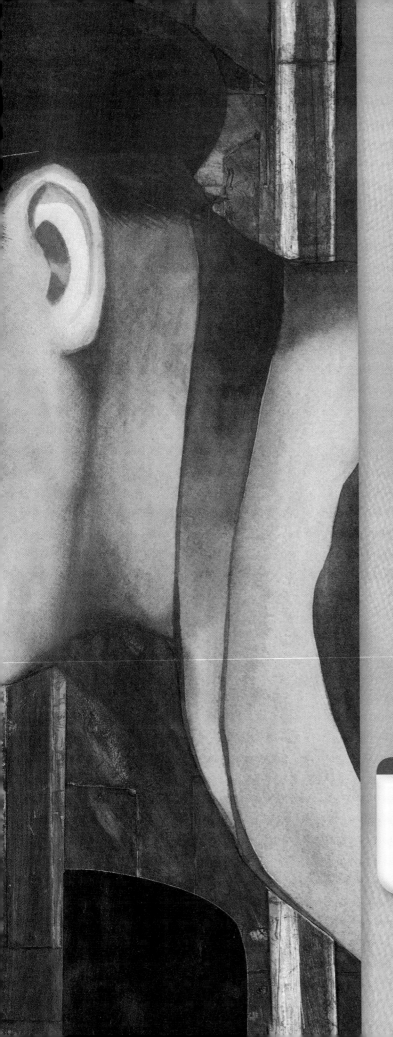

"I said give me those seats!" the bus driver bellowed. Mrs. Parks looked up in surprise. The two men on the opposite side of the aisle were rising to move into the crowded black section. Jimmy's father muttered, more to himself than anyone else, "I don't feel like trouble today. I'm gonna move."

Mrs. Parks stood to let him out, looked at James Blake, the bus driver, and then sat back down.

"You better make it easy on yourself!" Blake yelled.

"Why do you pick on us?" Mrs. Parks asked with that quiet strength of hers.

"I'm going to call the police!" Blake threatened.

"Do what you must," Mrs. Parks quietly replied. She was not frightened. She was not going to give in to that which was wrong.

STOP AND CHECK

Summarize Why would Mrs. Parks's actions lead the bus driver to call the police? Use the strategy Summarize to help you.

Some of the white people were saying aloud, "She ought to be arrested," and "Take her off this bus." Some of the black people, recognizing the potential for ugliness, got off the bus. Others stayed on, saying among themselves, "That is the neutral section. She has a right to be there."

Mrs. Parks sat.

As Mrs. Parks sat waiting for the police to come, she thought of all the brave men and women, boys and girls who stood tall for civil rights. She recited in her mind the 1954 Brown versus Board of Education decision, in which the United States Supreme Court ruled that separate is "inherently **unequal**."

She sighed as she realized she was tired. Not tired from work but tired of putting white people first. Tired of stepping off sidewalks to let white people pass, tired of eating at separate lunch counters and learning at separate schools.

She was tired of "Colored" entrances, "Colored" balconies, "Colored" drinking fountains, and "Colored" taxis. She was tired of getting somewhere first and being waited on last. Tired of "separate," and definitely tired of "not equal."

She thought about her mother and her grandmother and knew they would want her to be strong. She had not **sought** this moment, but she was ready for it.

When the policeman bent down to ask "Auntie, are you going to move?" all the strength of all the people through all those many years joined in her. Rosa Parks said no.

304

Jo Ann Robinson was at the Piggly Wiggly when she learned of the arrest. She had stopped in to purchase a box of macaroni and cheese. She always served macaroni and cheese when she baked red snapper for dinner. A sister member of the Women's Political Council approached her just as she reached the checkout lane.

"Not Mrs. Parks!" Mrs. Robinson exclaimed. She then looked furtively around. "Pass the word that everybody should meet me at my office at ten o'clock tonight," she said.

Mrs. Robinson was also Dr. Robinson, a professor at Alabama State, the college designated for "Colored" people, and she was the newly elected president of the Women's Political Council. She rushed home to put dinner on the table, cleaned up the kitchen, and put the kids to bed. She kissed her husband good-bye and hurried to the college. It was dark when they finally gathered.

The twenty-five women first held hands in prayer in hopes that they were doing the right thing. After all, they were going to use the stencil maker, printer, and paper of Alabama State without permission. If they were caught at the college, they all could be arrested for trespassing. But they were working to undermine a vicious law. They decided they would stand under the umbrella of courage Rosa Parks had offered, keeping off the rains of fear and self disgust.

The women quickly formed groups to carry out each task. Making the stencils was the most difficult because the machine keys had to be struck very hard so that the letters would be clearly readable. If a mistake was made, the whole page had to be thrown out; it took a lot of concentration.

STOP AND CHECK

Summarize How did the community respond to Mrs. Parks's arrest? Summarize the events to help you.

The posters read: NO RIDERS TODAY; SUPPORT MRS. PARKS— STAY OFF THE BUSES; WALK ON MONDAY. The women made enough posters for almost every citizen of color in Montgomery. The next morning, as people read the posters, they remembered the joy they felt when the Supreme Court declared that separate was not equal. They were sure that once the highest court in the land had spoken, they would not be treated so badly. But that was not the case.

Soon after the ruling, Emmett Till, a fourteen-year-old boy in Money, Mississippi, was viciously lynched. At his funeral, more than one hundred thousand people mourned with his mother. She left his casket open, saying, "I want the world to see what they did to my boy." Now, only weeks after his killers were freed, Rosa Parks had taken a courageous stand. The people were ready to stand with her.

They came together in a great mass meeting: the Women's Political Council, the NAACP, and all the churches. They needed someone to speak for them, to give voice to the injustice. Everyone agreed that the Reverend Martin Luther King, Jr., would be ideal. "We will stay off the buses," Dr. King intoned. "We will walk until justice runs down like water and righteousness like a mighty stream."

And the people walked. They walked in the rain. They walked in the hot sun. They walked early in the morning. They walked late at night. They walked at Christmas, and they walked at Easter. They walked on the Fourth of July; they walked on Labor Day. They walked on Thanksgiving, and then it was almost Christmas again.

They still walked.

People from all over the United States sent shoes and coats and money so that the citizens of Montgomery could walk. Everyone was proud of their nonviolent movement. And the soul force that bound the community together would sustain many marchers for the years of struggle that were yet to come.

STOP AND CHECK

Reread How does the author feel about the citizens' actions? Reread to check your understanding.

311

On November 13, 1956, almost a year after the arrest of Rosa Parks, the Supreme Court of the United States ruled that segregation on the buses, like segregation at schools, was illegal. Segregation was *wrong*.

Rosa Parks said no so that the Supreme Court could remind the nation that the Constitution of the United States makes no provision for second-class citizenship. We are all equal under the law and are all **entitled** to its protection.

The integrity, the dignity, the quiet strength of Rosa Parks turned her no into a YES for change.

About the Author and Illustrator

Nikki Giovanni was born in Tennessee and grew up in Lincoln Heights, Ohio. Today she lives in Virginia, where she is a professor of English at Virginia Polytechnic Institute and State University. However, being an educator is just one of the many hats Nikki wears. She is also a poet and writer of more than 30 books for children and adults. Many of her books and poems focus on the idea that an individual has the power to make a difference in the world.

Bryan Collier's interest in art began as a young child, when he admired the works of Ezra Jack Keats and Crockett Johnson. Bryan went on to develop his own style of painting, which combines watercolor and collage. To research *Rosa*, he traveled to Montgomery, Alabama. The heat during his visit inspired his use of different shades of yellows in his paintings. His artwork for *Rosa* has won the Caldecott Honor and the Coretta Scott King Honor awards.

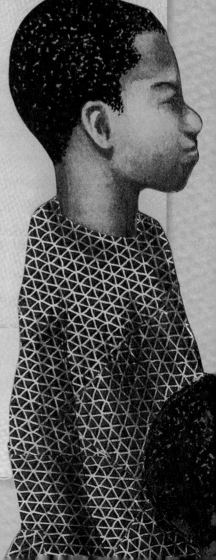

Author's Purpose

In *Rosa*, Nikki Giovanni describes Rosa Parks's thoughts. How does this help you understand her actions on the bus?

Respond to the Text

Summarize

Use the most important details from *Rosa* to summarize how Rosa Parks's actions brought about change. Details from your Author's Point of View Chart may help you.

Details	Author's Point of View
	→

Write

How does Nikki Giovanni use figurative language to help you understand the theme, or message, of this selection? Use these sentence frames to help organize your text evidence.

> Nikki Giovanni's description of Rosa helps me . . .
> She also uses similes to . . .
> This helps me understand her message by . . .

Make Connections

Talk about what Rosa and others in the community did to bring about positive change. ESSENTIAL QUESTION

Why is it important for people to stand up for what they believe to be right? TEXT TO WORLD

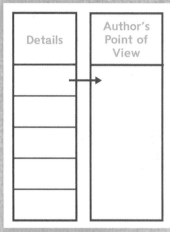

Genre • Expository Text

Compare Texts
Read to find out how groups of people took a stand to get the right to vote.

OUR VOICES, OUR VOTES

The United States of America was founded on the idea that people should have a say in how they are governed. However, not all people were granted this right at one time. It would take over a century for women, African Americans, and others to be allowed the right to vote.

The right to representation has been a central issue in America, even before it became a nation. In 1776, John Adams and other colonial leaders drafted a declaration of independence from Britain in revolt against voting laws they felt were unjust.

Abigail Adams, John's **outspoken** wife, saw an opportunity. "Remember the Ladies," Abigail wrote to her husband. They, too, did not want to be "bound by any Laws in which we have no voice, or Representation." But when the Constitution was created, and later amended by the Bill of Rights which guaranteed individuals' rights, the freedom to vote was **reserved** mostly for men who owned land. Women, among many others, were forgotten. That meant that over half of the people were not represented.

Abigail Adams supported women's right to vote.

Rights for African Americans

During the early 1800s, many women's groups joined with abolitionists to demand equal rights. Abolitionists were people who wanted to end slavery. They believed that freedom was a natural right. Women marched with them in protest. Some of them helped enslaved people escape to places where they could be free. Over 300 people gathered at a convention in Seneca Falls, New York in 1848. They discussed how women's rights were linked to other social and civil rights movements. Some speakers urged that suffrage, or voting rights, be a top priority for African Americans and women.

After the Civil War, the United States government added the Thirteenth Amendment, outlawing slavery. Three years later, the Fourteenth Amendment granted former slaves rights as citizens. Finally, in 1870, the Fifteenth Amendment gave male citizens of all races the right to vote. Though many women supported these causes, women still could not vote. Their fight was far from over.

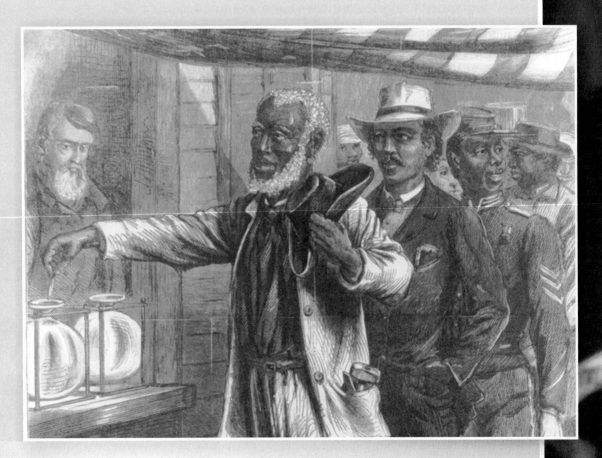

After the Civil War the government granted men of all races the right to vote.

Women's Suffrage

Women continued to fight for suffrage on the national, state, and local levels. Some were outraged enough to **defy** voting laws and attempt to cast ballots in elections. These acts of civil disobedience resulted in fines. In some cases, the women ended up in jail.

Women's suffrage remained unpopular with many men. Even so, the idea took hold in some areas. In 1869, Wyoming became the first state to allow women to vote in its elections. Over the next twenty years, four more states would grant women this right.

Susan B. Anthony was a leader of the suffrage movement.

Women began to join forces, borrowing ideas from women's groups in other countries. Some hired lobbyists, or people who tried to convince politicians to vote a certain way. Others held huge rallies to raise awareness. Petitions bearing thousands of signatures demanded that the country's laws be amended.

President Woodrow Wilson finally agreed that a true democracy should not deny women the right to vote. With his support, Congress drafted the Nineteenth Amendment to the Constitution. In 1920, it was approved.

Suffragettes held rallies to gain public support.

Protestors drew attention to unjust local voting laws.

The Final Act

Though the amendments granted voting rights, they still needed to be enforced. Local and state laws attempted to undermine federal law by requiring literacy tests or taxes to vote. For years, African Americans in Southern states were especially intimidated. In the face of strong, sometimes violent, opposition, they protested. In 1965, with the passing of the Voting Rights Act, the government stepped in to enforce the Fifteenth Amendment. Finally, people were able to exercise the rights granted to them nearly a hundred years earlier.

Extending the Vote

1848 The Seneca Falls Convention is held.

1872 Susan B. Anthony is arrested for voting.

1870 The 15th Amendment allows men of all races to vote.

1865 The 13th Amendment ends slavery in the United States.

1917 National Women's Party protest at the White House.

1965 Protestors march across Alabama to support voters' rights.

1965 The Voting Rights Act enforces the 15th Amendment.

1920 The 19th Amendment allows women to vote.

Make Connections

What actions did women and African Americans take to get the right to vote? ESSENTIAL QUESTION

How are the movements to change voting laws like other movements for change you have read about? TEXT TO TEXT

One Well

by Rochelle Strauss
illustrated by Rosemary Woods

Essential Question

Why are natural resources valuable?

Read about why water is a valuable natural resource.

Go Digital!

Imagine for a moment that all the water on Earth came from just one well.

This isn't as strange as it sounds. All water on Earth *is* connected, so there really is just one source of water—one global well—from which we all draw our water. Every ocean wave, every lake, stream and underground river, every raindrop and snowflake and every bit of ice in **glaciers** and polar icecaps is part of this global well.

So whether you are turning on a faucet in North America, pulling water from a well in Kenya or bathing in a river in India, it is all the same water. And because it is all connected, how we treat the water in the well will **affect** every species on the planet, including us, now and for years to come.

You need water, and so does every other living organism—every person, every plant and every animal. Without water, nothing can survive.

Earth is the only planet that has liquid water and is therefore the only planet that can support life. The amount of water on Earth hasn't ever changed.

One Well: The Story of Water on Earth written by Rochelle Strauss and illustrated by Rosemary Woods. Used by permission of Kids Can Press. Illustrations © 2007 Rosemary Woods

The Water in the Well

We live on a watery planet. Almost 70 percent of Earth's surface is covered with water. This surface water is found in oceans, lakes, rivers, streams, marshes, even in puddles and the morning dew. There is so much water that if you looked down at Earth from space, it would appear blue.

But there is also water we can't see, beneath the Earth's surface. This "groundwater" can be found just about everywhere—it fills the cracks in rocks and the spaces between rocks, grains of sand and soil. Most groundwater is close to the Earth's surface, but some of it is buried quite deep. Water is also frozen in glaciers and polar icecaps. And there is water in the atmosphere.

Every one of these water sources feeds Earth's One Well.

WHERE IS THE WATER ON EARTH?

Oceans	97.23 percent
Icecaps and glaciers	2.14 percent
Groundwater	0.61 percent
Freshwater lakes	0.009 percent
Inland saltwater seas	0.008 percent
Moisture in the soil	0.005 percent
Water in the atmosphere	0.001 percent
Rivers	0.0001 percent

Yes, there is more water in the atmosphere and soil than in all of Earth's rivers.

Recycling Water in the Well

The water you drank today may have rained down on the Amazon rainforest five years ago. A hundred years ago, it may have been steam escaping a teapot in India.

The amount of water on Earth doesn't change. The same water just keeps going through a **cycle** over and over again. This constant movement of water is called the water cycle.

During the water cycle, water evaporates from oceans, lakes, rivers, ponds and puddles, even from plants and animals. It rises into the air as water vapor.

As water vapor rises, it cools into tiny water droplets. This is called condensation. These droplets form clouds. Gradually, clouds collect more and more water droplets. The average white cloud weighs about twice as much as a blue whale.

When water droplets get too heavy, they fall from the clouds in the form of hail, snow or rain. This precipitation returns to oceans, lakes and rivers. It also **seeps** into the soil and down into the groundwater. Year after year, water continuously **circulates** through the water cycle.

The Water Cycle

STOP AND CHECK

Summarize How does water move from Earth's surface to the air and back? Use the strategy Summarize to help you.

In one year, an area of rainforest the size of a football field pumps over 75,000 L (19,700 U.S. gal.) of water vapor into the atmosphere—more than enough to fill a backyard swimming pool.

It takes about one million tiny water droplets to make just one raindrop.

Why are the oceans salty? Rivers flow into the sea, collecting salt from rocks and soil and adding it to the ocean. As ocean water evaporates, the salt is left behind.

How thirsty is a tree? On a summer's day, an average-sized birch tree can draw about 300 L (80 U.S. gal.) of water from the soil. That's almost enough water to fill two large bathtubs.

Many plants depend on water to disperse their seeds. A coconut (the seed of a palm tree) can spend weeks, months or even years drifting in the ocean before reaching land and sprouting.

The plants you eat are mostly water. Tomatoes are about 95 percent water. Apples are about 85 percent water. Seeds are among the driest foods—they contain only 5 to 10 percent water.

Plants at the Well

The first plants on Earth began life in the water. Some were washed ashore. At first they could live only in wet areas. Gradually they developed root systems that allowed them to tap into water in the soil.

Water is essential to plants. In fact, plants are mostly water. It's the water in their cells that gives them their shape and form—without it, they droop and shrivel.

Water also helps plants make food for themselves. Plants use the sun's energy to change water and carbon dioxide into simple sugars that feed the plant. This process is called photosynthesis. Water then helps carry this food throughout the plant.

During photosynthesis, plants also release water vapor into the air. Roots **absorb** water, which is carried to the stem. The stem acts like a water pipe in your house, moving water through the plant to the leaves. From the leaves, water is released back into the atmosphere. This is called transpiration. The water that is transpired is added to the cycle of water on Earth.

Water is important to plants, but plants are also important to water. Plant roots anchor soil and stop it from blowing or washing into lakes and rivers. Leaves and branches trap rainwater, allowing it to seep slowly into the soil instead of flowing quickly away. And trees provide shade, which helps keep moisture in the soil.

Plants depend on water from the well for survival, and the well depends on plants to help move water through its cycle. Without plants, the water cycle would be disrupted. Without water, plants could not survive.

Animals at the Well

Like plants, animals (including you) are mostly made of water. The water in animals is very important. It carries nutrients, helps digestion, removes waste, controls temperature, cleans eyes and lubricates (oils) joints.

Water habitats are also home to many of Earth's animals, and are where many animals find their food. Watery species, such as fish, crabs, shrimp and zooplankton, are an important part of food chains around the world. A food chain is the link that connects animals (and other species), based on who eats whom. Without water-based species, food chains and food webs (collections of food chains) would collapse. Animals would starve.

Animals not only need water to survive, they are also part of the water cycle. Animals add water to the atmosphere by breathing, sweating and even drooling. The water you brushed your teeth with today may have been the spray of a beluga whale ten years ago.

STOP AND CHECK

Summarize Why is water important to animals? Summarize the author's points to help you.

Some of the "wettest" animals on Earth are the jellyfish. They are about 95 percent water. Frogs and earthworms are about 80 percent water, while dogs, elephants and humans are about 70 percent water.

People at the Well

Since the beginning of time, people have depended on water—for drinking, for food, for bathing and for watering their crops. Water has always provided a highway to move people and products from place to place. As cities and societies grow, so does their need for water.

Today, water is essential in our homes, in industry and in agriculture. At home we use water for cleaning, cooking, drinking, flushing toilets and for bathing. But homes account for only 10 percent of all the freshwater used.

About 21 percent of the water we use goes to make everything from computers to cars. Water is used in hydroelectric plants to generate electricity and in petroleum plants to make gas. In factories, water is used to heat things up or cool things down and to wash away waste. Water vapor (steam) even runs machinery. Water is also an ingredient in many products, such as lotions, shampoos, chemicals and drinks.

The remaining 69 percent of the freshwater we use goes into agriculture. Farms use huge amounts of water for crops and livestock.

Look around—almost everything you see was made using water. It took about 130 L (34 U.S. gal.) of water to make your bike. Water was used to grow and make the food you eat and the clothes you wear. Water was even used to make the paper for this book—and the ink used to print the words.

It takes about 185 L (49 U.S. gal.) of water to produce just one glass of milk. This includes the water the cow drinks, the water used to grow food for the cow and the water needed to process the milk.

About 147,000 L (38,800 U.S. gal.) of water was needed to make your family's car.

In North American homes, the bathroom is where about three-quarters of all water is used. One flush of the toilet uses nearly 13 L (3 ½ U.S. gal.).

A lot of water is required to produce the food you eat. Approximately 5,200 L (1,375 U.S. gal.) of water is needed just to make one fast food lunch (burger, fries and a soda).

Nearly a billion people around the world depend on fish as their primary source of protein.

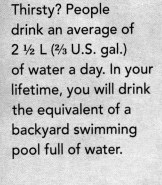

Thirsty? People drink an average of 2 ½ L (⅔ U.S. gal.) of water a day. In your lifetime, you will drink the equivalent of a backyard swimming pool full of water.

Pollution in the Well

The water cycle helps keep Earth's water clean. As water evaporates, minerals, chemicals and dirt are left behind. The water vapor that rises into the atmosphere is relatively clean. When rain falls back to Earth, some of it is filtered through rocks and sand and is further cleaned. Even plants play a role. As water travels through them, plants remove chemicals in the water. Then they transpire clean water back into the air.

But more and more waste from industry, agriculture and homes is getting into the water. Runoff from backyards, city streets and farms dumps dirt and chemicals (such as pesticides, fertilizers and detergents) into lakes, rivers, streams and ponds. Pollution in the atmosphere from cars and factories mixes with water vapor in the air. The rain that falls pollutes surface water and groundwater. Our actions may be overloading water's natural ability to clean itself.

As more water becomes polluted, there is less clean water available. Nearly 80 percent of all sicknesses in the world are caused by unsafe water. And wildlife suffers, too. Water pollution threatens the health of many species and habitats across the planet.

Because of water's self-cleaning powers, the effects of pollution can be stopped and quite possibly reversed. But to do so, we need to reduce the amount of pollution that gets into the water.

Water dissolves more things than any other liquid, so in nature, water is never really pure. It almost always has something dissolved in it.

Every day, 1.8 million tonnes (metric tons) (2 million tons) of garbage are dumped into Earth's water —enough to fill more than 15,000 boxcars.

STOP AND CHECK

Ask and Answer Questions How do people's actions affect the water cycle? Look for details in the text to help you.

Wetlands are nature's water treatment plants—they absorb chemicals and filter out pollution and waste.

When pollution in the air mixes with rain, it can turn into acid rain or even acid snow. This acid precipitation can fall thousands of kilometres (kilometers) (miles) from the source of the pollution, even reaching remote areas such as the Arctic.

333

Saving the Water in the Well

Water has the power to change everything. A single splash can sprout a seed, quench a thirst, provide a habitat, generate energy and sustain life. It also has the power to unite—or divide—the world. Water is the most basic and important need of all life on Earth.

But Earth's One Well is in trouble. There is simply not enough clean water to go around.

Taking actions to **conserve** water can help save the well. Conserving water means protecting both the quantity and quality of water on Earth. For example, using less water helps prevent water sources from drying up. And reducing water pollution protects the overall health of the well. Water conservation can help ensure there is enough clean water for everyone on the planet.

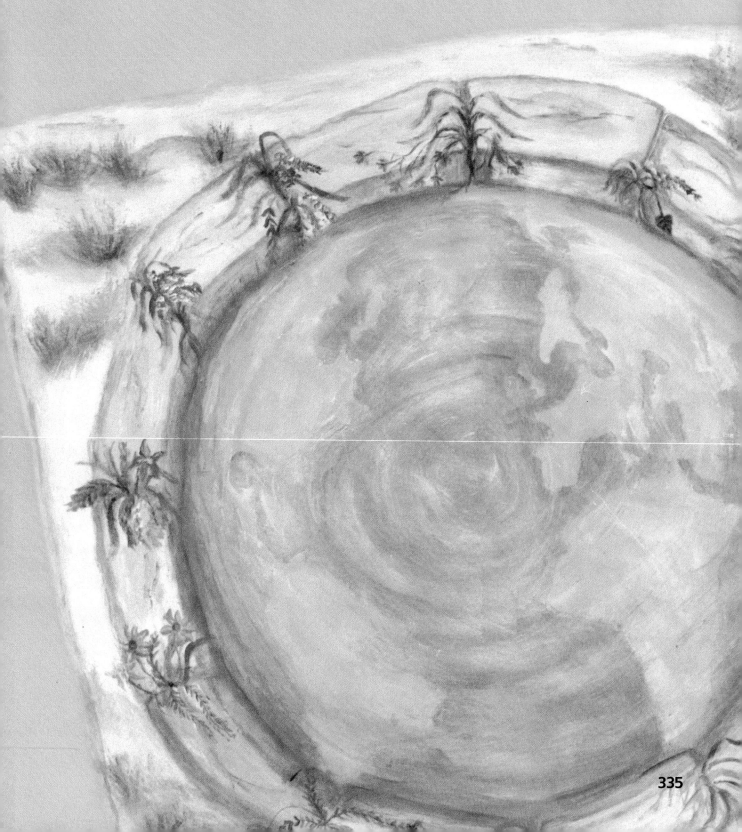

By becoming more aware of how you use water and by using less, you too can protect the water in Earth's One Well. Remember—every drop counts!

About the Author and Illustrator

Rochelle Strauss wants her readers to feel they have the power to change the lives of other living things for the better. That is why she is dedicated to writing, teaching, and consulting about the environment and natural history. Rochelle, who lives in Toronto, Canada, has worked as an educator and planner on national and international projects, and her award-winning books have been published around the world. She wrote *One Well* to help readers understand the importance of water. Her love of nature and her passion for teaching shine through in her writing.

Rosemary Woods lives in London, England, where she has created many of her illustrations. She grew up in Northern Ireland, where she lived by the sea and was surrounded by beautiful, watery landscapes. At night, she could see the glow of four different lighthouses. Her memories of the sea have influenced many of her illustrations.

Author's Purpose

In *One Well*, Rochelle Strauss wants readers to understand the importance of water. How do the captions and illustrations support the author's purpose?

(t) Felice Strauss; (b) Rosemary Woods

Respond to the Text

Summarize

Use the most important details from *One Well* to summarize what you learned about water. Details from your Author's Point of View Chart may help you.

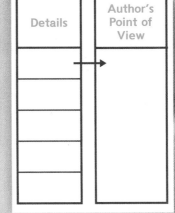

Details	Author's Point of View

Write

How does the author's use of text features support her message that water is valuable? Use these sentence frames to help organize your text evidence.

The author uses diagrams to . . .
The headings help me understand that . . .
This supports her message because . . .

Make Connections

Talk about why water is a valuable resource for people today. **ESSENTIAL QUESTION**

Tell the most interesting fact you learned about how we use water. What do you think communities could do to help protect or conserve water? **TEXT TO WORLD**

THE DIRT ON DIRT

In the 1930s, a drought struck the Great Plains, the central region of the United States. This area once was covered with tall grasses that anchored the soil. Over the years, farmers had cut these grasses and planted crops. The land was planted with the same crops year after year and the soil was not given a chance to restore its nutrients. By the time the drought struck, the soil was worn out. Soon the soil began to blow away in huge black clouds. These dust storms devastated the land, sending farmers and their families elsewhere. This area became known as the Dust Bowl.

Why did this happen? Soil helps store and move nutrients and water through the earth. Without these, soil cannot provide a habitat for other living things. The dust storms of the 1930s made people realize that healthy soil is a **necessity**.

A dust storm approaches Stratford, Texas. By the end of 1935, over 850 million tons of topsoil had been swept away.

Horizons of Soil

Soil is made up of particles of rock mixed with minerals, air, water, and specks of other matter. Soil consists of three major layers, called horizons. Soil's top layer contains a substance called humus. Humus contains bits of rock, animal waste, and rotting plants. This substance provides nutrients for plants and tiny organisms like worms and bacteria. The next layer has fine particles of rock. The layer below is harder and consists of more rocks. Below the soil is solid rock, called bedrock. These layers allow water to gradually seep into the earth, bringing nutrients to organisms and depositing minerals before it drains into nearby bodies of water.

Gaining Ground

People today are more aware of the importance of soil than they were in the 1930s so they have taken steps to **conserve** and protect it. Although current practices like the use of pesticides on crops can still pollute groundwater and harm organisms in the soil, governments and industries are working to develop safer chemicals. Many farmers take steps to keep soil healthy by alternating crops so soil nutrients are not used up. Others also plant trees as barriers that will keep the wind from blowing the soil away. The work of all these people helps to keep the soil safe, full of nutrients, and, most importantly, in place.

Make Connections

Why is soil an important natural resource? **ESSENTIAL QUESTION**

How can protecting soil help protect other natural resources you've read about? **TEXT TO TEXT**

Soil Horizons
Three major layers of soil rest on solid rock.

Topsoil

Subsoil

Substratum (sublayer)

Bedrock

Words Free as Confetti

Come, words, come in your every color.
I'll toss you in storm or breeze.
I'll say, say, say you,
Taste you sweet as plump plums,
bitter as old lemons,
I'll sniff you, words, warm
as almonds or tart as apple-red,
feel you green
and soft as new grass,
lightweight as dandelion plumes,
or thorngray as cactus,
heavy as black cement,
cold blue as icicles,
warm as *abuelita*'s yellowlap.
I'll hear you, words, loud as searoar's
Purple crash, hushed
as *gatitos* curled in sleep,
as the last goldlullaby.

Essential Question

**How do you express that something
is important to you?**

Read how poets express something
that is meaningful to them.

Go Digital!

Brad Wilson/Stone/Getty Images; TEXT: "Words Free As Confetti" from CONFETTI: POEMS
FOR CHILDREN Text copyright © 1996 by Pat Mora. Permission arranged with Lee & Low Books Inc.

I'll see you long and dark as tunnels,
bright as rainbows,
playful as chestnutwind.
I'll watch you, words, rise and dance and spin.
I'll say, say, say you
in English,
in Spanish,
I'll find you.
Hold you.
Toss you.
I'm free too.
I say *yo soy libre*,
I am free
free, free,
free as confetti.

— Pat Mora

Dreams

Hold fast to dreams
For if dreams die
Life is a broken-winged bird
That cannot fly.

Hold fast to dreams
For when dreams go
Life is a barren field
Frozen with snow.

— Langston Hughes

Respond to the Text

Summarize

Use important details from "Words Free as Confetti" to summarize the poem. Information from your Theme Chart may help you.

Detail
↓
Detail
↓
Detail
↓
Theme

Write

How do the poets use repetition and meter to help convey the theme of their poems? Use these sentence frames to organize your text evidence.

In her poem, Pat Mora . . .
Langston Hughes uses repetition to . . .
This helps me understand the poets' messages because . . .

Make Connections

How do both poets use figurative language to express what is important to them? **ESSENTIAL QUESTION**

What other forms of expression can people use to show that something is important? **TEXT TO WORLD**

Turtle Pond Publications

Permission granted by author, Simon J. Ortiz. Poem originally published in WOVEN STONE, University of Arizona Press. © 1992.

A STORY OF HOW A WALL STANDS

My father, who works with stone,
says, "That's just the part you see,
the stones which seem to be
just packed in on the outside,"
and with his hands puts the stone and mud
in place. "Underneath
what looks like loose stone,
there is stone woven together."
He ties one hand over the other,
fitting like the bones of his hands
and fingers. "That's what is
holding it together."

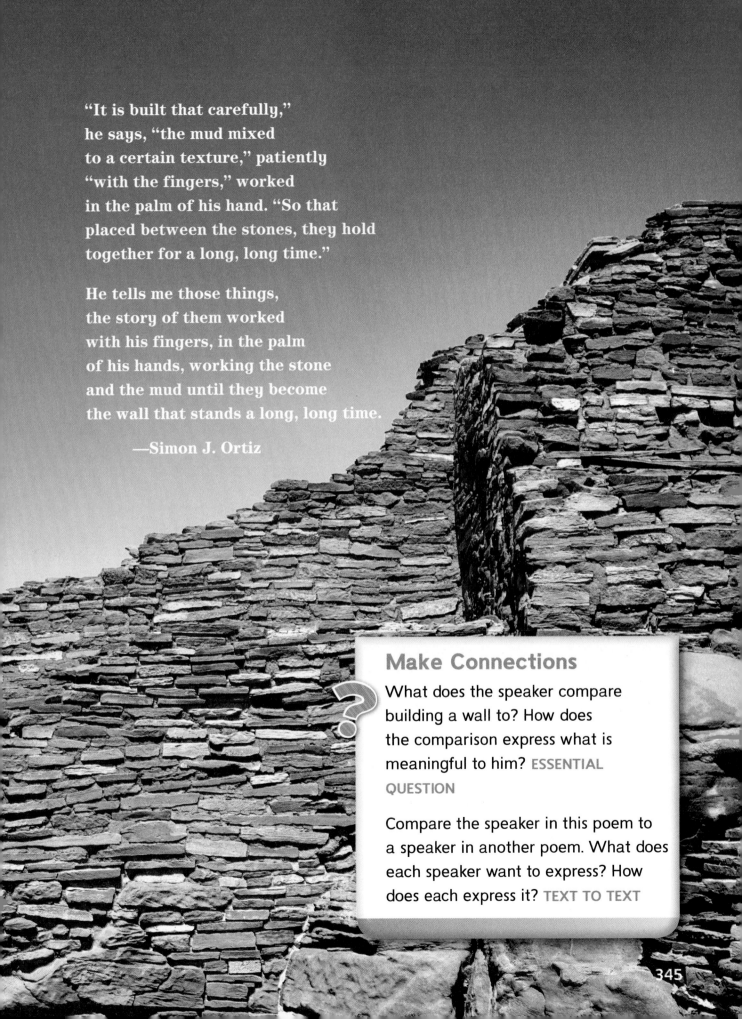

"It is built that carefully,"
he says, "the mud mixed
to a certain texture," patiently
"with the fingers," worked
in the palm of his hand. "So that
placed between the stones, they hold
together for a long, long time."

He tells me those things,
the story of them worked
with his fingers, in the palm
of his hands, working the stone
and the mud until they become
the wall that stands a long, long time.

—Simon J. Ortiz

Make Connections

What does the speaker compare building a wall to? How does the comparison express what is meaningful to him? **ESSENTIAL QUESTION**

Compare the speaker in this poem to a speaker in another poem. What does each speaker want to express? How does each express it? **TEXT TO TEXT**

Ida B

...and Her Plans to Maximize Fun, Avoid Disaster, and (Possibly) Save the World

by Katherine Hannigan
illustrated by Steven Mach

Essential Question

What experiences can change the way you see yourself and the world around you?

Read about how Ida B's experience at school gives her a new perspective.

Go Digital!

Ida B is an independent girl who loves spending time in her family's apple orchard. Unfortunately, Ida B's world turns upside down when her mother is diagnosed with cancer. Her parents are forced to sell part of the orchard to pay medical bills, which means that many of Ida B's beloved trees will be cut down to make room for houses. But that's just the beginning. Ida B finds out that her days of being home-schooled are coming to an end and that she must attend public school.

Upset by her mother's illness and her parents' decisions, Ida B stubbornly decides to distance herself from her parents and new classmates. Instead she chooses to spend time with her dog, Rufus, and cat, Lulu. But through the persistence and encouragement of her teacher, Ms. W., Ida B's iron will begins to dissolve.

$\bigcirc$ne day after lunch Ms. W. told the class, "I know it's time to read, but I don't think I can do it today. My voice is too tired."

She put her hand on her throat and scrunched up her face like something was paining her. It was the same face she'd make when Simone Martini was just about yelling across the room to Patrice Polinski, and Ms. W. would say, "Simone, use your inside voice. You are hurting my ears."

Everybody looked up from their chattering or worksheets at just about the same time, in exactly the same direction, with the same expression on their faces: a mix of thirty percent shock, twenty percent disbelief, and fifty percent plain old sad.

"Aw, man!" Matthew Dribble said right out loud.

I felt like the bottom had just dropped out of my stomach and everything I ate for lunch was tumbling around in my gut.

"Nope, my voice is just too tired," Ms. W. said, and, sure enough, it was sounding weak and raspy. "And we were going to read *Alexandra Potemkin and the Space Shuttle to Planet Z,* too. Well, that's disappointing."

Ms. W. sat down, put her head in her hand, and her body wilted. Like not only was her voice tired, but every bone in her body needed a rest.

"Please?" begged Alice Mae Grunderman.

"Please, Ms. Washington?" asked Patrice and Simone at the same time, with the same moon-eyed face.

And then everybody got the idea, and it became a sort of song with a verse of "Please, Ms. Washington" and a chorus of "Please, please, please."

But Ms. W.'s voice was deteriorating at an alarming speed, because now she could only speak in a hoarse whisper, and everybody had to stop with their "please"ing just to hear her.

"I'm sorry, but I can't."

She paused, and we could all tell by the look on her face that she was thinking hard. So we stayed quiet to give her some room.

"Maybe," she said, looking up and forcing a weak smile, "we could have a guest reader, just for today?"

Well, it was hard to imagine anybody but Ms. W. reading, and we all just sat there for a minute. Then one by one, people started nodding their heads and looking at each other and nodding more and smiling, because nobody wanted to miss story time, not even Tina Poleetie, who usually slept through it.

And after a couple of minutes of that, people started looking at Ms. W., nodding their heads real hard, sticking out their chests, and saying out loud, "I think that's a great idea" and "Yes, let's have a guest reader today," because they were realizing that maybe they could be the Guest Reader and Star Student of the Afternoon. They wanted to remind Ms. Washington that not only were they **superb** readers, but wonderful human beings, too.

Especially Calvin "Big-Headed" Faribault, who actually raised his hand, and I just knew it was to volunteer out of the kindness of his big, fat, big-headed heart.

But Ms. W. didn't even look in Calvin's direction. "Ida, since I know you've read the book," she said to me weakly, like it was her last request, "could you please read the first chapter today?"

Well, I was so shocked and embarrassed, sitting there with my mouth wide open, that I almost couldn't tell that all the other kids were staring at me with their mouths wide open, too. Making words into story music like Ms. W. did was the one thing I wanted to do more than just about anything in the world. But telling a story out loud in front of my class at Ernest B. Lawson Elementary School was nearly the last thing I'd want to do in my entire life. I was so confused about whether I should be happy or scared, I just sat there.

Ms. W. got up, walked over to me, put her face next to my **stunned** and frozen one, and whispered, "Ida, I need your help."

And there I was, hypnotized by that woman again. I was like a dog that would go fetch Ms. W.'s stick, even if it was in a snake's hole under a thorn bush that had just been sprayed by a skunk.

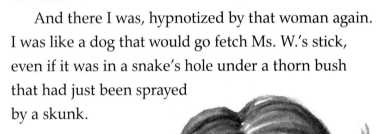

STOP AND CHECK

Make Predictions
How will Ida B respond to Ms. W.'s request? Look for details in the story to Make a Prediction.

350

I looked at Ms. W., just scared now, because I knew I was going to do it but I didn't know how.

"I know you'll be great," she croaked.

And in my head I was already trotting off, looking for that stick, even though I could smell the stink and the thorns were pricking me.

"Do you want to sit there, or in my chair?" Ms. W. asked.

"I'll sit here," I mumbled.

She set the book down on my desk, brought her chair over, sat down next to me, put her head back, and closed her eyes.

"Whenever you're ready, Ida," she rasped.

Ms. W. had given me quite a few books to read already because it only took me one or two days at the most to read them, unless I was working on my Terrify the People Who Bought Our Land Project. *Alexandra Potemkin and the Space Shuttle to Planet Z* was my favorite so far. It was Rufus's favorite, too.

I got tingly in my fingers thinking about opening up the book and reading those words out loud, making my voice go high and low, rough and smooth, like I did in my room. But my legs were shivering like they were out in a blizzard, and my stomach was flipping forward, then backward, forward, then backward, thinking about all of those people looking at me and hearing my voice.

I closed my eyes, put my right hand on top of the book, and passed it lightly across the cover. It was cool and smooth like a stone from the bottom of the brook, and it stilled me. A whole other world is inside there, I thought to myself, and that's where I want to be.

I opened the book and got ready to read the title, but I could feel everybody's eyes on me, crowding me so there was hardly any air. The only sounds that came out of me were little peeps, like a baby bird chirping "*Alexandra Potemkin and the Space Shuttle to Planet Z.*"

Ms. Washington, with her eyes still closed, leaned over and whispered, "You'll have to read louder, honey, so everyone can hear."

"Yes, ma'am," I whispered back. I took a deep breath, filled my stomach up with air, and then made my muscles squeeze it out, so it pushed a big gust of wind over my voice box and out my mouth.

"Chapter One," I bellowed. My voice was so loud it surprised me, and I jumped back a little in my chair.

But nobody laughed. They were listening.

The book is about Alexandra, and her parents think she is quite difficult, but actually she is a **genius** who is assisting the also-genius scientist Professor Zelinski in her quest to explore the lost planet Z. Alexandra gets into some trouble, but really she is just a very **focused** person.

At first, I was worrying about all of those people watching and listening. But after a few minutes, I left that classroom and went into the story. I was in Alexandra's laboratory instead of at school, and I was just saying out loud everything I saw her do or felt her feel. I let my voice tell the way she did it and saw it and felt it.

And I was so looking forward to seeing what happened next, I forgot that I was reading. All of a sudden it was the end of the chapter and it was like I was snatched out of a dream and couldn't quite recall where I was. I looked around and saw I was sitting at a desk, there was a book in front of me, kids were staring at me, and slowly I remembered.

I glanced over at Ms. W., and she smiled and whispered, "Thank you very much, Ida. That was lovely."

I handed Ms. W. the book, and we got back to work and everything was just like always, except that Ms. W. had to write all the instructions on the board instead of talking them.

At study time when I went to Ronnie's desk, he looked right in my eyes and said, "You read real good, Ida." And this time it was me staring down at my shoes like they might disappear if I didn't keep watching them.

My throat got stopped up so I could hardly say, "Thank you."

Nothing was different except the warm glow that was in my belly and my arms and my legs and my head and wouldn't go away. Even on the long, cruddy bus ride home.

> **STOP AND CHECK**
>
> **Confirm or Revise Predictions** How does Ida B respond to the challenge of reading in front of the class? What does this tell about her? Use the strategy Confirm or Revise Predictions.

"How was school today, Ida B?" Mama and Daddy would ask me every day after I first went back to Ernest B. Lawson Elementary School.

And every day I'd say, "It was O.K.," which now also stood for Overwhelming Kalamity.

"Well, what did you do?"

And I would just tell them the facts, hard and cold like my heart. "We had English, then we had science, then we went to the gym..." with no ups or downs or any part of the real me in there.

It was the same thing every day, and it was so boring and old and dry like stale bread I couldn't believe they kept trying for as long as they did.

After a while, though, they gave up. They'd just say, "How are you doing, Ida B?"

"O.K.," I'd mumble.

And that would be it. I didn't think they needed any more words than that to let them know that there was nothing close to joy floating around inside me.

But this day was different. The good feeling I had from reading that story out loud had been growing bit by bit all afternoon, till it ended up being a full-blown happiness by the time I got home. I'd keep thinking about what I did, and how it felt, and the warm brightness in me would get bigger and stronger and shinier every time.

My legs wanted to skip down the drive instead of walk. My mouth wanted to smile instead of scowl. My arms wanted to hug somebody instead of holding my backpack to my chest like a shield. My heart was horrified.

That happiness would not be satisfied staying inside me, either. It wanted to be shared. And it didn't mind who it shared itself with, including Mama and Daddy.

I could just imagine having dinner with the two of them and all kinds of good feelings spilling out of me. There I'd be, grinning and gabbing, and the next thing you'd know Mama and Daddy would be thinking that I had transformed into my old perky self, that school was the best thing that ever happened to me, and maybe everything had worked out just fine after all.

And that would not be acceptable.

I was not going to let that happiness compromise my stand that, even though good things might happen in the world from time to time, nothing was right in my family or in my valley.

So I tried to get rid of some of it before dinnertime by telling Rufus and Lulu about my Out Loud Reading Adventure. I sat them both on my bed, and while Lulu glared at Rufus with the deadliest **disdain**, I told them my story. Two thumps of Rufus's tail and a bored yawn from Lulu, though, didn't quiet that feeling down at all.

By the time I sat down to dinner, that happiness was doing somersaults of excitement in my stomach. It was jiggling with delight at the **prospect** of telling Mama and Daddy about my day. It was itching to talk about how pleased I was with Ms. W. and the stories she gave me, and reading *Alexandra Potemkin and the Space Shuttle to Planet Z* most of all. It even wanted to start chatting about Ronnie.

I tried to get away before any of the pleasure leaked out of me.

"I'm not hungry. Can I be excused?" I asked.

Daddy, however, was prepared to spoil my plan. "You need to eat your dinner, Ida B," he said.

"Eat a little bit, honey," Mama added.

Well, by that point my heart was beating extra hard trying to keep that happiness down and quiet, and it was losing ground fast. I realized I'd have to let some of it out so I could rein the rest of it in and get control of my insides again.

I focused on my carrots, lining them up with my fork vertically, then horizontally, then zigzag. And I released one tiny tidbit of cheer.

"I read a book out loud to my class today," I said, struggling to keep my voice low and even.

Daddy looked up and stared, like he didn't quite know what to do with a bit of conversation from me.

"Oh, Ida B, did you like it?" Mama asked, smiling at me.

I just nodded my head.

"What did you read?" Mama kept on.

"Just a book about a girl," I told those carrots.

"Did you know the book, or was that the first time you read it?"

"I read it before."

"Were you scared reading in front of all of those people, Ida B?"

I shrugged, like it was such a not-big-deal I could hardly recall. "Not really."

"Was it wonderful, baby?" Mama asked.

And as soon as Mama said it, I felt every drop of the goodness from reading that story. It flooded my insides, and I couldn't stop the happiness from pouring out of me.

"Yes," I said.

Then I looked right at Mama, for the first time in what seemed like forever, and she wasn't looking at me, but into me. She was pulling me to her with her eyes, like she used to do. All of a sudden I could see the light that was Mama's shining out of her eyes. I couldn't help smiling at it.

"Be careful," my heart warned me.

But I was having a hard time remembering that there was anything to be careful about. Because if I just looked at Mama's eyes, and not her bald head or her pale skin, I could tell that the part of her I thought had gone away forever was still there and glowing, only from deep down inside her.

STOP AND CHECK

Visualize How does Ida B's behavior toward her parents change? Visualizing her actions may help you.

About the Author

Katherine Hannigan spent her childhood in western New York, where she used her imagination to create stories with the dolls in her closet or paper characters cut from valentines. Years later, after earning a college degree in painting, she moved to Iowa to teach. Her new surroundings, which included several apple trees, inspired her to write *Ida B*.

Like Ida B, Katherine is an animal lover who owns a pet cat. However, the author doesn't see herself as being exactly like her storybook heroine. She says, "Hers is the life I would have chosen, if I could have. And I think I try to live up to her example—brave and true, full of fun, and fiercely loving."

Author's Purpose

Why do you think the author chose to write *Ida B* from Ida B's point of view? How did this help you understand the character?

LeAnn Guirud

Respond to the Text

Summarize

Summarize the events in the story that cause a change in Ida B. Details from your Venn Diagram may help you.

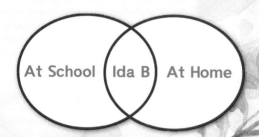

Write

The author includes many details in the story to help characterize Ida B. How do these details show how Ida B changes between the beginning and the end of the story? Use these sentence frames to organize your text evidence.

> At the beginning, the author describes Ida B . . .
> The author reveals a change in Ida's character by . . .
> At the end, the author's details show that Ida B is . . .

Make Connections

Talk about how Ida B's experience of reading in class gave her a new perspective on herself and others. **ESSENTIAL QUESTION**

What other kinds of experiences in school might help students see themselves or the world around them differently? **TEXT TO WORLD**

Genre • Realistic Fiction

Compare Texts

Read about how a boy changes when his family moves to a farmhouse.

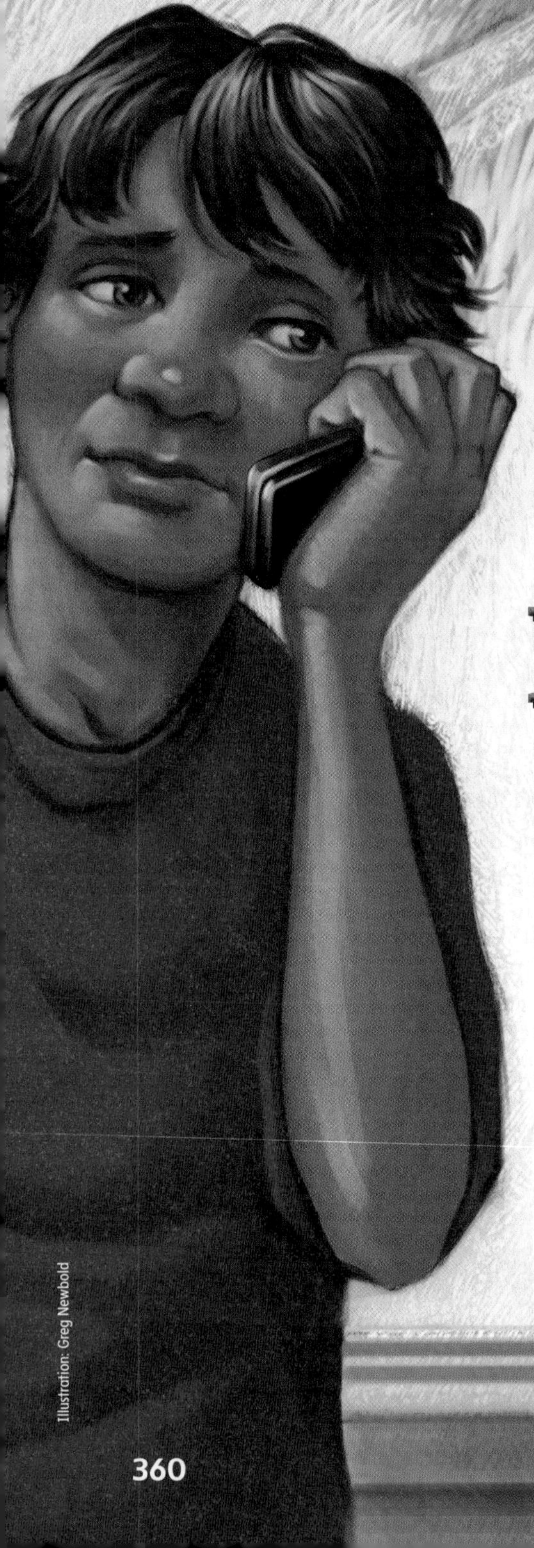

A DUSTY RIDE

Ravi drew back the curtains of his new bedroom, surveyed the view, and sighed into the phone. "Rob, there's nothing to do here," he told his friend. "There aren't even sidewalks!" As he spoke, he **focused** on a narrow dirt path near the shrubs, envisioning the city sidewalks he used to skateboard down.

"Look, it can't be that bad," Rob said on the other end of the phone, attempting to reassure him. "There are probably loads of things to do, and besides, I'll come visit soon."

Ravi was looking forward to it, but when he hung up he felt lonelier than before, so he headed downstairs to find his parents.

Illustration: Greg Newbold

"How's it going?" Ravi's mother asked, unpacking files in the office.

His dad adjusted a desk near the window, stood back to admire the room, and exclaimed, "What a change! To have fresh air right at my desk! Isn't it great, Ravi?"

Even though Ravi didn't agree, he didn't say so because it was his dad who had jumped at his company's offer to work outside the city. His mother, sharing his father's enthusiasm for a change, had decided to work from home, too, and before Ravi knew it, they had found a farmhouse to call home. Everyone, it seemed, had adjusted to the **transition** except Ravi.

He muttered a half-hearted reply, "Yeah, great," and then asked, "Can I go out for a little while?"

"Sure! Yes," his dad encouraged, "go explore!"

Outside, Ravi wondered, *Explore what?* Although he'd been there several weeks, he hadn't seen anything worth exploring. Then he remembered the dirt path he saw earlier and headed toward the side of the house.

Ravi had not gotten far down the path when he heard the hedgerow nearby rustle. As the shrubs began to shake, he detected heavy breathing and what sounded like a snort. Picturing a gigantic beast on the other side, Ravi retreated but then paused at the sound of a voice. He turned to see a woman on horseback emerge from the shrubs.

Seeing Ravi, the woman pulled the reins, stopping the horse in its tracks. He'd never seen a horse up close, and from his **perspective,** it was a towering giant.

"Hi!" the woman said, dismounting. "I hope we didn't scare you. I'm Lila, this is Dusty, and we live at the farm down the road. I was just coming by to welcome you!"

Sensing Ravi's hesitation, Lila explained, "No need to be scared of this old guy. In fact, Dusty is rather unique because he seems to sense your feelings: If you're scared, he gets nervous, but if you're calm, he's as cool as a cucumber." She gave him a wink, and added, "But Dusty has a way of calming people."

Ravi's parents came outside upon hearing Lila's voice, and, as the three introduced themselves, Ravi eyed the horse uneasily and noticed that the horse seemed to eye him, too.

Before Lila left, she said to them, "You should come on by! Maybe you'd even like to take a ride, Ravi? Dusty is a great tour guide."

"Yeah, maybe. Thanks," Ravi replied, but as he watched Lila ride away, the thought of being so high up on such an animal quickly turned his interest into doubt.

The next week, when he and his parents visited the farm, Lila and Dusty greeted them at the gate, eager for a ride. Ravi hadn't come up with a good excuse, and even if he had, Lila was hard to say no to. "C'mon up!" Lila said. "Grab my hand, set your left foot in that stirrup there, and then swing your leg over." Remembering what Lila had said the week before, Ravi took a deep breath to calm him, looked Dusty squarely in the eyes, and then climbed on.

As the horse settled under the added weight, Lila adjusted the reins and they took off at a measured trot.

Lila toured Ravi around the farm, telling him about raising chickens, pigs, and cows, and every now and then asking, "Right Dusty?" as if he would reply. Dusty seemed to nod knowingly.

When they passed the horse stables, Ravi was surprised, and asked, "You have more horses?"

"Oh, yes, I have many," Lila replied. "But Dusty's my favorite."

I'm beginning to see why, thought Ravi. Riding with Dusty made him forget he was so far away from his friends.

As they trotted back to Ravi's waiting parents, Ravi petted Dusty, looking forward to his next visit.

"So what do you think? Would you like to learn horseback riding?" Lila asked. "Eventually you could ride Dusty yourself."

"Wow, that would be great!" Ravi replied, then turned to his parents and asked, "May I?" At that, Dusty jerked his head up as if asking, too. They all burst into laughter.

"Who could say no to that?" his Dad answered.

Make Connections

How does Ravi's experience with Lila and Dusty change his view of his new home? **ESSENTIAL QUESTION**

Think of a character from another story who also adjusts to a change. How does each character's perspective change? **TEXT TO TEXT**

Essential Question

How do shared experiences help people adapt to change?

Read about how a band helps a boy adjust to a new home.

Go Digital!

Bud, Not Buddy

by Christopher Paul Curtis
illustrated by Floyd Cooper

Bud is a motherless ten-year-old boy growing up in Flint, Michigan during the Great Depression, shuttling between orphanages and foster homes. Bud doesn't have much, but he has a few special things. One is a set of rules—"Bud Caldwell's Rules and Things for Having a Funner Life"—about everything he's learned so far about surviving. He also has a suitcase full of treasured possessions: photos, a blanket, some special stones, and flyers advertising a famous band. While these items are the only mementoes Bud has of his mother, they also provide clues that Bud thinks may help him find a special man he's never met—his father.

Bud tracks down Herman E. Calloway, the well-known band leader who Bud believes to be his father. Calloway turns out to be a gruff old man who claims not to know anything about the boy. Fortunately, Calloway's band members, Grace Thomas, "Steady Eddie" Patrick, Jimmy Wesley, Chug "Doo-Doo Bug" Cross, Roy "Dirty Deed" Breed, and Doug "the Thug" Tennant, take a liking to Bud. After Bud joins the band for a meal at the Sweet Pea restaurant, where he breaks down and cries out of exhaustion and relief, Bud is invited to spend the night in a spare room at "Grand Calloway Station," Herman Calloway's large and busy home. The next morning, a still-tired Bud doesn't remember getting in bed, and wonders if he was put there by Miss Thomas. As Bud shakes off sleep, he hears voices in the house and follows them downstairs.

Right when I got near the kitchen door I could hear Herman E. Calloway saying, "...so that's how that cookie's going to crumble."

Miss Thomas said, "You have no idea how bad those orphanages can be, it's no place to be raised. I can't believe you, you'll take care of any stray dog wandering through this neighborhood, but when it comes to a child all of a sudden you have no **sympathy**. You might not have been paying attention, but we agreed last night what we were going to do about that boy, and that's what we're sticking to."

Uh-oh. I was glad I didn't take anything out of my suitcase, 'cause it looked like I might be making a break for the street again.

Herman E. Calloway said, "Like I said, I'ma find out what the real story is in Flint, and then we'll see."

Miss Thomas said, "That's fine, I believe the child. You, above all people, should know that I've got a sense about when someone is lying."

Uh-oh. I'd have to remember that.

She kept talking. "Until we've heard otherwise from Flint, he's staying right here."

A fourth voice said, "Well, I'm glad to hear it, that means I didn't go digging around in the basement for nothing. I think he's going to really like this."

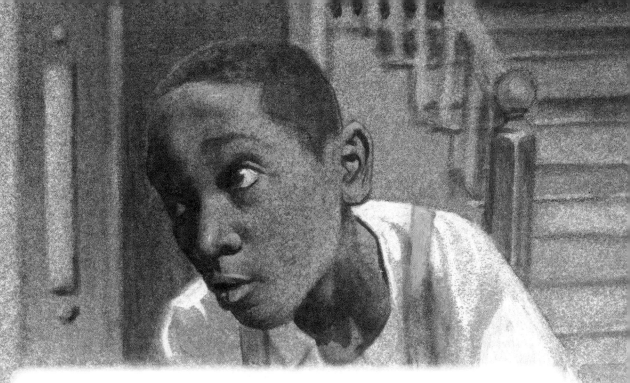

It was Steady Eddie and it sounded like he had something for me!

I ran back up the steps on my tiptoes and down the hall to the little dead girl's room. I stood outside the room and closed the door loud enough that they could hear it downstairs. I *clump-clump-clump*ed down the hall to the door that Miss Thomas said was the bathroom.

When I was done I pulled on a chain that made the water come down. The loud noise made me jump back.

Man, these inside-the-house outhouses were hard to get used to. I washed my hands with running hot water and closed the bathroom door kind of loud.

I *clump-clump-clump*ed down the steps, stopping a couple of times to yawn real loud.

When I walked into the kitchen they all had looks on their faces like they hadn't been talking about me at all.

I said, "Good morning, Mr. Calloway," but I didn't really mean it, then said, "Good morning, Miss Thomas, good morning, Mr. Jimmy, good morning, Steady Eddie."

STOP AND CHECK

Make Predictions Why does Bud go back upstairs? What do you think Steady Eddie will give him? Look for details in the story to Make a Prediction.

I noticed right away that Miss Thomas didn't have all her diamond rings on, I guess it would've been hard sleeping with them flashing lights up at you, she must have to keep them closed up in a box that the sparkles can't get out of. I noticed too that even without the rings Miss Thomas still had to be the most beautiful woman in the world.

They smiled and said, "Good morning, Bud." All except Herman E. Calloway. He got up from the table and said, "I don't like the way Loudean is sounding, I'ma have a look at her plugs."

He went outside through a door at the back of the kitchen.

Miss Thomas said, "Bud, we'd just about given up on you. Do you usually sleep until after noon?"

After noon? Man, I couldn't believe it, I'd slept as long as those rich folks in the moving pictures!

"No, ma'am, that's the first time I ever did that."

She said, "I know you must be starving, but if you can hold out for another half hour or so Mr. Jimmy's going to make everyone's lunch. Think you can wait?"

"Yes, ma'am." A half hour wasn't nothing to wait, no matter how hungry you were.

Mr. Jimmy said, "So what's the scoop, little man?"

I didn't know what that meant so I said, "Nothing, sir."

Steady Eddie said, "How'd you sleep, kiddo?"

"Great, sir." Oops, I forgot I wasn't supposed to call the band men *sir*.

He said, "Cop a squat." He pointed at a chair. I guessed that meant "sit down," so I did.

Miss Thomas said, "Were your ears burning last night, Bud?"

Man, all these Grand Rapids people really do talk funny. I only came from the other side of the state and it was like they talked some strange language out here. I said, "What, ma'am?"

She said, "There's an old saying that when people talk about you behind your back your ears start to get real warm, kind of like they were burning."

I said, "No, ma'am, my ears felt just fine."

She said, "Well, they should've been burning, you were the subject of a very long conversation last night. But as sound asleep as you were, I'm really not all that surprised you didn't notice. I had to check your pulse to make sure you were still alive!"

Shucks! I knew it. She did come in when I was conked out and took my doggone pants and shirt off and put me there. Man, this was real embarrassing.

Miss Thomas said, "Mr. Calloway and the band and I talked about you for a long time. We've come up with something we want to discuss with you, but we need your help in deciding what to do."

Uh-oh. That was Rules and Things Number 36, or something, that meant I was going to have to get ready to go fetch something for her.

I said, "Yes, ma'am?"

She said, "We've got to talk to some people in Flint first, but if they say it's all right, we were hoping that you'd stay here at Grand Calloway Station for a while."

A gigantic smile split my face in half.

Miss Thomas said, "I'm going to **assume** that that smile means yes."

I said, "Yes, ma'am! Thank you, ma'am!"

Miss Thomas said, "Before that grin gets stuck on your face, let me tell you you're going to have lots of chores and things to take care of around here, Bud, you'll be expected to pull your own weight the best you can. We all like a very clean house and none of us are too used to having children around, so we're all going to have to learn to be patient with each other. There's one person in particular that you're going to have to be very patient with. Do you know who I mean?"

I sure did. "Yes, ma'am, it's Mr. Calloway."

She said, "Good boy, give him some time. He really needs help with a lot of different things, he swears someone's adding weight onto that bass fiddle of his every year, but he's just getting older. He can use some young, wiry hands to help him around. Think you can handle that?"

Now I knew for sure she'd looked at my legs, she must've thought I was a real **weakling**.

I said, "Yes, ma'am, my legs are a lot stronger than they look, most folks are surprised by that."

Miss Thomas said, "I don't doubt that at all, Bud. I'm not worried about your body being strong, I'm more concerned about your spirit. Lord knows Mr. Calloway is going to give it a test."

I said, "Yes, ma'am, my spirit's a lot stronger than it looks too, most folks are really surprised by that."

She smiled and said, "Very good, but you know what, Bud?"

"What, ma'am?"

"I knew you were an old toughie the minute I saw you."

I smiled again.

She said, "Our schedule's pretty heavy for the next couple of months, and then come September we'll have to see about school for you, but we'll be doing a lot of traveling right around Michigan, so I hope you don't mind long car trips."

"No, ma'am."

She said, "That's great, Bud. Something tells me you were a godsend to us, you keep that in mind all of the time, OK?"

"Yes, ma'am."

Then she did something that made me feel strange. She stood up, grabbed both my arms and looked right hard in my face, just like Momma used to, she said, "Really, Bud, I want you to always keep that in mind, this might get hard for you some of the time and I don't always travel with the band, so I don't want you to forget what I'm telling you."

I said, "No, ma'am, I won't."

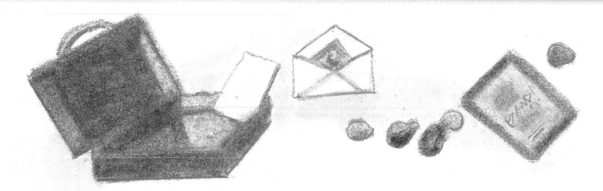

Steady Eddie said, "Since you're going to be part of the family there's some things we've got to talk about. Now I've noticed the tight grip you keep on that old suitcase of your'n. I need to know how attached to it you are."

"I carry it with me everywhere I go 'cause all my things are in there." I wasn't sure if I liked the way this talk was going.

Steady Eddie said, "That's what I need to know, are you attached to the suitcase, or is it the things inside that are important?"

I'd never thought about that before, I'd always thought of the suitcase and the things inside together.

I said, "The things I got from my mother are the most important."

He said, "Good, 'cause if you're going to be traveling with us it just wouldn't look too copacetic for you to be carrying that ratty old bag."

He reached under the kitchen table and pulled out one of those funny-looking suitcases that the band kept all their instruments in. This one looked like a baby one to his.

He put it on the table, opened it and said, "Since you're going to be traveling with Herman E. Calloway and the Worthy Swarthys, which is known far and wide as a very classy band, it's only fitting that you quit carrying your things in that cardboard suitcase.

"This is my old alto saxophone case, I've been hanging on to it for three years now, ever since the horn got stole right off the stage in Saginaw, but it doesn't look like I'm ever gonna get it back, so I figured you might as well keep your momma's things in it."

Wow! "Thank you, Steady Eddie!"

I pulled my new case over to me. The inside of it had a great
big dent where Steady Eddie's saxophone used to go, now
there wasn't anything in it but a little raggedy pink towel. The
case had some soft smooth black stuff all over the inside of it, it
covered everything, even the dent. There was a real old smell
that came out of it too, like dried-up slobber and something dead.
It smelled great!

The back kitchen door opened and I thought Herman E.
Calloway was coming back in to ruin everybody's fun, but it was
the rest of the band.

Everybody said hello, poured themselves some coffee, then sat
down at the table.

Doo-Doo Bug said, "I see Mr. C's got Loudean's carburetor tore
down again, anything wrong?"

Miss Thomas said, "There's lots wrong, but not with that car."

They all laughed so I joined in too.

I patted my new case and said, "This here's my case now, I'm
going to be going around with you."

They smiled and Dirty Deed said, "So we hear. Glad to have
you on board, partner."

Steady Eddie said, "I was just about to tell him some of the things Herman E. Calloway requires of anybody in his band."

The Thug said, "Otherwise known as Herman E. Calloway's Rules to **Guarantee** You Have No Female Companionship, No Alcohol, and No Fun at All."

"Rule number one, practice two hours a day."

Mr. Jimmy said, "That's a good one."

Steady Eddie said, "So I got you this, Bud."

Steady Eddie had another present for me! This was a long, brown, skinny wooden flute. I was going to have to learn music!

He said, "It's called a recorder. Once you've developed a little wind, and some tone and a embouchure we'll move on to something a little more complicated."

Those must've been more of those Grand Rapids words 'cause they sure weren't like any American talk I ever heard before.

I said, "Thank you!"

STOP AND CHECK

Confirm or Revise Predictions What does Steady Eddie give Bud? How does this make Bud feel? Confirming or Revising your Prediction may help you.

374

Steady Eddie said, "Don't thank me until you've been through a couple of hours of blowing scales. We'll see if you're still grateful then."

The Thug said, "Now all that's left is to give little stuff here a name."

Miss Thomas said, "You know, I don't like the way Loudean's been sounding, I think I'm gonna go check the air in the trunk." She picked her coffee up and started to leave the kitchen.

Doo-Doo Bug said, "You don't have to leave, Miss Thomas."

"Darling, I know that, it's just that this is one of those man things that you all think is so mysterious and special that I have absolutely no interest in. The only thing I can hope is that the process has improved since you four were given your names." Then she left the room.

As soon as she was gone Steady Eddie told me, "Hand me your ax and stand up, Bud." I was starting to catch on to this Grand Rapids talk, I remember that a ax was a instrument. I handed Steady my recorder and stood up in front of him.

He said, "Uh-uh, she was right, this is mysterious and special, so that grin's got to go, brother."

I tried to tie down my smile.

Steady said, "Mr. Jimmy, you're the senior musician here, would you proceed?"

Mr. Jimmy said, "Gentlemen, the floor's open for names for the newest member of the band, Bud-not-Buddy."

They started acting like they were in school. The Thug raised his hand and Mr. Jimmy pointed at him.

Thug said, "Mr. Chairman, in light of the boy's performance last night at the Sweet Pea, I **nominate** the name Waterworks Willie."

Shucks, I was hoping they'd forgot about that.

Mr. Jimmy said, "You're out of order, Douglas."

Steady raised his hand. "Mr. Chairman, this boy's **obviously** going to be a musician, he slept until twelve-thirty today, so I propose that we call him Sleepy."

Mr. Jimmy said, "The name Sleepy is before the board, any comments?"

Dirty Deed said, "Too simple. I think we need something that lets folks know about how slim the boy is."

Doo-Doo Bug said, "How about the Bone?"

Steady said, "Not enough class, he needs something so people will know right off that the boy's got class."

Mr. Jimmy said, "How do you say *bone* in French? French always makes things sound a lot classier."

The Thug said, "That's easy, *bone* in French is *la bone*."

Doo-Doo Bug said, "*La bone*, nah, it don't have a ring to it."

Steady Eddie said, "I got it, we'll compromise. How about Sleepy LaBone?"

I couldn't tie the smile down anymore, that was about the best name I'd ever heard in my life!

Mr. Jimmy said, "Let me try it out. Ladies and gentlemen, thank you very much for coming out on this cold November night, this night that will live in history, this night that for the first time on any stage anywhere, you have listened to the smooth saxophonical musings of that prodigy of the reed, Mr. Sleepy LaBone!"

The whole crowd broke out clapping.

The Thug said, "What can I say but *bang*!"

Dirty Deed said, "You nailed him!"

Doo-Doo Bug said, "That is definitely smooth."

Steady said, "My man!"

Mr. Jimmy said, "Kneel down, young man."

I got down on one knee.

Mr. Jimmy tapped me on the head three times with my recorder and said, "Arise and welcome to the band, Mr. Sleepy LaBone."

I got off my knee and looked at my bandmates.

Sleepy LaBone. Shucks, that was the kind of name that was enough to make you forget folks had ever called you Buddy, or even Clarence. That was the kind of name that was enough to make you practice *four* hours every day, just so you could live up to it!

STOP AND CHECK

Summarize How do the band members decide Bud's new name? How does Bud feel about becoming a part of the band? Summarizing the events may help you.

About the Author and Illustrator

Christopher Paul Curtis

says that good writers need to have "really good ears and really good eyes." He fills his books with sights and sounds to give readers a feel for what life was really like for the characters in a given place and time. Christopher's own grandparents lived through the Great Depression and became models for characters. His grandfather was the lead musician of Herman Curtis and the Dusky Devastators of the Depression.

Christopher won a Newbery medal award and a Coretta Scott King award for *Bud, Not Buddy.*

Floyd Cooper

was born and raised in Tulsa, Oklahoma but moved to New York as an adult to work as an illustrator. Floyd creates his award-winning illustrations using oil paint—and an eraser! Once the paint dries, Floyd erases some of the paint, leaving behind warm colors that illuminate the story. Floyd's illustrations have won him many honors, including the Coretta Scott King award for illustrators.

Author's Purpose

The author's main purpose for writing *Bud, Not Buddy* is to entertain. What other reasons do you think the author had in writing this story?

Respond to the Text

Summarize

Use key events and details to summarize Bud's experience with the band in *Bud, Not Buddy*. Information from your Character Web may help you.

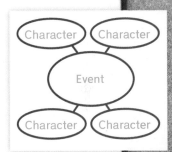

Write

How does the author show how the significance of Bud's set of rules changes and plays a role in the message of the story? Use these sentence frames to organize your text evidence.

> The rules change . . .
> This is important because . . .
> This affects the story . . .

Make Connections

Talk about how becoming a member of the band helps Bud adapt to life at "Grand Calloway Station." ESSENTIAL QUESTION

How will the band members' lives change once Bud joins them? Give an example of another kind of change that a group of people might face together. What benefit would come from sharing the experience? TEXT TO WORLD

Genre • Expository Text

Compare Texts
Read about how music provided hope
for people during the Great Depression.

MUSICAL IMPRESSIONS
of the Great Depression

In the 1930s, a downturn in the economy caused hardship for
millions of people that lasted for years. This period became known as
the Great Depression. To some, it seemed the difficult times might
never end. Others remained hopeful that good times were just around
the corner. The music of this era reflected both perspectives.

The Great Depression

After a decade of prosperity called the Roaring Twenties, economic progress in the United States changed abruptly. In October of 1929, the stock market collapsed and left thousands of investors broke. In turn, many companies laid off workers that they could no longer afford to pay. Around the same time, a massive drought destroyed crops and also left many farmers penniless. With so few resources, people across the country struggled to get by.

Sympathy through Song

Many songs of the 1930s, particularly in folk and country music, recounted people's stories of loss and hardship. The songwriter Woody Guthrie followed farm workers who traveled west to California hoping to find work. He saw that they often encountered new and tougher challenges. Guthrie expressed **sympathy** for them through songs like "Dust Bowl Blues" and "Goin' Down the Road Feeling Bad." He hoped to restore people's sense of dignity.

Meanwhile, across the country, The Carter Family performed similar songs, such as "Worried Man Blues," describing life in the Appalachian Mountains where resources were scarce. Listeners found comfort in the knowledge that they were not alone in their struggles.

During the 1930s, bands like this one (left) lifted people's spirits. Woody Guthrie (right) toured the country and composed songs about the challenges people faced.

A popular style of music called
swing inspired people to dance.

On the Up-Swing

Times were certainly hard in the country. In the nation's cities,
the situation was equally difficult. In some African-American
communities, unemployment soared above fifty percent. These
challenges reminded some of earlier times of slavery, and many found
comfort in the musical styles of that era: gospel and blues.

Jazz, a newer form of music with upbeat rhythms, lifted people's
spirits. Band leaders like Duke Ellington and Count Basie created
a new, high-energy style of jazz called swing. Around the country,
people of all races responded to these positive rhythms. People left
their problems behind and escaped onto the dance floor.

In New York, Broadway musicals delighted theatergoers. Many
musicals offered light entertainment, while others addressed the
current hardships through songs, such as "Brother, Can You Spare a
Dime?" Radio helped spread these songs beyond the city, connecting
people across the country and creating nationwide hits.

Reaction from the Government

While some blamed the government for hard times, President Franklin Delano Roosevelt (FDR) created programs the public could **rely** on for assistance and new opportunities. This legislation became known as the New Deal. As part of a program called the Works Progress Administration, FDR initiated the Federal Music Project in 1935. His wife, Eleanor, promoted its main goals. These were to help musicians find work and to **guarantee** all people access to the arts, regardless of their financial situation.

Eleanor Roosevelt (standing, center) supported the work of musicians.

Before long, federally supported concerts and shows played on the radio and in music halls across the country. Throughout the nation, teachers provided free voice and instrument lessons to help promote participation and music appreciation. The government's **supportive** programs also paid musicians to travel and record styles of folk music from different regions. These recordings were preserved in our country's Library of Congress.

By the end of the 1930s, the hardest days of the Great Depression had passed. Times had been tough, but music had offered a way for people to share their fears and keep up their hopes. The music remains a legacy of this era that has inspired musicians to this day.

A poster for a government-funded performance

Make Connections

How did the shared experience of music help people adapt to the changes caused by the Great Depression? ESSENTIAL QUESTION

How have characters in a story helped each other adapt to a change? How are their actions similar to the way people helped each other get through the Great Depression? TEXT TO TEXT

GLOBAL WARMING

by Seymour Simon

Essential Question

What changes in the environment affect living things?

Read about how a change in climate can affect living things.

Go Digital!

Thousands of years ago, large parts of the land mass on Earth were covered by ice. Since then, Earth has been getting warmer. In recent decades, the rise in average temperature has been particularly rapid. "Global warming" is the term that has been used to describe these changes.

Weather and climate are different. Weather is what happens every day. Climate is the average weather over a period of years. For example, it's possible that the weather on any day might be cool but the average weather, the climate, is getting warmer.

Why is the climate changing? Could Earth be getting warmer by itself? Are people doing things that make the climate warmer? What will be the **impact** of global warming? Can we do anything about it?

Global warming is happening because of the greenhouse effect. A greenhouse is a house made of glass. The glass lets in sunlight but keeps warm air from escaping. Earth is not a greenhouse, but certain gases in the **atmosphere** act like the glass in a greenhouse. Sunlight passes through Earth's atmosphere and warms the ground. Some of the heat bounces back into space, but much of it remains trapped near the ground by carbon dioxide, water vapor, and other greenhouse gases in the atmosphere.

The greenhouse effect helps make Earth warm enough for life to exist. But if greenhouse gases are released into the atmosphere in larger amounts much faster than before, then the warming will get much stronger and the climate will **noticeably** change.

In 2007, a report by 2,500 scientists from 130 countries concluded that humans are responsible for much of the current warming. No *one* person causes global warming. But there are billions of people on Earth. We cut down huge numbers of trees, drive hundreds of millions of cars and trucks, and burn vast amounts of coal and oil. All these activities contribute to a huge increase in greenhouse gases. Even if we decreased the amount of gases we now produce, it would not immediately stop the warming because greenhouse gases stay in the atmosphere for years.

The Earth's climate is very complex, and many factors play important roles in determining how the climate changes. Natural **variations** in Earth's orbit around the sun change the amount of sunlight we receive and thus the temperature. Earth has had much warmer and much colder climates in the distant past.

Most scientists agree that something different is happening now. While Earth's climate has always varied, it is now changing more rapidly than in any other time in recent centuries. Since we have been keeping weather records, nineteen of the twenty hottest years *ever* have happened since 1980.

For thousands of years, the balance of greenhouse gases in the atmosphere had not changed much. But now we burn huge amounts of coal, oil, and natural gas to generate energy. Every year, billions of tons of carbon dioxide pour out from the exhausts of cars, trains, trucks, airplanes, buses, and ships and from the chimneys of factories. There is 30 percent more carbon dioxide in the air than there was 150 years ago.

Trees, like other green plants, convert carbon dioxide into oxygen.

But trees and forests are cut down in huge numbers. When wood burns or **decays**, even more carbon dioxide is released. Carbon dioxide enters into the atmosphere much faster than the remaining forests and oceans can absorb it.

The release of other greenhouse gases adds to the speed at which the world's climate is changing. Methane is released by millions and millions of cattle and other farm animals. Nitrous oxide comes from chemicals used in soil fertilizers, as well as from automobiles.

STOP AND CHECK

Ask and Answer Questions According to the author, why has the atmosphere changed? Go back to the text to find the answer.

Bernhard Edmaier/Photo Researchers, Inc.

The Arctic is already showing the effects of global warming. Average temperatures in the northern regions of Alaska, Canada, and Russia have risen twice as fast as in the rest of the world. The Ward Hunt Ice Shelf, the largest single sheet of ice in the Arctic, started to crack in 2000. By 2002, it had split. Now it is breaking into smaller pieces.

The Arctic Ocean is the great body of sea ice that covers the North Pole. Satellite photographs show that the ice pack has been shrinking and thinning in depth since the early 1990s. Scientists say that for the first time in human history, ice may disappear from the Arctic Ocean every summer.

Global warming has also changed the feeding patterns and behaviors of polar bears, walruses, seals, and whales. It may even impact their survival.

Polar bears live only in the Arctic. They are completely dependent on the sea ice for all their life needs. In the winter, females give birth to cubs. The mother polar bear eats little or no food during the winter.

As spring approaches, the bear family makes a run onto the sea ice to feed on seals, their main source of food. If the ice melts, their food supply will be cut off and this will impact their survival.

Glaciers and mountain snow covers are rapidly melting. Almost every glacier in Alaska is **receding**. A few decades ago, huge rivers of ice stretched over the land. Now hundreds of feet or sometimes miles of bare rock and soil are exposed. In 1963, the Mendenhall Glacier Visitor Center in Juneau opened, very close to the glacier. Today, it is a mile or more away from the frozen edge of the retreating glacier.

In the 1850s, there were 150 glaciers in Montana. By 1968, there were 37. In 2008, there were fewer than 24. Glaciers that have lasted for thousands of years may be gone in two decades.

The icy coverings on tall mountain peaks are also disappearing. Each year, there is less snow remaining on the mountains during the summer. The snow melts earlier by a week or more in the spring, and snow falls later by a week or more in the autumn.

Grinnell and Salamander Glaciers,
1957

Grinnell and Salamander Glaciers,
2004

As temperatures rise, the level of the oceans will rise. A recent study found that if average temperatures rise by 3° Celsius (5.4° Fahrenheit), Greenland's enormous ice sheet will begin to melt and sea levels all over the world may rise by a half foot to 3 feet or more.

This may happen over years or decades or may take longer than a century. A 3-foot rise in sea level would swamp the Gulf Coast and every East Coast city from Boston to Miami. Rising water would cover low-lying areas such as the Nile Delta and countries such as Bangladesh. Millions of people would be forced to move.

The Antarctic ice cap holds about 90 percent of the world's ice and about 70 percent of its freshwater. It does not look as if the entire ice cap will melt anytime soon, but if it does happen, sea levels would rise 20 or more feet. Now, *that* would cause major flooding in coastal areas.

Atmospheric warming can cause a rise in ocean temperatures and place coral reefs in jeopardy. Coral reefs are huge branching structures made of the limestone skeletons of tiny animals called coral polyps. Coral reefs are found in warm, clear, shallow oceans. They are home to many kinds of fishes, jellyfish, anemones, crabs, turtles, sea snakes, clams, and octopuses and the algae that give the reefs their stunning colors.

Most coral reefs are highly sensitive. Even small changes in water temperature and in the amount of carbon dioxide in the water can kill algae in a reef. When the coral dies, it bleaches white. In 1998, a weather pattern called El Niño warmed the seas. In just one year, about one in every six of the world's reefs was lost. If coral reefs die, then much of the animal life they support will be wiped out as well.

Changing climate affects every ocean and every continent. Rising temperatures add heat energy and water vapor to the atmosphere. That can lead to heavier rainfalls and more powerful storms in some places, and long droughts in others. The changes will differ depending upon the location.

Many tropical areas may have greater rainfall. But in dry regions, even less rain may fall. Higher temperatures will cause the soil to dry up, and terrible droughts may ensue.

STOP AND CHECK

Ask and Answer Questions How might a warmer climate affect life in the oceans and on land? Look for details in the text to help you.

393

Wildfires may increase in forested areas as timberlands grow drier. The fires are likely to be bigger and more frequent and to burn longer. They would also release more carbon dioxide into the atmosphere and could lead to more warming.

Climate changes are not as easy to notice as changes in the weather. For example, a particular storm or a number of warm days during a winter is not really evidence of anything. We can all see day-to-day weather changes. But climate changes are noticeable as well. Plants and animals are already showing the effects of Earth's warming. Cold places, such as the North and South Poles and mountaintops, have been the first to feel the heat. Spring has come earlier, the ice has melted sooner, and there are fewer days where the temperatures are below freezing.

Many kinds of wildlife need the cold to survive. Some animals have adapted to the warmer weather by migrating to colder places. As the climate has warmed over the past century, the colorful checkerspot butterfly of the American West has moved northward or to higher elevations. The checkerspot butterfly has almost completely disappeared from its original home in Mexico and has adjusted to its new northern home in Canada. But not every animal can travel as easily. Scientists worry that crowding on mountaintops and colder places will cause some species to become extinct.

We can't do anything about some changes in our environment. Our planet may be going through a natural cycle of getting warmer. However, most scientists say that humans are at least partly responsible for climate change. That means it may be possible for people to slow down the change.

There is a debate about what we can do about our changing climate. Here's what people in some nations are trying to do:

- Improve fuel and energy economy so that people use less energy for vehicles, schools, offices, homes, and factories.
- Encourage the use of wind and solar power.
- Explore alternative ways of producing energies that do not directly release more greenhouse gases into the atmosphere.
- Protect and plant trees to increase forestlands.

Lisa J. Goodman/Photographer's Choice/Getty Images

Nations and governments can do certain things to slow down dramatic climate changes. People can help, too. They can choose to use less energy to heat and cool their houses or use less fuel when getting around. Here are some things we might consider:

- Walking, biking, or using public transportation. One school bus can carry the same number of children as 30 or more cars.

- Using sturdy reusable bags for shopping and reusable cups and glasses is less wasteful than using disposable bags and cups.

- Taking short showers uses less energy than long showers.

- Planting a single tree can make enough oxygen for the lifetimes of two people. If one million trees are planted, the trees would eventually absorb more than one million tons of carbon dioxide.

Here's what some families are doing to slow down rapid climate change:

- Using fans instead of air conditioners. They may set a house air conditioner slightly higher in the summer, and slightly lower their heaters. They may lower a water heater's thermostat from "hot" (about 135° F.) to "warm" (about 120° F.).

- Using energy-saving fluorescent lightbulbs instead of incandescent lightbulbs. Fluorescent lightbulbs are more energy efficient and save on electricity costs.

- Turning off electric appliances and lights when they are not being used.

- Installing double-paned windows, extra insulation, good weather stripping, and solar panels to houses also saves energy.

Global warming isn't just about the Arctic Ocean melting and distant deserts becoming drier and hotter. Climate change impacts all of us. It can affect the world's food supply and the economic **stability** of countries.

The people and governments of the world are developing the tools and the scientific know-how to meet these challenges. As Earth's climate continues to change, we all want to find ways to safeguard our own and future generations.

STOP AND CHECK

Summarize How are some people trying to slow climate change? The strategy Summarize may help you.

Bloomimage/Corbis

About the Author

Seymour Simon was born and raised in New York City, but he learned a lot about the natural world from exploring parks and vacant lots near his home and taking trips to nearby mountains and seashores. Before turning to full-time writing, he taught science and creative writing in the New York City public school system.

From space to snakes, from wolves to whales—if it's a fascinating scientific subject, chances are that Simon has written a book about it. He has written more than two hundred science books for children, many of them award-winning. Simon not only writes about science, he also photographs nature. He uses photographs to illustrate many of his books.

Author's Purpose

Simon features photographs in many of his books. How does the author's use of photographs in this selection support the information?

Respond to the Text

Summarize

Use the most important details from *Global Warming* to summarize what you learned about changes in the environment. Details from your Venn Diagram may help you.

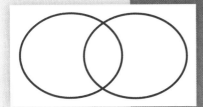

Write

How do the photographs in this selection help you understand how living things are affected by climate change? Use these sentence frames to organize your text evidence.

> The author uses photographs that show . . .
> The photographs are important because . . .
> This helps me understand . . .

Make Connections

How has a change in climate affected wildlife in different locations? **ESSENTIAL QUESTION**

Give one example of what some nations are doing about climate change. How might this activity affect the environment? **TEXT TO WORLD**

Compare Texts
Read about how volcanic
eruptions affect living things.

WHEN VOLCANOES ERUPT

On the morning of May 18, 1980, gray ash drifted from the
sky near Mount Saint Helens, Washington, turning day into
night. A volcano had erupted, sending an ash cloud thousands
of feet into the sky. Rock debris and ice fell from the mountain
and was pushed by the eruption across nearby lakes and ridges.
The eruption went on for just nine hours, but in that time the
surrounding landscape completely changed.

A column of ash and gas rose 15 miles into the air
when Mount Saint Helens erupted.

Cascades Volcano Observatory

VENTS IN THE EARTH

What causes a volcano like Mount Saint Helens to erupt? Beneath Earth's rocky crust, there is a layer that consists partly of hot, melted rock. This molten rock is called magma. A **gradual** buildup of pressure caused by gases within Earth can cause magma to burst or seep through vents, or openings, in Earth's surface.

Magma that has escaped to the surface is called lava. Depending on the type of volcano, lava can explode upward or flow slowly outward. As it hardens, lava forms into solid rock.

An active volcano is one that is currently erupting, has recently erupted, or is about to erupt. An eruption can last days, weeks, months, or years. A dormant volcano has been quiet for many years, yet is still capable of erupting. An extinct volcano hasn't erupted in perhaps thousands of years and is not expected to erupt again.

A vent is also called the mouth of a volcano.

A lava flow is a stream of molten rock.

THE IMPACT OF VOLCANOES

There are about 50 volcanic eruptions that occur somewhere in the world every year. Many are concentrated in an area of the Pacific Ocean known as the "Ring of Fire." The most frequent volcanoes in the United States occur in Hawaii and in the southwestern island chain off of Alaska. Volcanoes in the Cascade Range, the mountain range that runs from western Canada south through California, are less frequent but can be more dangerous.

Eruptions can devastate surrounding areas. An eruption can spew lava, ash, rocks, mud, and poisonous gases into the air and harm nearby plants, animals, and people. Crops and property can be destroyed.

Eruptions can even have a global **impact** on the environment. Winds can move clouds of ash and gas far from an eruption site. Gases from an eruption can absorb heat and warm temperatures. At other times a volcanic cloud can block sunlight and cool temperatures. Over time, these atmospheric changes can affect a region's climate. The gases in a volcanic cloud can also combine with water vapor to make acid rain. This rain can harm plants and soil in other parts of the world.

Fortunately, scientific predictions of volcanic activity can help people escape the dangers of eruptions. Scientists monitor tremors in the earth and changes in gases emitted from a volcano. These signals of an impending eruption allow scientists to give advance warning.

The eruption of Mount Pinatubo in the Philippines in 1991 caused a haze that cooled temperatures worldwide. It also dusted the area with ash.

Philippe Bourseiller/The Image Bank/Getty Images

A FORCE OF NATURE

Volcanic eruptions can cause damage to the environment, but they are part of Earth's natural cycles. Volcanic activity has shaped and reshaped more than 80 percent of Earth's surface. It has produced mountains, plateaus, and plains. Widely scattered volcanic ash also has benefits. It can make soil fertile, eventually promoting the growth of living things. Although the immediate effects of volcanic eruptions can be dangerous and destructive to the environment, over time nature rebounds.

A mudflow (right) covered the area after Mount Saint Helens erupted. Decades later, the area has shown signs of recovery (below).

Make Connections

Talk about ways that a volcano affects living things. ESSENTIAL QUESTION

Think of another change in the environment that affects living things. How are the effects of volcanoes different? TEXT TO TEXT

Genre • Expository Text

When Is a Planet Not a Planet?

The Story of Pluto

by Elaine Scott

Essential Question

How can scientific knowledge change over time?

Read about how knowledge about our solar system has changed over time.

Go Digital!

(bkgd) Hubble Heritage Team/NASA, (c) NASA/JPL

My very eager mother just served us nine pizzas.

A silly sentence, yet schoolchildren have memorized it for years, because it helps them remember the planets in our solar system. The first letter of every word stands for a planet, in the order of how close it is to the Sun. *My very eager mother just served us nine pizzas.* Mercury, Venus, Earth, Mars, Jupiter, Saturn, Uranus, Neptune, and Pluto. Mercury is the planet closest to the Sun, and tiny Pluto is the farthest away. That is, until recently.

Pluto is still there, of course. Along with the planets, asteroids, comets, meteors, and bits of space rock and ice, Pluto is part of our solar system. Pluto and all those other objects orbit, or travel around, the Sun.

My very eager mother just served us nine pizzas. This is a composite of photos taken on many different NASA missions. It illustrates our solar system. Our star, the Sun, is at the far left; Pluto is at the far right. The wispy tail of a comet is shown in the lower left, and the Southern Ring Nebula is near the lower right. The other faint objects in the image are artistic additions, created with a computer.

However, on August 24, 2006, the International **Astronomical** Union (IAU), a group of individual astronomers and astronomical societies from around the world, made an announcement. They declared that Pluto was not a planet. Suddenly, "My very eager mother just served us nine pizzas" didn't work anymore, because now there are only eight major planets orbiting the Sun. Perhaps someone will create a new sentence to help us remember their names and order.

Names are important, but they are not the only things to know about the planets. Learning how planets form, where they are located, and what they are like is the kind of activity that makes science exciting and fun.

PLUTO'S PROBLEMS

There are two groups of planets in our solar system. The planets closest to the Sun—Mercury, Venus, Earth, and Mars—have a solid surface made of a mix of rocks, dirt, and minerals. The planets farthest away from the Sun—Jupiter, Saturn, Uranus, and Neptune—don't have a solid surface. They are made up mostly of gas, with a rocky core. Scientists have a theory about why some planets are terrestrial, or made of rocks and dirt, and why some are composed primarily of gas.

Most scientists believe that our solar system began as a space cloud, called a nebula. The nebula was made up of bits of space dust, rocks, ice, and gas. A tiny star, not yet ready to give light, began to form in the center of the nebula. The star was our Sun. As years passed, the Sun grew big enough that high temperatures and extreme pressure caused hydrogen at the center of the Sun to begin to fuse into helium and release energy as light—sunshine!

Meanwhile, the nebula continued to orbit the new Sun until it formed a large flat ring around it. Scientists call this ring a "protoplanetary disk." The disk, or ring, was hottest where it was closest to the Sun, and coolest at its outer edge. As the disk swirled around the Sun, the Sun's gravity went to work. It pulled and tugged at the bits of rock, dust, ice, and gas until they came together in clumps of material we now call the planets.

An artist's conception of a protoplanetary disk forming around a star.

407

NASA/JPL–Caltech/T. Megeath(University of Toledo) & M. Robberto(STScI)

A small portion of the Orion Nebula, 1,500 light years away from Earth. At least 153 stars in this region have protoplanetary disks swirling around them, forming new solar systems. Scientists believe our solar system formed in just this way.

The planets that were closest to the Sun didn't keep much of their gas. The Sun's heat blasted it away, leaving behind solid **spheres** of matter, with only a little gas. Those spheres became the terrestrial planets—Mercury, Venus, Earth, and Mars. But on the outer edges of the disk, far away from the Sun's heat, it was much cooler. The clumps of rock and dirt there still had their thick layers of gas; they didn't burn away. The planets farthest from the Sun became the gas giants—Jupiter, Saturn, Uranus, and Neptune.

Because astronomers still believed this theory about how our planets formed, they had a problem with Pluto. When it was first discovered in 1930, astronomers assumed Pluto was made of ice and gas because of its great distance from the sun. However, by 1987, Pluto had moved into a position that only occurs twice in its 248-year orbit and scientific instruments had improved. Astronomers were able to study Pluto and the light that reflected off it. Their instruments told them that Pluto was dense and must have a rocky core. That new information raised questions. If the planets closest to the Sun were rocky and the planets farthest away from the Sun were mostly made of gas, why was Pluto—the most distant planet of all—made of rock?

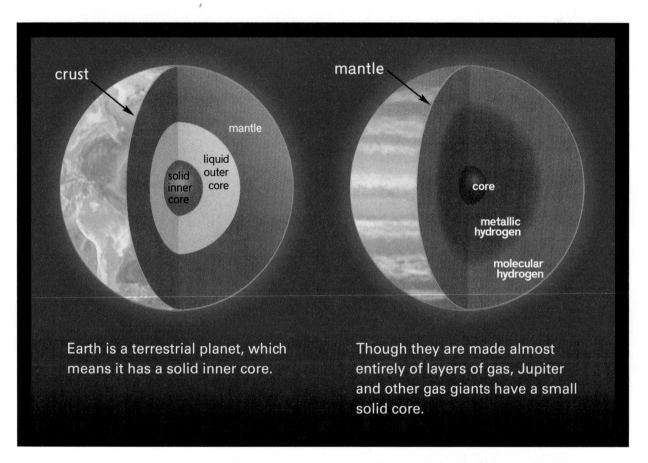

crust

mantle

mantle

liquid outer core

solid inner core

core

metallic hydrogen

molecular hydrogen

Earth is a terrestrial planet, which means it has a solid inner core.

Though they are made almost entirely of layers of gas, Jupiter and other gas giants have a small solid core.

Michelle Gengaro-Kokmen

STOP AND CHECK

Ask and Answer Questions According to theory, why are some planets mostly made of gas and others mostly made of rock? Go back to the text to find the answer.

There were other questions as well. Pluto's orbit is different from the orbits of the planets. Think of an orbit as a lane on a racetrack. Just as runners have their own lanes on the track, each planet has its own orbit around the Sun. For the runners, all the lanes together make up the racetrack. For the planets, all their orbits, taken together, make up the "orbital plane." Just as runners don't run outside their individual lanes, planets don't travel around the Sun outside their individual orbits. Except for Pluto. Pluto crosses Neptune's orbit.

Pluto's orbit

Neptune's orbit

All of the planets, comets, and asteroids in the solar system are in orbit around the Sun. Their orbits line up with each other, creating an imaginary flat disk called the orbital plane. Pluto's orbit, which takes 248 Earth years to complete, brings it outside the orbital plane. For 20 years of each orbit, Pluto moves inside the orbit of Neptune, making Neptune farther from the sun than Pluto. Pluto was inside Neptune's orbit from 1979 to 1999.

Pluto and its moon, Charon. Pluto was 2.6 billion miles from Earth when the Hubble Space Telescope took this photo.

Dr. R. Albrecht, ESA/ESO Space Telescope European Coordinating Facility; NASA

The shape of Pluto's orbit is different, too. The larger planets travel around the Sun in an oval-shaped orbit. Pluto's orbit is more of a stretched-out oblong. The other planets' orbits are level with the Sun. Pluto's is tilted. Comets' orbits are often tilted, so astronomers wondered, Could Pluto be a comet?

And of course there is Pluto's size. Astronomers knew Pluto was tiny when it was discovered in 1930. But because it was so far away, it was hard to see the planet clearly. Pluto appeared as a tiny dot of light in the night sky. Then telescopes improved. In 1976, American astronomer James Christy discovered that the tiny dot everyone thought was Pluto was really two objects: Pluto had a moon— Charon (CARE-en). Once astronomers discovered that Charon was separate from Pluto, they realized that Pluto was even smaller than they had originally thought. Pluto is only 1,440 miles in **diameter.** (Charon's diameter is 790 miles.) They began to ask, Is Pluto too small to be a planet? And since they had found Charon, they wondered, Were there more objects out there the size of Pluto? Were *they* planets, too?

FINDING PLANETS

In 1992, astronomers made an amazing discovery: 9.3 *billion* miles away from our sun is another region of space, shaped like a disk. Astronomers believe it contains approximately 70,000 icy objects, including Pluto.

This area of space was named the Kuiper Belt, after the Dutch-American astronomer Gerard Kuiper (KI-per) who lived from 1905 to 1973. In 1951, more than forty years before its discovery, Kuiper actually predicted that a region like this might exist.

Michael Brown, Chad Trujillo, and David Rabinowitz are planetary astronomers who study Kuiper Belt Objects, or KBOs. People often call these men "the Planet Finders." Together, they hunt for planets at the outer edges of our solar system using the Samuel Oschin Telescope at the Palomar Observatory in California. The Oschin telescope is a wide-field telescope, which means it views broad regions of the sky at once. When paired with a camera at the observatory, it can take pictures of these large areas.

In the past, astronomers had to spend their evenings peering through telescopes in order to study the night sky. Now things have changed. Robots control the Oschin telescope and its camera.

In the evenings, the cameras in the telescope at the Palomar Observatory are at work. They take three photographs over three hours of the part of the night sky the men want to study. Any object moving across the background of billions of stars and galaxies will be captured in pictures. The pictures are then sent from the telescope's cameras to a bank of ten computers at the California Institute of Technology. Next, the computers decide which objects appear to be moving and therefore might be a planet. Usually, the computers select about 100 objects; when the men arrive at work each morning, the pictures are ready for them to view.

Objects in the Kuiper Belt are so far away, it takes them hundreds of Earth years to orbit the Sun.

They call David Rabinowitz (left), Chad Trujillo (upper left), and Mike Brown (center) "the Planet Finders." The team used the Oschin telescope (right) to discover Eris.

(l) Courtesy of Caltech, Palomar Observatory, (c) Courtesy of Chad Trujillo, (r) Courtesy of Caltech, Palomar Observatory

Mike Brown says most of the objects he looks at on his computer screen are not planets. Many are caused by some kind of flaw in the telescope's camera. But every once in a while, an astronomer will get very lucky and something new and exciting will appear. That's how Mike and his team discovered 2003UB313, or Xena (ZEE-nah), as it was nicknamed, on October 21, 2003. Mike says, "The very first time I saw Xena on my screen, I thought that there was something wrong. It was too big and too bright. Then I did a **calculation** of how big it was and how far away it was. Xena is the most distant object ever seen in orbit around the Sun."

Pluto is 3.6 billion miles away, but Xena is 10 billion miles away and is approximately 400 miles bigger in diameter than Pluto. It takes Xena more than twice as long as Pluto to orbit the Sun.

Xena was always a nickname. On September 13, 2006, the newly discovered celestial body officially became Eris (AIR-is), for the Greek goddess of strife and discord. It seems an appropriate name, since there was a lot of strife and discord surrounding Eris. Was it a planet, or not?

An artist's conception of the Milky Way, our home galaxy. A galaxy is a group of billions of stars and their solar systems. The Milky Way is a spiral galaxy that contains 200 billion stars.

WHAT IS A PLANET?

Because scientists always check and recheck their work, Mike Brown and his team of astronomers didn't announce their discovery of Eris until January 5, 2005, after they had had a chance to verify their information. When they revealed their discovery, many people thought the solar system had gained its tenth planet. But others disagreed. Soon an argument was raging among astronomers all over the world. And the argument came down to one question. What, exactly, is a planet?

It seems surprising, but until August 24, 2006, science had never had a definition for the word "planet." Dictionaries had definitions, of course, but most said something similar to "A large celestial body that circles around the Sun or another star." For a scientist, that definition had problems. For one thing, what is meant by "large body"? Jupiter, the largest planet in our solar system, is 88,700 miles in diameter, and it is a planet. Pluto is only 1,440 miles in diameter and—at the time—it was a planet, too. The question "What is a planet?" needed an answer, and the International Astronomical Union decided to create not one definition but three.

The IAU came up with three classes of objects that orbit the Sun: planets, dwarf planets, and small solar-system bodies.

The IAU decided that a celestial body is a planet if it:

1. orbits the Sun
2. is round or nearly round, because its gravity has pulled it into that shape
3. is big enough and has enough gravity to "clear the neighborhood" around its orbit

The first two qualifications for planethood, orbiting the Sun and a round shape, are easy to understand. The concept of "clearing the neighborhood" is a little more difficult.

It might help to think of planets as the schoolyard bullies of the solar system. In order to clear the neighborhood, a planet has to be big enough, and have enough gravity, to get rid of any celestial objects in its way. A large planet might clear its orbit by using its gravity to pull other, smaller, objects toward it and destroy them, the way asteroids are destroyed when they hit Earth.

A cosmic collision. Planets often "clear their neighborhoods" in this manner.

Or a planet might clear its orbit by attracting smaller objects toward it, then turning them into moons that remain in orbit around the planet.

Sometimes a planet will simply push a smaller body into a completely different orbit and get rid of it that way. But no matter how it does the clearing, according to the IAU definition, a planet must travel in its orbit by itself.

The secondary category of planets, called "dwarf planets," have the following characteristics. They must:

1. orbit the Sun
2. be round
3. not be a moon or satellite of another planet

By this definition, Pluto is a dwarf planet. And although Charon, its former moon, is still locked in an orbit with Pluto, it is a dwarf planet, too. Now they are known as a double-planet system. Ceres is a dwarf planet, also, and Mike Brown's discovery, Eris, is one as well. They are dwarf planets because they orbit the Sun, they are round, and they are not moons of another planet—but they're too small to have enough gravity to clear their neighborhood. Pluto, Charon, Ceres, and Eris are all KBOs—orbiting far out in space with other objects in the Kuiper Belt.

STOP AND CHECK

Ask and Answer Questions How does the size and gravity of a planet affect other objects around it? Look for details in the text to find the answer.

NASA/JPL

Everything else—asteroids, comets, meteors—are now members of the third class of objects that orbit the Sun and are called "small solar-system bodies."

Some astronomers think the definition of a planet will change again in the future. Others think the current definition is a good one and will last.

Science is exciting, because it continually changes as new information is discovered. A long time ago, we thought there were six planets. Then we thought there were eight. For a while, there were nine. Then it was back to eight. Then, with Pluto, the number jumped up to nine again. And now it's back to eight. And that is just in *our* solar system!

An artist's conception of the New Horizons spacecraft as it arrives at Pluto. Charon is visible in the distance.

We know our Sun is not the only star that has planets in orbit around it. New planets are forming around other stars, making new solar systems. There are 200 billion stars in the Milky Way galaxy alone. And there are billions of galaxies, full of stars, in the universe. As we study those planets and the stars they orbit, we ask questions. Are there other planets like Earth somewhere in the universe? Does life exist on them? We ask questions as we study the planets in our own solar system, too. Does life exist on one of them, or even one of their moons? Did life ever exist on any of them? Is Earth the only planet with life? Are we alone in the universe?

In January 2006, NASA launched the New Horizons mission to Pluto. If all goes well, the New Horizons spacecraft will reach Pluto and Charon sometime in the summer of 2015. Then instruments aboard the spaceship will begin to get a close look at these distant worlds. As the information beams back to Earth, scientists here will study it, trying to learn more about the origins of our solar system and what lies at its outer edges. Pluto still has a story to tell. There are questions that need answers, and the answers will come through science. New information is just waiting to be discovered.

STOP AND CHECK

Reread Why do some astronomers think the definition of a planet will change in the future? The strategy Reread may help you.

About the Author

Elaine Scott's first published work was a poem she wrote in the sixth grade that made it into the local newspaper. Twenty-five years later, she returned to writing as a career. At first, she wrote for adults but soon got hooked on the fun of writing for children. Elaine knows that young people are perfectly capable of grasping difficult ideas as long as the subject is explained clearly. Sometimes she visits schools, where she talks with the students about how she researches and writes her books.

Elaine likes to get information for her books first hand. As she was writing *When Is a Planet Not a Planet?*, astronomers were still arguing over whether Pluto was or wasn't a planet. Elaine interviewed experts and checked their Web sites to stay tuned to the latest developments in scientific discovery.

Author's Purpose

In this selection, the author often ends a paragraph with a question. Identify one example. Why do you think she does this?

(t and cl) NASA/JPL; (cr) Cynthia S. Oualline; (b) Johns Hopkins University Applied Physics Laboratory/Southwest Research Institute —

Respond to the Text

Summarize

Use the most important details from *When Is a Planet Not a Planet?* to summarize how scientific knowledge about planets has changed. Details from your Cause and Effect Chart may help you.

Cause	→	Effect
	→	
	→	
	→	
	→	

Write

Think about how the author supports her ideas. How does she use organization and text features to explain Pluto's status as a planet? Use these sentence frames to organize your text evidence.

The author uses text features to . . .
She organizes information to . . .
The way she supports her ideas helps me to . . .

Make Connections

How did astronomers get more information about Pluto over time? How did technology help them? **ESSENTIAL QUESTION**

Why is it important for scientists to check their own work and the work of others? **TEXT TO WORLD**

Compare Texts
Read about how a mission to the Moon leads to a surprising discovery.

New Moon

On July 20, 2069, a team of four students and their professor leave Earth, heading for the Moon to study its composition.

Dr. Sirius

Ling

We are **approximately** 300 kilometers from the surface of the Moon. Prepare for lunar landing.

Based on its movements, it seems to be held in **orbit** by Earth's gravitational pull.

Luis

Wait! Hold this course! I am getting another reading—there appears to be another object just beyond the Moon.

What could it be?

Dr. Sirius

Hmmm...if we know the distances between the object, the Moon, and our ship, we should be able to calculate the object's **diameter** and mass. Then we can run this data through the supercomputer and compare it against information about all known objects in our solar system.

Dr. Sirius inputs the numbers into the computer. Luis reviews the printouts.

I've managed to **evaluate** the results which, based on the **criteria** for space object classification, indicate that the object is a moon—but one belonging to Mars, not Earth!

Luis

How can that be?

Unlike Earth, Mars has two moons. A strong force would have had to knock one of Mars's moons out of orbit—another object might have collided with it!

Like an asteroid?

Precisely.

Look! We are approaching the moon from Mars!

BEEP! BEEP!

I'm getting emergency messages from Earth! The tides are rising rapidly!

Rising tides? I bet this moon from Mars is the cause!

That's right, Luis. The Moon affects tides on Earth. A new object entering Earth's orbit would change the gravitational pull between the Earth and the Moon and alter the tides.

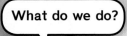

What do we do?

We need to force this moon back into Mars's gravitational field before there is a real disaster. Mark, fire up the Asteroid Simulator Beam!

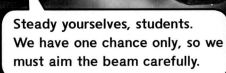

Steady yourselves, students. We have one chance only, so we must aim the beam carefully.

Great Job!

The messages from Earth indicate that the tides are receding! We did it!

Make Connections

How did the team's discovery change their understanding of the solar system? ESSENTIAL QUESTION

How is the team's discovery similar to another team's scientific discovery? How does each team make their discovery? TEXT TO TEXT

Illustration: Ralph Voltz

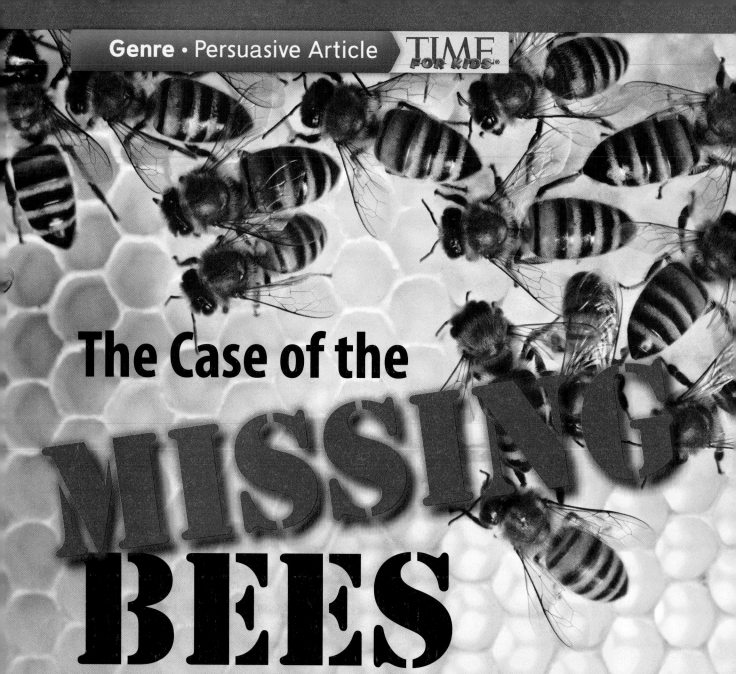

The Case of the MISSING BEES

Essential Question

How do natural events and human activities affect the environment?

Read two views about how natural events and human activities have affected honeybee colonies.

Go Digital!

POINT / COUNTERPOINT

A Germ of an Idea

An infection seems to have caused the decline of honeybee populations.

Where have all the honeybees gone? Over the past few years, billions of honeybees have disappeared. They fly away from their colonies and seem to never return. This **widespread** problem is called Colony Collapse **Disorder** (CCD). It's the main reason the honeybee population in the U.S. today has **declined** to half of what it was 50 years ago. Because one-third of crops in the U.S. require honeybees to help pollinate them, some experts predict CCD could create an **agricultural** catastrophe.

What's responsible for the **unexpected** disappearance? There are several suspects, including stress on bees from overcrowded hives, lack of pollen, parasites, and pesticides. Scientists have yet to identify any one of these as the definite cause of CCD. But recently, researchers have found two **probable** causes: a fungus and a virus. A fungus is an organism that breaks down matter; some fungi can cause infection. A virus is a microbe, or germ.

A Deadly Combination

Bees infected with either the fungus or the virus separately could become sick, but they probably would survive. Bees infected with the fungus and the virus at the same time would most certainly die. That is what scientists who did research in Montana concluded. They tested samples of empty hives against hives that **thrive**, a control group that was unaffected by CCD. They compared their findings and discovered the virus and fungus in every empty hive they tested.

Though the fungus and virus combination is the most probable cause so far, investigations into CCD continue. Other scientists are investigating whether CCD could have been caused by a combination of many factors: pesticides, parasites, fungus, and virus. Each of these can weaken a bee's immune system and make it sick. A combination could be deadly.

Only when scientists find the cause of CCD can they find the cure to saving the bees.

STOP AND CHECK

Ask and Answer Questions
According to the author, why are honeybees disappearing? Find the answer in the text.

Don Farrall/Digital Vision/Getty Images

425

Farmers use pesticides to keep away insects that will damage crops. Some pesticides can harm beneficial insects, like honeybees.

Pointing to Pesticides

Lately, honeybees have not been very busy. Are pesticides to blame?

It's a honey of a mystery. In recent years, beekeepers in many countries have lost thousands of colonies and billions of bees. The insects would suddenly disappear and not return to their hives. This condition, called Colony Collapse Disorder (CCD), has caused 20 to 40 percent of U.S. honeybee colonies to die out. Unfortunately, the reduction in the bee population could affect the country's food production. That's because honeybees pollinate crops of flowering plants. Without these insects, the production of fruits and vegetables would be threatened.

The Unusual Suspects

Most scientists believe the probable cause of CCD is a fungus or a virus, working alone or in combination. But some experts have reached a different conclusion. Their main suspect is pesticides. Pesticides are chemicals sprayed on crops to keep away pests. Researchers in France managed to **identify** one pesticide as harmful to bees. This has led other scientists to investigate how other pesticides affect bees.

Pesticides can be absorbed by pollen that the bees consume or that drifts into the hive. Some studies have shown that even small amounts of certain pesticides can affect bee behavior, such as how they search for flower nectar. Sick bees may not be able to figure out where they're going, get lost, and never return to their colonies. This would explain the decline in honeybee populations.

Are Pesticides to Blame?

A study of hives hit by CCD in Florida and California found 50 different human-made chemicals in the samples. The study could not confirm that the pesticides had directly caused CCD, but other scientists are still investigating whether pesticides are at least partly to blame. At the least, the chemicals may weaken bees enough to allow infection by a virus or a fungus. Until scientists know the exact cause of the honeybee disappearance, the use of these harsh poisons should be cut back.

Beekeepers examine hives to make sure the honeybee colonies are healthy.

Respond to the Text

1. Use details from the selection to summarize. SUMMARIZE

2. Think about how each persuasive article is organized. Which author's style is more convincing and why? WRITE

3. What do you think caused the bees to disappear? Support your answer with reasons. How could people help honeybees? TEXT TO WORLD

427

Compare Texts

Read how honeybees affect humans and the environment.

Busy, Beneficial BEES

Billions of honeybees are disappearing from a **widespread** mysterious condition called Colony Collapse **Disorder**. The disappearance of honeybees is bad news for two big reasons. Obviously, without honeybees, there would be no honey. Worse, many important foods wouldn't make it to our supermarkets or tables.

Honeybees are responsible for about one-third of the food in the human diet, including vegetables, fruits, seeds, and nuts. Honeybees help many crop plants **thrive**. They pollinate flowering plants, which allows the plants to produce the foods we eat and the seeds that will grow into new plants.

Tinke Hamming/Ingram Publishing

Crops Depend on Honeybees

Many crops depend on insects to pollinate them. For some crops, honeybees make up a large percentage of those pollinators.

Numbers based on estimates in 2000. Source: Compiled by CRS using values reported in R. A. Morse, and N.W. Calderone, *The Value of Honey Bees as Pollinators of U.S. Crops in 2000, March 2000,* Cornell University.

Crop	Dependence on Insect Pollination	Proportion That Are Honeybees
Alfalfa, hay & seed	100%	60%
Apples	100%	90%
Almonds	100%	100%
Citrus	20–80%	10–90%
Cotton	20%	90%
Soybeans	10%	50%
Broccoli	100%	90%
Carrots	100%	90%
Cantaloupe	80%	90%

Honeybees use nectar from flowers to make honey, their winter food source. When the bees visit flowers to get nectar, tiny grains of pollen cling to their bodies. The bees carry the pollen from flower to flower and plant to plant. This process of pollination makes flowers turn into fruits. For farmers, this means a harvest!

Honeybees were brought to the U.S. from Europe about 400 years ago for **agricultural** purposes. Beekeepers today still maintain hives. Some sell honey. Others may rent hives to farmers to pollinate crops. In addition to honeybees, there are about 4,000 species of native "wild" bees in North America which also pollinate flowering plants. Most of these bees do not live in colonies and have not been affected by CCD.

In the U.S., honeybees pollinate about $15 billion worth of crops a year. That's on top of the $150 million worth of honey they produce annually. Although some crops can be pollinated by other nectar-feeding insects, many crops depend specifically on honeybees for pollination. Without honeybees, our crops and our economy would really feel the sting!

Make Connections

How do honeybees affect the environment? ESSENTIAL QUESTION

Think of an agricultural activity you've read about that affects the environment. How are the effects of beekeeping different? TEXT TO TEXT

The UNBREAKABLE Code

by Sara Hoagland Hunter ◆ illustrated by Julia Miner

Essential Question
How do different groups contribute to a cause?

Read about how a group of Navajos helped the American military during World War II.

Go Digital!

430

John raced up the trail, sending pebbles skidding behind him. When he reached his favorite hiding place, he fell to the ground out of breath. Here between the old piñon tree and the towering walls of the canyon, he felt safe. The river full of late-summer rain looked like a silver thread winding through his grandfather's farm land. They would be looking for him now, but he was never coming down.

His mother had married the man from Minnesota. There was nothing he could do about that. But he was not going with them. He closed his eyes and rested in the stillness. The faint bleat of a mountain goat echoed off the canyon walls.

431

Suddenly a voice boomed above him: "Shouldn't you be packing?"

John's eyes flew open. It was his grandfather on horseback.

"Your stepfather's coming with the pickup in an hour."

"I'm not going," John said.

"You have to go. School's starting soon," said Grandfather, stepping down from his horse. "You'll be back next summer."

John dug his toe deeper into the dirt. "I want to stay with you," he said.

Grandfather's soft, brown eyes disappeared in the wrinkles of a smile. John thought they were the kindest eyes he had ever seen.

"You're going to be all right," Grandfather said. "You have an unbreakable code."

"What's that?" asked John.

Grandfather sat down and began to speak gently in Navajo. The sounds wove up and down, in and out, as warm and familiar as the patterns of one of Grandmother's Navajo blankets. John leaned against his grandfather's knee.

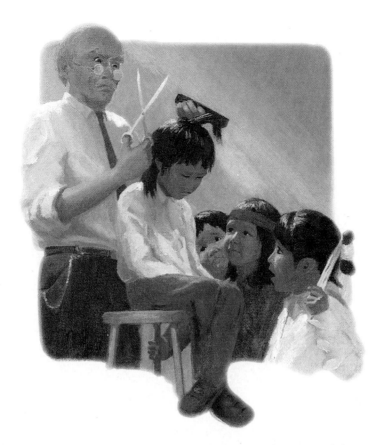

"The unbreakable code is what saved my life in World War II," he said. "It's the Navajo language."

John's shoulders sagged. Navajo couldn't help him. Nobody in his new school spoke Navajo.

"I'll probably forget how to speak Navajo," he whispered.

"Navajo is your language," said his grandfather sternly. "Navajo you must never forget."

The lump in John's throat was close to a sob. "You don't know what it's like there!" he said.

His grandfather continued quietly in Navajo. "I had to go to a government boarding school when I was five. It was the law.

"They gave me an English name and cut my hair off. I wasn't allowed to speak my language. Anyone who spoke Navajo had to chew on squares of soap. Believe me, I chewed a lot of soap during those years. 'Speak English,' they said. But Navajo was my language and Navajo I would never forget.

"Every summer I went home to herd the sheep and help with the crops. I cried when the cottonwoods turned gold and it was time to go back.

"Finally, one night in the tenth grade, I was working in the kitchen when I heard a bulletin on the school radio: 'Navajo needed for special duty to the Marines. Must be between the ages of seventeen and thirty-two, fluent in English and Navajo, and in excellent physical condition.'

"Just before lights out, I snuck past the bunks and out the door towards the open plain. I felt like a wild horse with the lasso finally off its neck. Out in the open, the stars danced above me and the tumbleweeds blew by my feet as I ran. The next day, I enlisted."

"But you weren't seventeen," said John.

"The reservation had no birth records," Grandfather said with a grin. "Two weeks later I was on a bus headed for boot camp with twenty-eight other Navajos. I stared out the window into the darkness. I was going outside of the Four Sacred Mountains for the first time in my life."

STOP AND CHECK

Summarize Why does Grandfather leave the boarding school? Summarizing the events may help you.

"Were you scared?" asked John.

"Of course," said his grandfather. "I didn't know where I was going or what our mission was. Most of all, I didn't know how I would measure up to the people out there I had heard so much about."

"How did you?" asked John, chewing his fingernail.

His grandfather began to laugh. "We were known as the toughest platoon at boot camp. We had done so much marching at boarding school that the drills were no problem. Hiking in the desert of California with a heavy pack was no worse than hauling water in the canyon in midsummer. And I'd done that since I was four years old.

"As for the **survival** exercises, we had all gone without food for a few days. A Navajo learns to survive.

"One weekend they bused us to a new camp in San Diego. On Monday we were marched to a building with bars on every window. They locked us in a classroom at the end of a long, narrow corridor. An officer told us our mission was top secret. We would not even be allowed to tell our families. We were desperately needed for a successful invasion of the Pacific Islands. So far the Japanese had been able to **intercept** and decode all American messages in only minutes. This meant that no information could be passed between American ships, planes, and land forces.

"The government thought the Navajo language might be the secret weapon. Only a few outsiders had ever learned it. Most importantly, the language had never been written down, so there was no alphabet for the Japanese to discover and decode.

"He gave us a list of more than two hundred military terms to code. Everything had to be memorized. No trace of the code could ever be found in writing. It would live or die with us in battle.

"When the officer walked out of the room, I looked at the Navajo next to me and began to laugh. 'All those years they told us to forget Navajo, and now the government needs it to save the country!'

"We were marched every day to that classroom. We were never allowed to leave the building. We couldn't even use the bathroom by ourselves. Each night, an officer locked our notes in a safe.

"The code had to be simple and fast. We would have only one chance to send each message. After that, the Japanese would be tracing our location to bomb us or trying to record the code.

"We chose words from nature that would be easy to remember under fire. Since Navajo has no alphabet, we made up our own.

"'A' became *wollachee*."

"Ant?" asked John in English.

Grandfather nodded.

"'B' was *shush*."

"Bear," said John.

"'C' was *moasi*. 'D', *be*. 'E', *dzeh*." His grandfather continued through the alphabet. Each time he named the Navajo word, John answered with the English.

"We named the aircraft after birds. The dive-bomber was a chicken hawk. The observation plane was an owl. A patrol plane was a crow. Bomber was buzzard.

"At night we would lie in our bunks and test each other. Pretty soon I was dreaming in code.

STOP AND CHECK

Summarize How do the Navajo soldiers create a code? Summarizing what they did may help you.

437

"Since we would be radiomen, we had to learn all kinds of radio **operations**. We were taught how to take a radio apart and put it together blindfolded. The Japanese fought at night, so we would have to do most of our work in complete darkness. Even the tiniest match flame could be a target.

"When the day came for the code to be tested in front of the top Marine officers, I was terrified. I knelt at one end of a field with our radio ground set. The officers marched towards me. Behind a building at the other end of the field, another code talker sat under military guard waiting for my transmission. One officer handed me a written message:

"'Receiving steady machine gun fire. Request reinforcements.'

"It took only seconds for me to speak into the microphone in Navajo code. The officer sent a runner to the end of the field to check the speed and accuracy of the message. The Navajo at the other end handed him the exact message written in English before he even came around the corner of the building! They tested us over and over. Each time, we were successful. The government requested two hundred Navajo **recruits** immediately. Two of our group stayed behind to train them. The rest of us were on our way."

"Tell me about the fighting!" said John.

Suddenly Grandfather's face looked as creased and battered as the canyon walls behind him. After a long pause he said, "What I saw is better left back there. I would not want to touch my home or my family with those pictures.

"Before we invaded, I looked out at that island. It had been flattened and burned. 'Let this never happen to a beautiful island again,' I thought. I just stayed on the deck of the ship thinking about the ceremonies they were doing for me at home. We invaded at dawn.

"I almost drowned in a bomb crater before I even got to shore. I was trying to run through the water and the bullets when I felt myself sinking into a bottomless hole. My eighty-pound radio pack pulled me straight down. I lost my rifle paddling to the surface.

"On the beach, it was all I could do just to survive. I remember lying there with gunfire flying past my ears. A creek that ran to the beach was clear when I first lay there. By noon it was blood red.

"The worst were the fallen soldiers I had to run over to go forward. I couldn't even stop to say I was sorry. I just had to run over them and keep going.

"I had to move through the jungle at night, broadcasting in code from different locations. One unit needed medical supplies. Another needed machine-gun support. I had just begun broadcasting to another code talker. 'Arizona! New Mexico!' I called. The next thing I knew, an American soldier behind me was yelling, 'Do you know what we do to spies?'

"'Don't shoot!' I said. 'I'm American. Look at my uniform.' He didn't believe me. He had just heard the foreign language. He had seen my hair and my eyes. Japanese spies had been known to steal uniforms from fallen soldiers.

"One of my buddies jumped out of the bushes right at that moment and saved my life."

"How did you stay alive the rest of the time?" asked John.

"My belief was my shield," Grandfather answered.

He drew a ragged wallet from deep inside of his shirt pocket. "Inside of this, I carried corn pollen from the medicine man. 'Never be afraid,' he said. 'Nothing's going to touch you.' And nothing ever did. More than four hundred code talkers fought in some of the bloodiest battles of World War II. All but a few of us survived.

"The Japanese never did crack the code. When they finally discovered what language it was, they captured and tortured one poor Navajo. He wasn't a code talker and couldn't understand the message they had intercepted. He told them we were talking about what we ate for breakfast. Our code word for bombs was 'eggs.'

"Six months before the war ended, Navajo code talkers passed more than eight hundred messages in two days during the invasion of Iwo Jima.

"When the American flag was raised on top of Iwo Jima's mountain, the victory was announced in code to the American fleet. 'Sheep-Uncle-Ram-Ice-Bear-Ant-Cat-Horse-Itch' came the code."

John tried to spell out the letters.

"Suribachi?" asked John.

"Yes," said Grandfather. "Mount Suribachi.

"When I came home, I walked the twelve miles from the bus
station to this spot. There weren't any parades or parties.

"I knew I wasn't allowed to tell anyone about the code.
I looked down at that beautiful canyon floor and thought,
'I'm never leaving again.'"

"But why did you leave in the first place?" asked John.

His grandfather lifted him gently onto the horse. "The answer to that is in the code," he said. "The code name for America was 'Our Mother.' You fight for what you love. You fight for what is yours."

He swung his leg behind John and reached around him to hold the reins.

"Keep my wallet," he said. "It will remind you of the unbreakable code that once saved your country."

John clutched the wallet with one hand and held the horse's mane with the other. He wasn't as scared of going to a new place any more. His grandfather had taught him who he was and what he would always have with him. He was the grandson of a Navajo code talker and he had a language that had once helped save his country.

STOP AND CHECK

Ask and Answer Questions How does Grandfather's story affect John? Go back to the text to find the answer.

ABOUT THE AUTHOR AND ILLUSTRATOR

Sara Hoagland Hunter traveled to the Southwest to write this story. There, she interviewed some of the Navajo people who had served in World War II. After much discussion, the tribal elders finally agreed that Sara should tell their story. The Navajo men were eager to pass along their experiences to their own children and grandchildren, and a children's book would be a fine way to achieve that.

Sara wanted to represent Navajo culture accurately. She respected the generosity and peaceful wisdom of the people she interviewed. During the writing process, she even shared drafts with the people she had met. *The Unbreakable Code* turned into one of Sara's favorite works.

Julia Miner is an artist and architect who enjoys illustrating stories with a regional or historical focus. For that reason, she was eager to accompany Sara Hoagland Hunter on her research trip to the Southwest. Julia fell in love with the landscape and was excited to draw and paint the scenery. When she shared her artwork with the Navajos, they were delighted by her realistic drawings.

Author's Purpose

Sara Hoagland Hunter found the Navajo people she interviewed to be generous, peaceful, and wise. How does she show these characteristics in *The Unbreakable Code*?

Respond to the Text

Summarize

Summarize how Grandfather helped the military in *The Unbreakable Code*. Details from your Theme Chart may help you.

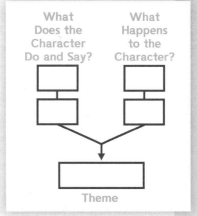

What Does the Character Do and Say?

What Happens to the Character?

Theme

Write

How does the author use dialogue and Grandfather's story to teach John about the strengths of his Navajo culture? Use these sentence frames to organize your text evidence.

The author includes Grandfather's stories to . . .
John's reaction to these stories shows that . . .
In the end, John . . .

Make Connections

Talk about how the Navajo code talkers and other people in the military contributed to a cause. ESSENTIAL QUESTION

Give another example when people of different backgrounds worked together for a cause. How does a group benefit from the contributions of different people? TEXT TO WORLD

Compare Texts
Read about how groups of people contributed to one effort during World War II.

Allies in Action

During the 1930s, many countries faced hard economic times. Leaders of two nations, Germany and Japan, saw an opportunity and invaded neighboring countries to expand their power. Other countries, such as Italy, joined them. These forces were called the Axis powers. In response, a number of countries including Great Britain, France, and later the Soviet Union, joined together. This group came to be known as the Allied forces. The conflict worsened and expanded, eventually involving over fifty nations. It became known as World War II.

Keystone/Hulton Archive/Getty Images

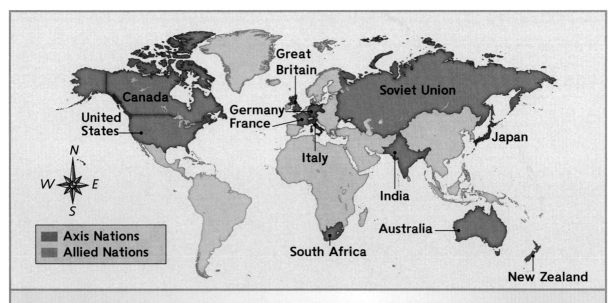

By 1941, Germany and Japan had invaded a number of countries. In response, the United States, the Soviet Union, France, and Great Britain (and countries that were part of its commonwealth) joined together to oppose them.

Joining the Allies

At first the United States tried to remain neutral. However, after Japan attacked Pearl Harbor in December of 1941, the U.S. had to act. The country joined the Allies and sent troops to fight in the Pacific and in Europe.

Many men left the United States to fight in the war. Women also **enlisted**, often serving in the Army Nurse Corps. The large number of **recruits** that went overseas caused a worker shortage back home. In response, many women took jobs previously held by men. They held positions in government and worked in factories. They also raised funds and collected materials that would be recycled into supplies for the troops.

The shortage of workers in agriculture led the United States to institute the Bracero Program with Mexico. *Bracero* is the Spanish word for laborer. This program encouraged Mexican workers to offer assistance to farm owners in the United States. These skilled workers helped maintain crops, keeping the country's economy productive during the war.

Though women could enlist in the army reserve, most were not sent directly into battle.

(r) Hulton Archive/Getty Images

447

The Tuskegee Airmen

By the start of the war, a number of African American men were already active in the military. However, their positions were limited. They were rarely given opportunities for advancement and special military **operations**.

Many civil rights groups had protested these restrictions on African Americans. In response, the U.S. Army Air Corps began a new training program in 1941. They taught African Americans how to become pilots and navigators. This program was based in Tuskegee, Alabama. Those who completed aeronautic, or pilot, training there became known as "The Tuskegee Airmen."

The Tuskegee Airmen flew many missions during World War II. Over time, they gained a strong reputation for their skills. Their success would lead the U.S. military to recognize African American service and offer them more training opportunities in different fields.

Nearly 1,000 African Americans completed the pilot training program in Tuskegee, Alabama.

The Navajo Code Talkers

One group's unique skill played a major role in the U.S. military's success during the war. Philip Johnston, a World War I veteran and son of a missionary at a Navajo reservation, learned that soldiers from the Choctaw tribe had been able to encode, or put into a code, Army messages. He thought the Navajo could help out the same way during World War II.

Johnston was right. He demonstrated how quickly the Navajo could encode and decipher messages. They were far faster than the machines being used. In addition, the complex Navajo language was not a written language. This made coded messages that the enemy might **intercept** even more difficult to figure out.

In 1945 the Allied forces won the war against the Axis powers. Victory required the **contributions** of many people from a **diversity** of backgrounds, both on the battlefield and on the home front. Some offered their skills and abilities. Others made sacrifices, large and small, to support the war effort. Whether in action or in support, these various groups' efforts led to an important achievement in world history.

The Tuskegee Airmen flew more than 15,000 missions between 1943 and 1945.

The Navajo code stumped the Japanese, who had deciphered many other codes.

Make Connections

How did different groups support the United States' efforts during World War II?
ESSENTIAL QUESTION

How are the Tuskegee airmen like another group from a story you've read? How are each group's skills and purpose different? TEXT TO TEXT

(t) U.S. Marine Corps Photograph

449

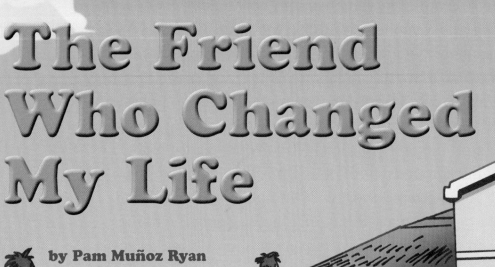

The Friend Who Changed My Life

by Pam Muñoz Ryan

illustrated by Carl Pearce

Essential Question

What actions can we take to get along with others?

Read about how one girl's confrontation with a bully changes her life.

Go Digital!

450

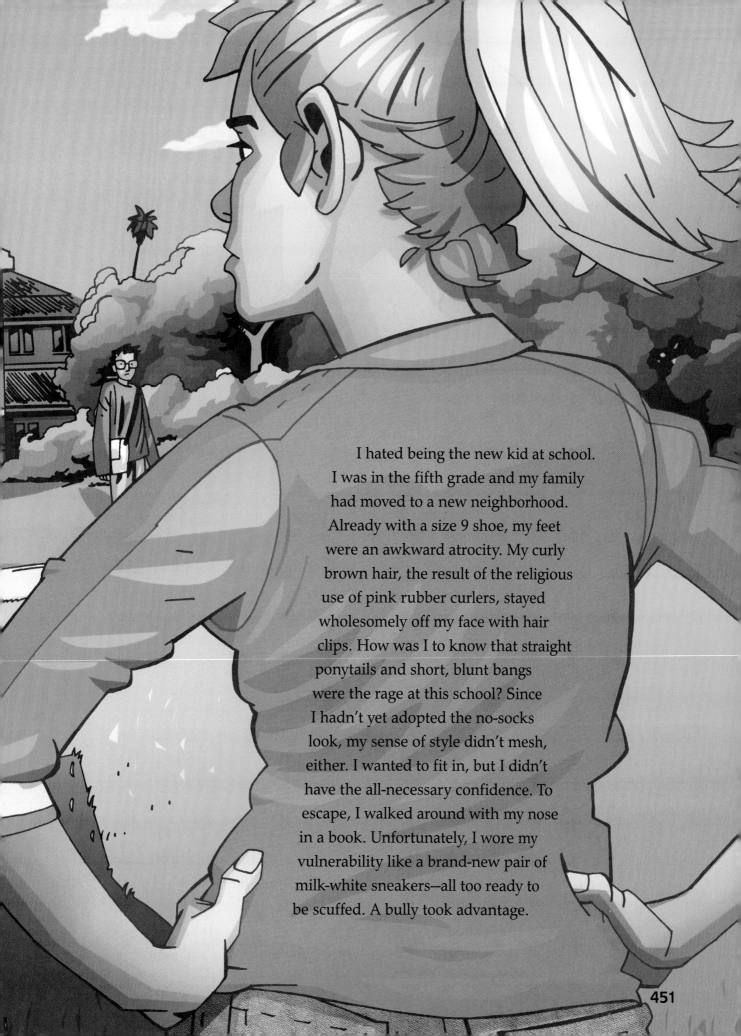

I hated being the new kid at school. I was in the fifth grade and my family had moved to a new neighborhood. Already with a size 9 shoe, my feet were an awkward atrocity. My curly brown hair, the result of the religious use of pink rubber curlers, stayed wholesomely off my face with hair clips. How was I to know that straight ponytails and short, blunt bangs were the rage at this school? Since I hadn't yet adopted the no-socks look, my sense of style didn't mesh, either. I wanted to fit in, but I didn't have the all-necessary confidence. To escape, I walked around with my nose in a book. Unfortunately, I wore my vulnerability like a brand-new pair of milk-white sneakers—all too ready to be scuffed. A bully took advantage.

Her name was Theresa. She was tiny, wiry, and loud, with blond bangs and the mandatory tightly-pulled-back ponytail. I swore she walked with a deliberate swagger just to get her ponytail to swing back and forth. For a reason unknown to me, she decided that I was worthy of her undivided attention, and every day she waltzed up to me and kicked me in the shins or the back of the legs. I could expect a wallop any time I was off guard, while I was standing in line to go to class after a recess, on my way out of the girls' bathroom, or as I pushed my lunch tray along the counter in front of the cafeteria ladies. *Bam!* Theresa was smart and quick. No teacher ever saw her, and my legs were black, blue, purple, and green within a week.

My mom noticed the marks, but I pacified her by saying that I played on the jungle gym at recess and had bruised them on the bars. I could tell from my mom's expression that she was suspicious of my story. She made me promise I'd play somewhere else. I knew that if I kept coming home with mottled legs one of my parents would eventually go to my teacher. I could only imagine the price I'd have to pay among the other kids if I was seen as both the new kid *and* a crybaby tattletale.

I used to lie in bed every night dreading school and trying to figure out complicated routes to walk from one place to another so Theresa couldn't get to me easily. I had a convoluted method of getting to my classroom, which involved walking outside the fenced school yard and entering the grounds at the opposite end of the campus, then working my way through the kindergarten playground. At recess and lunch I stayed in the open spaces on the grassy field because if I saw Theresa coming, I could at least run.

One day, Theresa chased me on the playground, about to close in with yet another successful attack. Frantically, I ran away from her, glancing back every few seconds to see where she was. I looked to one side and was relieved when I didn't see her. Thinking she had given up, I stopped **abruptly** and turned around, unaware that Theresa had been running full-speed toward me from the other side. She didn't expect my sudden stop and **collided** into me and bounced toward the ground. A group of kids standing nearby laughed. Angry, Theresa got up and began kicking me with a fury, over and over. A scrape on my knee reopened and blood trickled down my leg. As much as I wanted to, I didn't cry. I just stood there and took it.

Mary Lou, also in the fifth grade, was the tallest and biggest girl in the entire school, including the sixth graders. She wasn't fat but was sturdy and big-boned and strong.

Her red hair, thousands of freckles, and fair skin gave her a gentle giant appearance. Still, no one ever messed with her. When Mary Lou shoved her way through the crowd of kids and took my elbow, everyone backed away, including Theresa.

Mary Lou ushered me to the girls' bathroom. As I stood there, shaking, she took a wad of paper towels, wet them, handed them to me, and pointed to my bloodied leg.

"So, Theresa's been bothering you."

I nodded, hoping that the next words out of Mary Lou's mouth would be, *Well, I'm going to take care of her for you.* I had visions of having a personal hero to protect me—fantasies of Mary Lou escorting me around the school with a **protective** arm over my shoulder, clobbering anyone who came near me.

Instead Mary Lou said, "You can't let her keep doing this to you. She's never going to stop unless you make her stop. Get it?"

I didn't really get it, but I nodded.

"Listen, she's a pain. But if you don't stick up for yourself, things will get worse. You know that, don't you?"

How could it get worse? I was already paralyzed with fear and had turned into a whipping post for some girl who was half my size. Besides, what did Mary Lou mean about sticking up for myself? Did she want me to *fight* Theresa? That idea terrified me more than being kicked every day.

"I'm not kidding," said Mary Lou. "And if you don't *do* something, I'm going to start hitting you, too. Understand?" She made a fist and held it in front of my face.

I thought about Mary Lou's size and weight and gulped. Things could *definitely* get worse. "Yes," I whispered.

"Okay then, get back out there."

Now? Did she mean stand up for myself right now?

I walked back to the playground with Mary Lou smugly following behind. I couldn't see a way out of the situation. In front of me was Theresa and in back of me was Mary Lou. The first bell rang and kids began to assemble in their assigned lines on the blacktop in front of the classrooms. In a few minutes, the second bell would ring and teachers would walk out and get their students for class. The yard duty teacher was out on the grassy field blowing her whistle and rounding up the stragglers. As usual, no teachers would be around to witness my destruction.

Theresa stood in a huddle of girls. Mary Lou nudged me toward her. I had never started a fight before in my life. I had never hit anyone and didn't have an inkling of what to do. My insides shook worse than my outsides. When Theresa saw me approaching, she set her mouth in a grim line, marched toward me, and swung her leg back to haul off and kick me. I jumped back to avoid the kick. I made a fist and flailed my arm wildly, in some sort of ridiculous motion. *Pop!* In a miraculous blow, I caught Theresa in the nose and blood sprayed across her clothes. I don't know which of us was more surprised.

STOP AND CHECK

Summarize **Why does the narrator confront Theresa? Summarizing the events may help you.**

I don't remember what happened next. I know we brawled on the blacktop. Gritty sand scraped the bare skin on my arms. (I would notice the burns later.) As we rolled over and over, tiny pebbles embedded in my face. One of them made a substantial puncture that didn't heal for weeks. (The pock remained for years.) I'm not sure who separated us and broke it up. In a matter of minutes, someone retrieved the yard duty teacher, and she corralled and ceremoniously walked us to the principal's office. I, the nice girl, the good girl, was going to the principal's office for fighting. Devastated, I hung my head.

Sitting on the bench outside the principal's office and waiting to be called in, I worried about several things. Would the school tell my parents? What would my punishment be? What would Theresa do to get back at me? What would the other kids think? Branded, I was now a bad girl.

The yard duty teacher deposited us in two chairs, side by side, in the principal's office and placed the referral slip on his desk. Our principal was a balding man, with glasses and a kind, grandfatherly face. He seemed happy to see us.

Smiling, he said, "Well, girls, I want you to put your heads together and decide what your punishment should be while I make a phone call."

He picked up the phone, and as he made his call, I stared at his desk. I realized I could read the referral slip upside down. The yard duty teacher had written: *Benched for one week.*

Theresa leaned toward me and whispered, remorsefully, "I guess we should be benched for two weeks." She felt worse than I had suspected.

I glared at her and shook my head no.

The principal put down the phone. "Well, young ladies?"

"We should be benched for a week," I blurted.

"I agree...and I don't want to see you back here anytime soon." He signed the referral and sent us back to class.

"How did you know to say one week?" Theresa asked on our way back to class.

"I could read what the yard duty teacher put on the slip. Upside down," I told her.

"Wow, you can read upside down?" Theresa said, her ponytail swinging like a pendulum.

I didn't answer her.

That night I told my mother that I fell, trying to jump rope double Dutch.

Theresa and I were confined at every recess and lunchtime to the same green bench next to the stucco wall of the cafeteria building. It was indisputably the Bad Kids' Bench. Kindergartners and first graders had to file by to get to their classrooms and they always gave us a wide berth, their orderly line snaking away from us, then back in formation, as if our badness might be contagious. The bench faced the playground so the entire recess population could see who was *not privileged* enough to play. The yard duty teacher could keep an eye on us, too, in case we decided to jump up and sneak in a hopscotch game. Indignant and humiliated, I refused to talk to Theresa, who didn't seem to have any inhibitions about being chatty.

She bragged to me about all sorts of things, but I was aloof until she said, "My mom takes me to the *big* downtown library every Tuesday after school."

I rode my bike to the small branch library near my house every weekend, but my parents both worked full-time and couldn't always manage after-school activities or driving to the main branch. The *big* library had a hundred times the selection of the branch library and a huge children's room with comfy pillows. They sometimes had puppet shows, story times, free bookmarks, and writing contests.

"Yep, every single Tuesday I go to the *big* downtown library to check out as many books as I like."

Before I could pretend I didn't care, I said, "You're lucky." I was suddenly jealous of Theresa, but I didn't want her to know how much. So I returned to my determined martyrdom. Instead of listening to her, I stared at the dirt and ignored her prattle.

The week was over soon enough. The principal never called my parents. The other kids didn't seem to care that I had been disciplined on the Bad Kids' Bench. In fact, I actually detected a subtle reverence from some of my classmates. From then on, Theresa left me alone and Mary Lou was my widely acknowledged **ally**. I didn't know how I'd ever repay her.

STOP AND CHECK

Summarize **How do the narrator and Theresa behave while they are benched? Summarize to help you.**

A few weeks passed and one of the girls in our class had a slumber party. All the fifth-grade girls were invited. The barrage of females descended on the birthday girl's house with sleeping bags, pillows, and overnight cases. Mary Lou and I set up our sleeping bags right next to each other. The night progressed happily... until someone suggested we tell ghost stories.

I hated ghost stories. I had far too active an imagination, which always took me much farther than the storytelling. I couldn't seem to turn off the dark, scary world. If I saw even a slightly scary movie on television, my stomach would churn for days and I'd have to sleep with my bedside lamp on all night. Mary Lou must have felt the same, because she moved closer to me. We huddled together behind the avid listeners with our pillows almost covering our faces. There was no way *not* to listen. One girl told a particularly gruesome tale about a tree whose giant branches turned into fingers and could grab and capture children. Most of the girls squealed and clutched one another in mock terror before they ended up giggling. Already fraught with anxiety, I couldn't imagine how I would get through the night. I suddenly wanted to be in my own house, in my own bed, with my parents down the hall and my trusty bedside lamp. There

didn't seem to be any way out of the situation that wasn't humiliating. At least Mary Lou was by my side.

Suddenly, Mary Lou started crying. "I'm scared," she said. "I want to go home."

Mary Lou had read my mind but had voiced it with her own tears.

One of the girls said, "Don't be such a baby!"

Others chimed in, "Mary Lou's a scaredy-cat!"

"I'm calling my parents," said Mary Lou through her giant sniffles.

"The baby's calling her mommy and daddy," the girls chanted.

I shivered in my sleeping bag, my stomach sick with fear. Sick that Mary Lou was leaving. Sick that I was next to a window, with a tree looming on the other side.

Mary Lou headed toward the phone and didn't seem to care about the **taunting**. She called her parents with her chin up, set down the phone, and methodically began packing up her things.

My sleeping area looked bare without Mary Lou's sleeping bag and blanket. A tree branch brushed against the window from the wind. I was convinced it was the same tree from the story and that I would be its next victim.

I stood up and began rolling up my sleeping bag. "I'm going home, too. Mary Lou, can your dad give me a ride?"

I heard more giggles.

Then, from across the room, a small voice said, "Me, too?"

Mary Lou nodded.

I secretly celebrated. I knew that we'd suffer the consequences of the gossip and finger-pointing at school on Monday, but now I didn't care. There was safety in numbers. As I dragged my things into the hallway, I saw the third person.

It was Theresa.

The three of us huddled on the front porch waiting for Mary Lou's dad. In a final gesture of belittlement, one of the girls turned off the porch light so we had to wait on the front steps in the dark, directly under the tree with the sprawling branches. On the other side of the door, the party howled with laughter. I was never so grateful to see station wagon headlights.

Mary Lou's dad headed toward Theresa's house first. On the way, we were mostly quiet, but I felt happy. Happy I was going home to my own room. Happy that Mary Lou's tearful exit scene had been watered down by our group departure. I was puzzled, though, that Theresa had been frightened, too. She always seemed so **confident**, so tough.

In front of Theresa's house, she climbed out of the car and said, "So do you guys want to go to the *big* library with me after school on Tuesdays? My mom drives me and she could drive you, too."

I would love *to go to the* big *downtown library on Tuesdays after school,* I thought. *But with Theresa?* My mind battled with my emotions.

Theresa eagerly continued. "My mom can call your moms to... you know...make sure it's okay and everything."

I hesitated. "Are *you* going?" I asked Mary Lou.

"I can't," she said. "But you should go if you want to."

Theresa sounded sincere enough.

Mary Lou nudged me in the backseat as if to say, *Go!*

I finally nodded.

It was a strange camaraderie, given our history. Theresa and I shared many trips to the library together on Tuesdays. I've often wondered if, in some convoluted way, Theresa's abuse had been an attempt to get my attention. She liked the library and I always had my nose in a book, so she targeted me. Too bad for my legs that she didn't have better social skills!

Mary Lou is still my hero. If a person believes in the domino effect, the premise that one action triggers another, then I am deeply indebted to her. If she had never made me stand up to Theresa, I would have existed on the outskirts of fifth-grade society, always defenseless. I would have never gained Mary Lou's respect or become her friend. I wouldn't have gone home with her that night at the slumber party. Instead, I would have suffered through my worst imaginings. And if it weren't for Mary Lou, I might not have had the opportunity or courage to accept Theresa's invitation to the *big* library on Tuesdays, which fueled my affection for books in a dramatic way. After all, I was entering the enemy's camp.

It's sometimes easier to be brave if you have someone with whom you can stand beside or who you know is always standing behind you. Being Mary Lou's friend was always comforting, even when she

revealed her own vulnerability. Big, strong people have fears (as do tiny, wiry people), and it often takes more courage to reveal a weakness than to cover it up. She was confident, determined, fair-minded, and unafraid of her emotions. I was her antithesis: naive, insecure, and desperately wanting to be a part of something. Mary Lou fit in because she didn't try to be anything but herself.

I wanted to be just like her.

STOP AND CHECK

Reread Why is Mary Lou the narrator's hero? Reread to check your understanding.

About the Author and Illustrator

Pam Muñoz Ryan knows what it feels like to be the new kid in school. When she was in fifth grade, her parents moved to a new neighborhood. Pam faced the challenge of making new friends and fitting in. What helped her adjust? Reading books! Like reading, Pam says that writing is also a journey—but one she can create. She says writing can help her "sort out the issues of life." Pam has written over 30 books and won many awards, and her journey as a writer continues.

Carl Pearce lives in Wales in the United Kingdom. He sometimes uses scenes from local places to help him illustrate settings in books. His work is also influenced by his love of movies. Carl brings characters and events described in books to life through his colorful drawings.

Author's Purpose

Why do you think the author chose to write the story in first-person? How does this point of view help you understand the events?

Respond to the Text

Summarize

Summarize what happened to the characters in *The Friend Who Changed My Life* that led them to get along. Details from your Theme Chart may help you.

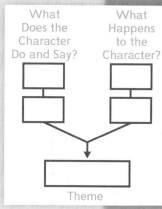

Write

Why is *The Friend Who Changed My Life* a meaningful and appropriate title for this story? Use these sentence frames to organize your text evidence.

The author helps me understand the characters by . . .

She organizes the story to show me how . . .

This is important because it helps me understand that . . .

Make Connections

Talk about what leads the characters in this story to get along. **ESSENTIAL QUESTION**

Give an example of one action that a character from the story takes to get along with others. In what other ways can people get along? **TEXT TO WORLD**

Compare Texts

Read about actions people can take to get along with others.

CHOOSE YOUR STRATEGY:
A Guide to Getting Along

Tap. Tap. Tap.

Your classmate is tapping her foot on your desk and you are—tap, tap, tap—having a hard time concentrating. *What do you do?*

Ha. Ha. Ha. Your mismatched socks sent your friends into giggles, and the teasing hasn't stopped. Now your face is turning pink and red too. *What can you do?*

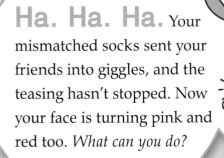

Silence. You and your best friend were chatting all morning, but at lunch, she is silent and decides to sit with another group. *What will you do?*

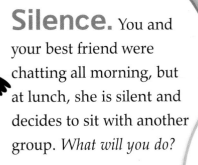

Snap. You hear the sharp snap of a pencil behind you. Those two boys have started to pick on your classmate again. *What do you decide to do?*

Sound like problems? You can probably imagine what it's like to be in each circumstance, because, unfortunately, problems do happen. What you decide to do and how you respond in these kinds of situations is important: Your reaction can affect how you feel about yourself and others, and how others feel about you.

Because each person and problem is different, the strategies you use to resolve problems will be different, too. These are just some of the ways people can get along with others.

Consider Other Perspectives

A good way to approach any problem is to think about the other person's perspective of a situation. Have you ever heard the expression, "Put yourself in someone else's shoes"? No, you will not be slipping on another person's pair of shoes. It means to imagine what it might be like to be in someone else's position. After all, maybe your classmate was concentrating and didn't realize her tapping was affecting you. Considering the other possibilities and points of view can help you decide how best to respond. Also, before you react impulsively, stop and ask yourself: Is this a *big* problem? Then you can decide whether it's worth saying or doing something.

Talk it Out

Problems often arise when people misunderstand each other. Sometimes it's difficult to know how another person is feeling, and you may not be able to guess what's wrong. Talking things through is one way to solve the problem. But where do you begin? A simple "What's up?" can open up discussion. For example, if a friend is suddenly avoiding you, asking her what's wrong might clue you in. Maybe you didn't realize you made a remark that hurt her feelings. Having a simple conversation can help you to see each other's point of view and clear up misunderstandings.

Adjust Your Attitude

One of the best ways to get along with others is to have a positive attitude. Remember, your attitude and your tone of voice affect those around you. If you respond to your classmate by yelling, it is likely that your classmate will react negatively, too, and this can escalate a minor problem to a major one. If you ask politely, you may get a better result.

Finding a little humor in a situation can also make it less tense. So you are mortified by your mismatched socks, but stop and consider whether it is really worth getting angry. On second thought, it *is* funny. Sometimes laughter can be the best medicine, and a change of attitude can change your day.

Extra Help

When a serious **conflict** arises between friends or classmates, you may need to ask for some extra assistance. Problems that do not go away using other strategies may require an adult, such as a parent or teacher, to **intervene**. Some situations may get worse or become a repeated problem, in which case it is better to get help. If those two boys bother your classmate every day, you may want to suggest that your classmate ask an adult for help.

Remember, there may not be one way to solve a problem. Like a game, getting along involves strategy, and what works for one person or in one situation may not work for another. Each situation is unique—it's up to you to decide what to do.

Make Connections

What are some strategies that can help people get along? **ESSENTIAL QUESTION**

Think of a character you've read about who has a conflict with another character. What actions does the character take to get along? What other actions could he or she have taken?

TEXT TO TEXT

SURVIVAL AT 40 BELOW

by Debbie S. Miller,
illustrated by Jon Van Zyle

Essential Question

How are living things adapted to their environment?

Read about how some animals are adapted to the Arctic environment.

Go Digital!

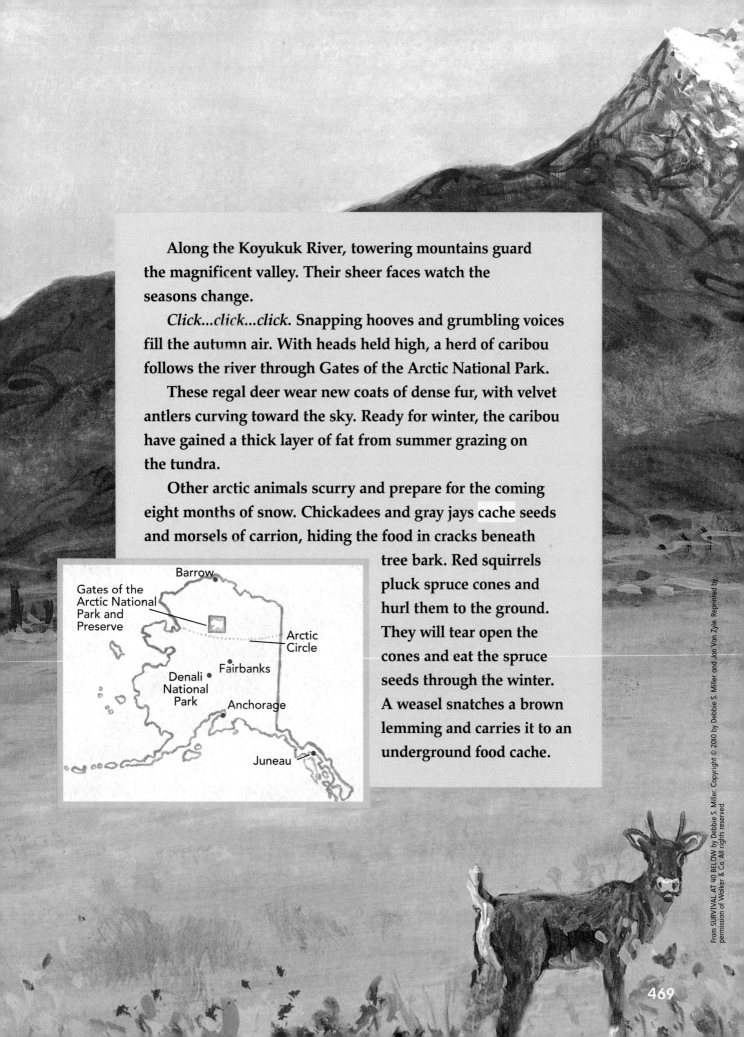

Along the Koyukuk River, towering mountains guard the magnificent valley. Their sheer faces watch the seasons change.

Click...click...click. Snapping hooves and grumbling voices fill the autumn air. With heads held high, a herd of caribou follows the river through Gates of the Arctic National Park.

These regal deer wear new coats of dense fur, with velvet antlers curving toward the sky. Ready for winter, the caribou have gained a thick layer of fat from summer grazing on the tundra.

Other arctic animals scurry and prepare for the coming eight months of snow. Chickadees and gray jays cache seeds and morsels of carrion, hiding the food in cracks beneath tree bark. Red squirrels pluck spruce cones and hurl them to the ground. They will tear open the cones and eat the spruce seeds through the winter. A weasel snatches a brown lemming and carries it to an underground food cache.

Barrow

Gates of the Arctic National Park and Preserve

Arctic Circle

Fairbanks

Denali National Park

Anchorage

Juneau

Nights grow colder. A thin layer of ice creeps across a pond near the river. Snug in their lodge, beavers rest after cutting many saplings for their underwater cache. Near their food pile, an Alaska blackfish paddles slowly through pond vegetation, searching for insect larvae. This bottom dweller can survive the winter in shallow frozen ponds with little oxygen. Along with gills, the blackfish has an unusual esophagus that can work like a lung, absorbing oxygen from the air. During the winter, this fish will find holes in the ice and breathe through its mouth.

Leaves rustle softly as a wood frog burrows into the duff of the forest floor. Suddenly, the frog feels its skin freezing. Its heart begins to beat rapidly. The frog's liver quickly produces lots of glucose. This sugary fluid, which the frog pumps through its body for several hours, will protect the insides of the cells from ice crystals. When more than three-quarters of its body freezes, the frog stops breathing and its heart stops beating.

But, like magic, the frog is still alive. Beneath the insulating layers of duff and snow, this frozen amphibian will hibernate until spring. It's a live frogsicle!

Farther up the valley, a small golden mammal is plump after a summer diet of tundra plants and seeds. As days grow shorter, the male arctic ground squirrel tunnels into the earth to prepare its burrow. He digs an underground chamber, about the size of a basketball, and stuffs it with grasses and tufts of caribou fur. Then he collects and stores seeds and berries.

Sik...sik...sik. The squirrel chatters a warning signal. Across the river, a grizzly bear browses on berries and digs up thick potato-like roots with her sharp claws. Alarmed by this huge predator, the squirrel dashes beneath the tundra. Like the squirrel, this grizzly will soon dig her winter den on a mountain slope.

STOP AND CHECK

Ask and Answer Questions How does the change in season affect the arctic ground squirrel? Go back to the text to find the answer.

As snowflakes swirl, the squirrel is ready to hibernate. He curls into a ball in his burrow, then slowly supercools his body, lowering his temperature to just below the freezing point of water. His heart rate gradually drops to three beats per minute, and his brain activity ceases. This ice-cold furry squirrel looks dead, but, amazingly, he is only in the inactive state of torpor.

After three weeks, something triggers the squirrel to wake up. His heart rate increases. He warms his body by burning brown fat. This insulating fat protects his vital organs and acts like a heating pad. Within several hours, his heartbeat and temperature are normal.

After rearranging his nest, the squirrel curls back into a ball and falls asleep. He dreams and sleeps soundly for about twelve hours. Then his body supercools again. Like a yo-yo, the squirrel warms himself, sleeps, and supercools about a dozen times during the winter to conserve enough energy to survive.

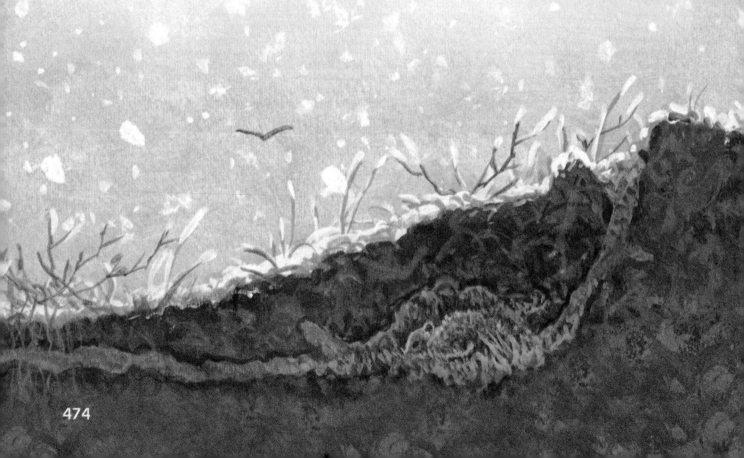

Above the squirrel's burrow, an arctic fox searches for prey. The fox picks up the scent of voles beneath the snow. These mouselike animals are huddling in their nest to keep warm. Like an acrobat, the fox springs high in the air and pounces on the voles. Breaking through the snow, he traps one by surprise.

The arctic fox keeps warm in frigid temperatures because he wears two winter coats. His dense underfur insulates him like the down in a fluffy sleeping bag. His thick outer coat has tiny air pockets inside the hair shafts, instead of color pigment. The snow-white coat perfectly camouflages the fox for hunting prey and escaping predators. Fur also covers the soles of his paws, and his big, bushy tail provides extra warmth.

Inch by inch, the layer of snow deepens with each winter
storm. On a frigid January day, the temperature plummets to
40 below zero. Thick pond ice cracks and makes eerie sounds.
The fluffy quilt of snow insulates and protects the many
animals, plants, and insects beneath it. It is much warmer under
the snow layer than in the open air.

Other animals are well adapted to survive the colder air
temperatures above the ice and snow. Snowshoe hares and
ptarmigan zigzag between the willow bushes. Both animals
can travel lightly across the snow with insulated feet that help
spread out their weight. But the ptarmigan can't survive the
lethal night temperatures and fly off at dusk to seek shelter.

Puff! They dive into a drift of powdery snow. Invisible to the world, the ptarmigan roost inside their snow burrows, protected from predators and the extreme cold.

Another bird combats the deep freeze. A black-capped chickadee flits from tree to tree, eating his cached food. He must gain enough fat each day to survive the night.

But this small bird needs more than food to survive. He fluffs up his dense feathers for better insulation. Tiny muscles control the angle of each feather, while other muscles shiver to produce heat. The chickadee can also lower his temperature and metabolism to save energy. He roosts in a thick forest or in tree cavities that give him the best shelter.

While birds roost beneath a full moon, all is not quiet. A wolf howls on a distant ridge as caribou crunch through the snow with their broad hooves. These deer are well insulated for the Arctic by dense fur and hollow guard hairs. They sniff the snow and detect the smell of ashes from an old forest fire. Turning away, the caribou avoid this burned area.

Muzzles to the ground, the caribou later detect the mushroomlike scent of lichens. They dig craters and forage on clumps of these rootless plants. Their hooves and thin legs are well adapted for digging. A special liquid fat protects their joints. Blood traveling directly to the hooves helps warm the returning blood to the heart. This circular flow protects the legs and reduces heat loss.

STOP AND CHECK

Ask and Answer Questions How are the caribou adapted to a cold environment? Go back to the text to find the answer.

While caribou wander, the grizzly bear is snug in her den with two newborn cubs. The drowsy bear nurses them and rests to save energy. The three survive off her large storehouse of fat. As she sleepily feeds her fast-growing cubs, she doesn't notice the faint sound of steps across the snow.

Sure-footed and agile, Dall sheep pick their way across the mountain slope. Fierce winds have blown snow off the alpine tundra, exposing frozen grasses and sedges. The sheep graze on these withered plants, then seek shelter from the wind by bedding down in the lee of some rocky crags.

Month by month, winter passes slowly. Backs to the wind, a group of musk oxen stands on the snow-covered tundra, conserving energy. Short legs, small ears, and fluffy underwool, known as *qiviut*, insulate musk oxen from even the deepest cold. One musk ox sees wolves approaching and senses danger. Immediately, the musk oxen gather together. Shoulder to shoulder they form a circular wall of thick fur and horns. As one wolf draws near, a large bull lowers his deadly sharp horns. With a sudden burst, he charges the wolf.

Wheeling away, the wolf quickly retreats. The musk oxen continue to work as a team, charging and driving off the hungry wolves.

Trickle...tinkle...drip. The snow and ice begin to melt. As temperatures rise, bumblebees, butterflies, and other dormant insects begin to stir. A woolly bear caterpillar basks in the sun after being snow-covered for eight months. His dark, furry body traps the sun's heat. Inching his way to a budding willow, he chews on a tiny leaf.

These fuzzy creatures, and other northern insects, have antifreeze substances that prevent ice crystals from forming in their bodies. The woolly bear will spend up to fourteen winters in the Arctic as a caterpillar. Then this amazing survivor will transform into a moth, but for only one short summer!

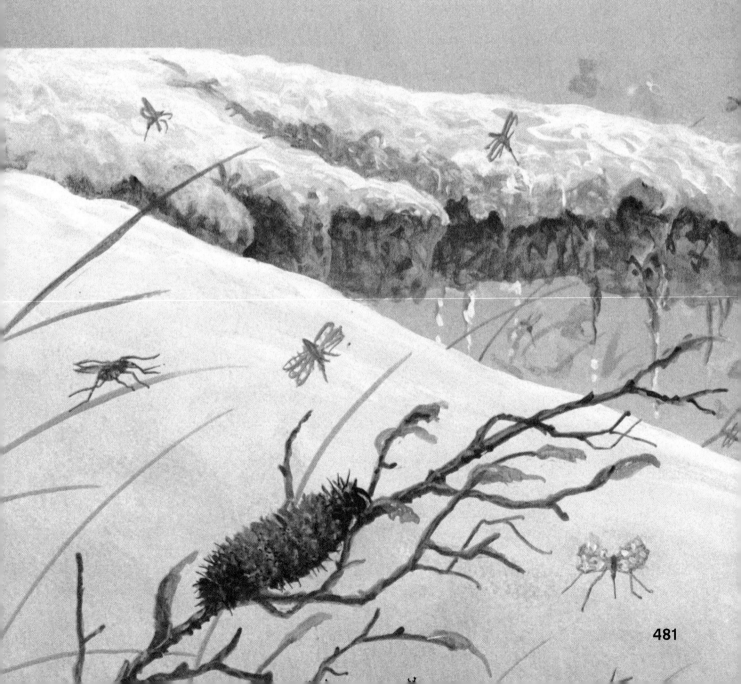

One by one, moist leaves rustle near the pond. The wood frog slowly thaws out, and its heart beats once again. *rrrrRuk... rrrrRuk.* The frog begins calling for a mate, making a ducklike sound near the pond's edge. Slapping their tails in the open water, the beavers dive while the blackfish dart after prey on the pond's bottom. Farther up the valley, the male ground squirrel eats his stored cache of food, then leaves his burrow in search of a mate.

Hour by hour, day by day, the pulse of life increases with warmer June days and greening plants. Caribou feast upon a summer buffet, while playful grizzly bear cubs tussle and explore the tundra as their mother searches for prey. Birds that migrated south for the winter return to their birthplace, building nests on the tundra and filling the air with music. For more than two months the days will be endless, as the top of the world tilts toward the sun and the magical Land of the Midnight Sun explodes with life.

STOP AND CHECK

Visualize How does the warmer weather affect life in the Arctic? Visualizing the animals and their actions may help you.

483

ABOUT THE AUTHOR AND ILLUSTRATOR

Debbie S. Miller first moved to Alaska to teach in a community of Athabaskan people native to the Arctic. Once there, Debbie explored the nearby Arctic National Wildlife Refuge and learned about the environment and its inhabitants. Alaska's wildlife and landscape have inspired many of her award-winning books. She hopes her books help to build an appreciation for the natural environment.

Jon Van Zyle has illustrated nine of Debbie S. Miller's picture books. He lives near Eagle River, Alaska, where he and his wife raise Siberian huskies. Jon has participated in the Iditarod sled-dog race twice and has created a new poster for the race each year since 1979. In addition to painting dog teams, Jon paints Alaska's people, landscapes, and wildlife.

Author's Purpose
In *Survival at 40 Below,* the author writes about a variety of animals through the course of four seasons. Why do you think she arranged the text in this way?

Respond to the Text

Summarize

Use details from *Survival at 40 Below* to summarize how Arctic animals adapt to their environment during the winter. Your Cause and Effect Chart may help you.

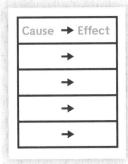

Cause ➡ Effect
➡
➡
➡
➡

Write

How does the author express her point of view about the animals that live and adapt to the Arctic environment? Use these sentence frames to organize your text evidence.

> The author uses words and phrases to help me understand . . .
> She uses figurative language to compare . . .
> I know how she feels about animals because . . .

Make Connections

 Talk about how Arctic animals adapt to their environment during the winter. **ESSENTIAL QUESTION**

Which animal's adaptation did you find the most unusual or interesting? What might people learn by studying this animal? **TEXT TO WORLD**

Why the Evergreen Trees Never Lose Their Leaves

The approach of winter brings changes to many northern environments that can send animals on the move, seeking warmer regions. Other animals stay, but they must **hibernate** *or seek out food and shelter that will keep them warm through the cold winter months. Each animal has an* **adaptation** *that helps it survive.*

Winter was coming, and the birds had flown far to the south, where the air was warm and they could find berries to eat. One little bird had broken its wing and could not fly with the others. It was alone in the cold world of frost and snow. The forest looked warm, and it made its way to the trees as well as it could, to ask for help.

First it came to a birch-tree. "Beautiful birch-tree," it said, "my wing is broken, and my friends have flown away. May I live among your branches till they come back to me?"

Illustration: Richard Downs

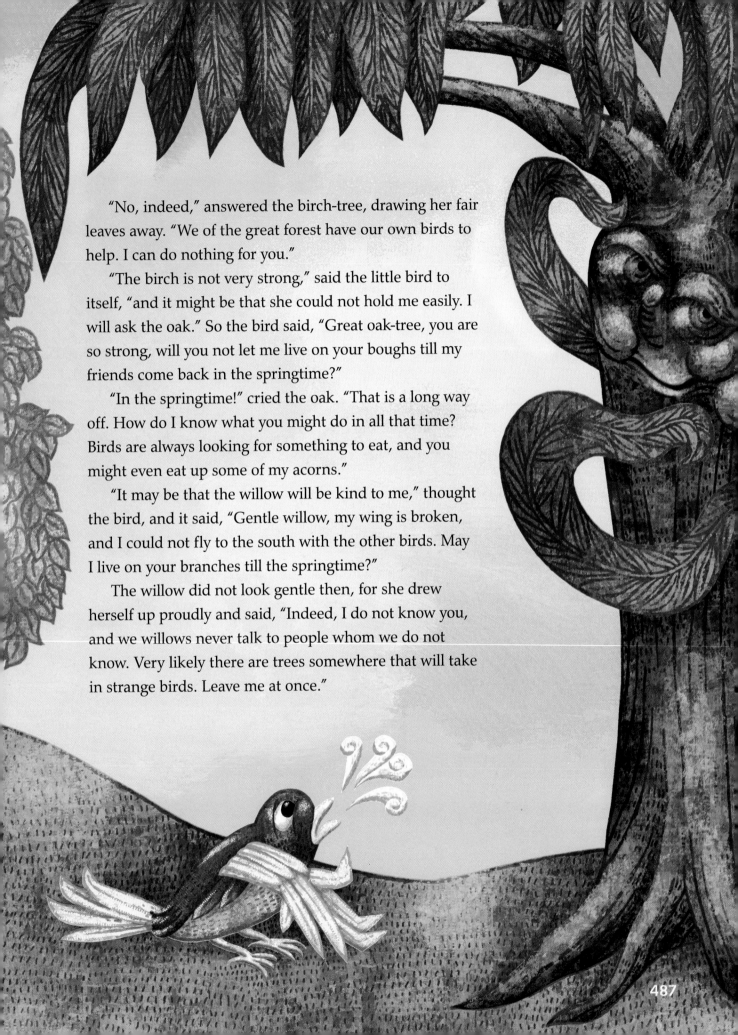

"No, indeed," answered the birch-tree, drawing her fair leaves away. "We of the great forest have our own birds to help. I can do nothing for you."

"The birch is not very strong," said the little bird to itself, "and it might be that she could not hold me easily. I will ask the oak." So the bird said, "Great oak-tree, you are so strong, will you not let me live on your boughs till my friends come back in the springtime?"

"In the springtime!" cried the oak. "That is a long way off. How do I know what you might do in all that time? Birds are always looking for something to eat, and you might even eat up some of my acorns."

"It may be that the willow will be kind to me," thought the bird, and it said, "Gentle willow, my wing is broken, and I could not fly to the south with the other birds. May I live on your branches till the springtime?"

The willow did not look gentle then, for she drew herself up proudly and said, "Indeed, I do not know you, and we willows never talk to people whom we do not know. Very likely there are trees somewhere that will take in strange birds. Leave me at once."

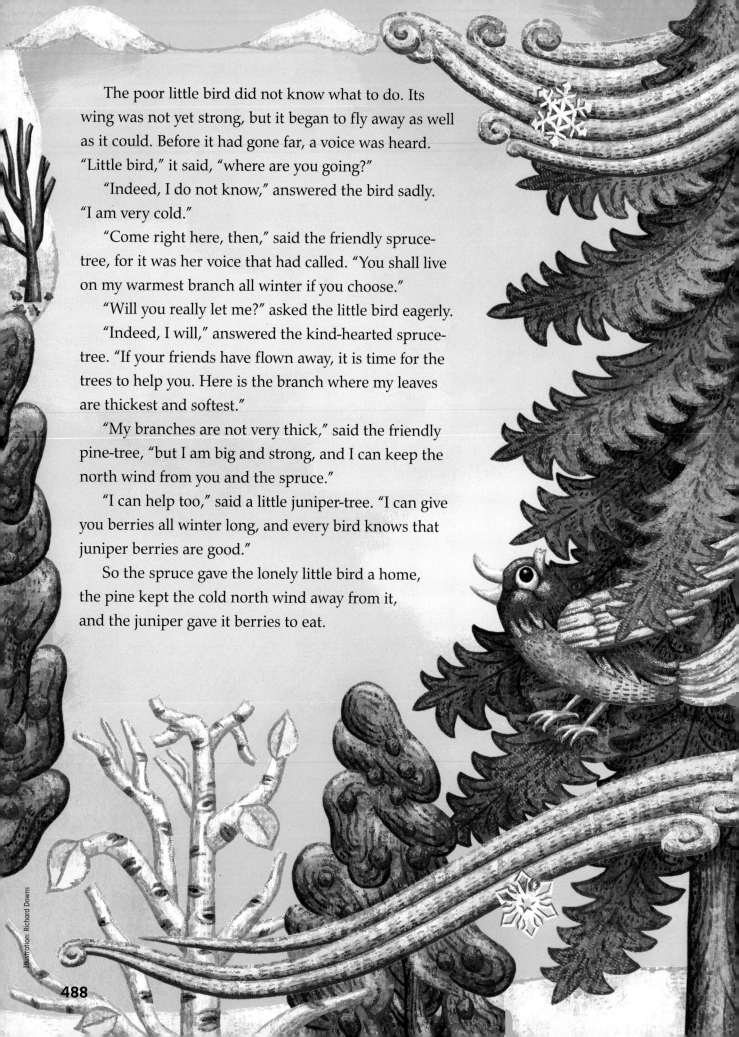

The poor little bird did not know what to do. Its wing was not yet strong, but it began to fly away as well as it could. Before it had gone far, a voice was heard. "Little bird," it said, "where are you going?"

"Indeed, I do not know," answered the bird sadly. "I am very cold."

"Come right here, then," said the friendly spruce-tree, for it was her voice that had called. "You shall live on my warmest branch all winter if you choose."

"Will you really let me?" asked the little bird eagerly.

"Indeed, I will," answered the kind-hearted spruce-tree. "If your friends have flown away, it is time for the trees to help you. Here is the branch where my leaves are thickest and softest."

"My branches are not very thick," said the friendly pine-tree, "but I am big and strong, and I can keep the north wind from you and the spruce."

"I can help too," said a little juniper-tree. "I can give you berries all winter long, and every bird knows that juniper berries are good."

So the spruce gave the lonely little bird a home, the pine kept the cold north wind away from it, and the juniper gave it berries to eat.

The other trees looked on and talked together wisely.

"I would not have strange birds on my boughs," said the birch.

"I shall not give my acorns away for any one," said the oak.

"I never have anything to do with strangers," said the willow, and the three trees drew their leaves closely about them.

In the morning all those shining leaves lay on the ground, for a cold north wind had come in the night, and every leaf that it touched fell from the tree.

"May I touch every leaf in the forest?" asked the wind in its frolic.

"No," said the frost king. "The trees that have been kind to the little bird with the broken wing may keep their leaves."

This is why the leaves of the spruce, the pine, and the juniper are always green.

Make Connections

How does the bird adapt to changes in its environment? What happens as a result? ESSENTIAL QUESTION

How is the bird's adaptation in this story different from other animal adaptations you've read about? TEXT TO TEXT

Essential Question

What impact do our actions have on our world?

Read about how one woman made a difference in her country.

Go Digital!

Planting *the* Trees of Kenya

The Story of Wangari Maathai

written and illustrated by
Claire A. Nivola

As Wangari Maathai tells it, when she was growing up on a farm in the hills of central Kenya, the earth was clothed in its dress of green.

Fig trees, olive trees, crotons, and flame trees covered the land, and fish filled the pure waters of the streams.

The fig tree was sacred then, and Wangari knew not to disturb it, not even to carry its fallen branches home for firewood. In the stream near her homestead where she went to collect water for her mother, she played with **glistening** frogs' eggs, trying to gather them like beads into necklaces, though they slipped through her fingers back into the clear water.

Her heart was filled with the beauty of her **native** Kenya when she left to attend a college run by Benedictine nuns in America, far, far from her home. There she studied biology, the science of living things. It was an inspiring time for Wangari. The students in America in those years dreamed of making the world better. The nuns, too, taught Wangari to think not just of herself but of the world beyond herself.

How eagerly she returned to Kenya! How full of hope and of all
that she had learned!

She had been away for five years, only five years, but they might
have been twenty—so changed was the **landscape** of Kenya.

Wangari found the fig tree cut down, the little stream dried up,
and no trace of frogs, tadpoles, or the silvery beads of eggs. Where
once there had been little farms growing what each family needed
to live on and large **plantations** growing tea for **export**, now
almost all the farms were growing crops to sell. Wangari noticed
that the people no longer grew what they ate but bought food from
stores. The store food was expensive, and the little they could afford
was not as good for them as what they had grown themselves, so
that children, even grownups, were weaker and often sickly.

She saw that where once there had been richly wooded hills with grazing cows and goats, now the land was almost treeless, the woods gone. So many trees had been cut down to clear the way for more farms that women and children had to walk farther and farther in search of firewood to heat a pot or warm the house. Sometimes they walked for hours before they found a tree or bush to cut down. There were fewer and fewer trees with each one they cut, and much of the land was as bare as a desert.

Without trees there were no roots to hold the soil in place. Without trees there was no shade. The rich topsoil dried to dust, and the wind blew it away. Rain washed the loose earth into the once-clear streams and rivers, dirtying them with silt.

> **STOP AND CHECK**
>
> **Ask and Answer Questions**
> How has Kenya changed since Wangari left? Find details to support your answer.

495

"We have no clean drinking water," the women of the countryside complained, "no firewood to cook with. Our goats and cows have nothing to graze on, so they make little milk. Our children are hungry, and we are poorer than before."

Wangari saw that the people who had once honored fig trees and now cut them down had forgotten to care for the land that fed them. Now the land, weak and suffering, could no longer take care of the people, and their lives became harder than ever.

The women blamed others, they blamed the government, but Wangari was not one to complain. She wanted to do something. "Think of what we ourselves are doing," she **urged** the women. "We are cutting down the trees of Kenya.

"When we see that we are part of the problem," she said, "we can become part of the solution." She had a simple and big idea.

"Why not plant trees?" she asked the women.

She showed them how to collect tree seeds from the trees that remained. She taught them to prepare the soil, mixing it with manure. She showed them how to wet that soil, press a hole in it with a stick, and carefully insert a seed. Most of all she taught them to tend the growing seedlings, as if they were babies, watering them twice a day to make sure they grew strong.

It wasn't easy. Water was always hard to come by. Often the women had to dig a deep hole by hand and climb into it to haul heavy bucketfuls of water up over their heads and back out of the hole. An early nursery in Wangari's backyard failed; almost all the seedlings died. But Wangari was not one to give up, and she showed others how not to give up.

Many of the women could not read or write. They were mothers and farmers, and no one took them seriously.

STOP AND CHECK

Ask and Answer Questions Why was it difficult to plant trees? Find details in the text to help you.

But they did not need schooling to plant trees. They did not have to wait for the government to help them. They could begin to change their own lives.

All this was heavy work, but the women felt proud. Slowly, all around them, they could begin to see the fruit of the work of their hands. The woods were growing up again. Now when they cut down a tree, they planted two in its place. Their families were healthier, eating from the fruit trees they had planted and from the vegetable plots filled again with the yams, cassava, pigeon peas, and sorghum that grew so well. They had work to do, and the work brought them together as one, like the trees growing together on the newly wooded hills.

The men saw what their wives, mothers, and daughters were doing and admired them and even joined in.

Wangari gave seedlings to the schools and taught the children how to make their own nurseries.

She gave seedlings to inmates of prisons and even to soldiers. "You hold your gun," she told the soldiers, "but what are you protecting? The whole country is disappearing with the wind and water. You should hold the gun in your right hand and a tree seedling in your left. That's when you become a good soldier."

And so in the thirty years since Wangari began her movement,
tree by tree, person by person, thirty million trees have been
planted in Kenya—and the planting has not stopped.

"When the soil is exposed," Wangari tells us, "it is crying out for help, it is naked and needs to be clothed in its dress. That is the nature of the land. It needs color, it needs its cloth of green."

STOP AND CHECK

Reread How did Wangari get people to join her movement? Use the strategy Reread to help you.

About the Author and Illustrator

Claire A. Nivola grew up in New York City. The daughter of two artists, she drew pictures and created sculptures starting from early childhood. She also loved to read. After studying literature and history in college, she began to illustrate children's books, including one titled *Messy Rabbit* written by her mother. Other children's books she has written and illustrated include *Elisabeth* and *The Forest*.

Claire was inspired to write about Wangari Maathai after hearing her speak on the radio about her tree-growing project in Kenya, called the Green Belt Movement. Claire wanted children to understand how people's actions can harm the environment, which provides for everyone. However, she wanted her message to be hopeful. "A child is just beginning in life and needs to have hope," she said. She hopes her biography of Wangari inspires readers to make positive changes in the world.

Author's Purpose

Claire A. Nivola wrote and illustrated *Planting the Trees of Kenya*. How did the author's illustrations help you understand the changes that took place in Kenya?

Respond to the Text

Summarize

Use the most important events from *Planting the Trees of Kenya* to summarize how Wangari Maathai helped her country. Details from your Problem and Solution Chart may help you.

Problem	Solution

Write

How does the way the author uses language show how Wangari helped the land and the people of Kenya? Use these sentence frames to organize your text evidence.

In the beginning, the author introduces the ideas . . .
The author develops these ideas by . . .
The author uses figurative language to . . .
This is important because I can see how . . .

Make Connections

Talk about how the actions of the people of Kenya affected the land before and after Wangari's movement. **ESSENTIAL QUESTION**

Why is it important for people to take care of the land? **TEXT TO WORLD**

503

Compare Texts

Read about how students at one elementary school made a difference in their community.

THE PARK PROJECT

Two third-grade students Adeline Dixon and Sophia Kimbell, saw that Letty Walter Park, a park in their Indiana community, was in poor condition and needed repairs. The students wanted to plant new trees along the park's creek, but that project required money, which the students did not have. So they decided to write a letter asking a community organization for money to **restore** the park.

"We wrote it by ourselves," Sophia said. "Our parents spell-checked, but that was it."

Happily, the money was granted. The two students and their classmates bought and planted trees along the park's creek. One tree was named The Survivor Tree because it had grown from a seed taken from a tree that survived the Oklahoma City bombing in 1995.

Sophia Kimbell worked to improve Letty Walter Park in New Albany, Indiana.

Unfortunately, the park improvements did not last long. Later that year, powerful storms caused by a nearby hurricane destroyed most of the trees the students had planted. Only two trees remained standing, including The Survivor Tree. The third graders were saddened by the destruction, but they held on to their dream of improving the park.

Two years later, Adeline and Sophia, now fifth graders, wrote another letter to the same community organization. Again they **urged** the group to donate money so students could fix up Letty Walter Park. Again money was granted for planting trees and for further improvements, such as adding two park benches and spreading mulch—a mix of leaves and straw—on the playground.

Once they had supplies, there was plenty of work to do. More than 60 students from the local school pitched in to help. They performed a variety of tasks for their park project. Some planted trees or repainted wooden stalls. Others trimmed bushes, dug up weeds in the playground area, and removed garbage from the creek. The students even managed to **influence** their parents and others in their community to help around the park as well.

Teacher Scott Burch and students take a break beside the park's creek.

By the time all the work was completed, the park looked much greener and cleaner. Scott Burch, a teacher who helped organize the project, praised the students for what they had done. He believed that the children had learned an important lesson. "It shows the students that they can accomplish anything," he declared.

Make Connections

? How did the students' actions have an impact on their community? ESSENTIAL QUESTION

Think of another person or group you've read about who has restored a place. In what ways are the girls' actions different? Explain how each achieved results. TEXT TO TEXT

(t) Kevin McGloshen/News and Tribune; (r) C Squared Studios/Photodisc/Getty Images

You Are My Music
(Tú eres mi música)

My older sister Ana's hands dance as she asks,
"Are you ready to go?" Down five flights and out
onto our cheerful street, a summer Saturday chorus
of honks and shouts. Hand in hand we walk four blocks

to the Pappas Family Music Store. "*Kalimera*, Mr. Pappas.
I am here to buy the guitar I have admired for so long."
How proud I feel with my savings from a year of walking
Mrs. Birnbaum's dog. Mr. Pappas's face becomes a frown.

"I am sorry, Aida, I sold it yesterday. In a week
I will have another, please come back then, *mikro pouli*,
little bird." "Be patient," Ana tells me with her hands,
"just a few more days. Let's go to Mr. Kim's for flowers."

The florist's shop smells cool and fresh, like one big rose.
"*Annyeonghaseyo*, Mr. Kim. I'd like sunflowers, please."
His smile also disappears. "Someone bought them all
this morning. I'll have more on Monday, *chamsae*, little bird."

Back outside we go into the August heat, where a siren shrieks,
every radio blares a different tune. My feet feel heavy,
my shoulders droop. Ana and I have one sweet errand more,
across the street at Castelli's Bakery. But even here,

Essential Question

What can our connections to the world teach us?

Read about how poets reflect on the connections people make with others.

Go Digital!

something isn't right. A note taped to the door reads,
"Closed today, cannoli tomorrow." Too many horns,
too many trucks, too hot, the worst Saturday ever.
As we walk home, Ana signs, "You will be happy soon,"

but I can't think about a time called "soon." I unlock
the door to our apartment and suddenly—what is this?
Mamá, papá, Mrs. Birnbaum, the Castellis too,
my friends Jenny Kim and Voula Pappas, cousins Raul and Rai,

a cake with icing roses, four vases full of sunflowers!
"*Feliz cumpleaños*," my family exclaims.
Voula hugs me, whispers "Happy Birthday."
Then Jenny, "*Saengil chukha hae*." "Yes, Happy Birthday!"

Mr. and Mrs. Castelli add. And everyone says, "Oooooh"
as Ana brings in my dream guitar tied with a pink ribbon
and a card: "For Aida's eleventh birthday. *Tú eres mi música*."
Ana's hands say "Happy, happy," circles in the air.

We all make the sign for "happy," and the room
is filled with dancing hands, a world of music,
my cousins eating too much cake, my beautiful sister
smiling, her hands quiet now, held over her beautiful heart.

— Jean LeBlanc

You and I

Only one I in the whole wide world
And millions and millions of you,
But every you is an I to itself
And I am a you to you, too!

But if I am a you and you are an I
And the opposite also is true,
It makes us both the same somehow
Yet splits us each in two.

It's more and more mysterious,
The more I think it through:
Every you everywhere in the world is an I;
Every I in the world is a you!

— Mary Ann Hoberman

Respond to the Text

Summarize

Use important details from "You Are My Music" to summarize the poem. Think about the connection the speaker makes with others. Details from your Point of View Chart may help you.

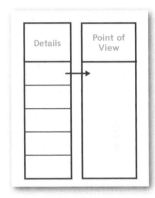

Write

Think about the figurative language in the poems. How do the poets use it to communicate a message about people and the connections they make? Use these sentence frames to organize your text evidence.

> The metaphors in the first poem . . .
> The figurative language in the second poem . . .
> These techniques show that people can connect with each other by . . .

Make Connections

What do connections mean to each of the poets?
ESSENTIAL QUESTION

What can people learn by making connections with different people? TEXT TO WORLD

Compare Texts

Read about how a poet reflects on a friendly exchange.

A Time to Talk

When a friend calls to me from the road
And slows his horse to a meaning walk,
I don't stand still and look around
On all the hills I haven't hoed,
And shout from where I am, "What is it?"
No, not as there is a time to talk.
I thrust my hoes in the mellow ground,
Blade-end up and five feet tall,
And plod: I go up to the stone wall
For a friendly visit.

— Robert Frost

(bkgd) RDImages/Epics/Getty Images; TEXT: "A Time to Talk" from the book THE POETRY OF ROBERT FROST edited by Edward Connery Lathem. Copyright © 1916, 1969 by Henry Holt and Company. copyright © 1944 by Robert Frost Reprinted by permission of Henry Holt and Company, LLC.

Make Connections

Why does the speaker stop to visit with his friend? What lesson does this teach? Use details from the poem to support your ideas. **ESSENTIAL QUESTION**

Think of another poem in which a speaker makes a connection with another person. How is each speaker's experience different? **TEXT TO TEXT**

Glossary

A glossary can help you find the meanings of words in a book that you may not know. The words in the glossary are listed in alphabetical order.

Guide Words

Guide words at the top of each page tell you the first and last words on the page.

anticipation/barbecue

First word on the page

Last word on the page

Sample Entry

Each word is divided into syllables. The way to pronounce the word is given next. You can understand the pronunciation respelling by using the pronunciation key.

Pronunciation

Part of speech

Main entry & syllable division

am·bu·lance (am′byə ləns) *noun.*
A special vehicle that is used to carry sick or injured people to a hospital.
*My neighbor once called an **ambulance** to take him to the hospital.*

Definition

Example sentence

Pronunciation Key

You can understand the pronunciation respelling by using this **pronunciation key**. A shorter key appears at the bottom of every other page. When a word has more than one syllable, a dark accent mark (') shows which syllable is stressed. In some words, a light accent mark (') shows which syllable has a less heavy stress.

Phonetic Spelling	Examples	Phonetic Spelling	Examples
a	**a**t, b**a**d, pl**ai**d, l**au**gh	d	**d**ear, so**d**a, ba**d**
ā	**a**pe, p**ai**n, d**ay**, br**ea**k	f	**f**ive, de**f**end, lea**f**, o**ff**, cou**gh**, ele**ph**ant
ä	**fa**ther, c**a**lm		
âr	c**are**, p**air**, b**ear**, th**eir**, wh**ere**	g	**g**ame, a**g**o, fo**g**, e**gg**
e	**e**nd, p**e**t, s**ai**d, h**ea**ven, fr**ie**nd	h	**h**at, a**h**ead
ē	**e**qual, m**e**, f**ee**t, t**ea**m, p**ie**ce, k**ey**	hw	**wh**ite, **wh**ether, **wh**ich
i	**i**t, b**i**g, g**i**ve, h**y**mn	j	**j**oke, en**j**oy, **g**em, pa**g**e, e**dge**
ī	**i**ce, f**i**ne, l**ie**, m**y**	k	**k**ite, ba**k**ery, see**k**, ta**ck**, **c**at
îr	**ear**, d**eer**, h**ere**, p**ier**ce	l	**l**id, sai**l**or, fee**l**, ba**ll**, a**ll**ow
o	**o**dd, h**o**t, w**a**tch	m	**m**an, fa**m**ily, drea**m**
ō	**o**ld, **oa**t, t**oe**, l**ow**	n	**n**ot, fi**n**al, pa**n**, **kn**ife, **gn**aw
ô	c**o**ffee, **a**ll, t**au**ght, l**aw**, f**ou**ght	ng	lo**ng**, si**ng**er
ôr	**or**der, f**or**k, h**or**se, st**or**y, p**our**	p	**p**ail, re**p**air, soa**p**, ha**pp**y
oi	**oi**l, t**oy**	r	**r**ide, pa**r**ent, wea**r**, mo**r**e, ma**rr**y
ou	**ou**t, n**ow**, b**ou**gh	s	**s**it, a**s**ide, pet**s**, **c**ent, pa**ss**
u	**u**p, m**u**d, l**o**ve, d**ou**ble	sh	**sh**oe, wa**sh**er, fi**sh**, mi**ss**ion, na**ti**on
ū	**u**se, m**u**le, c**u**e, f**eu**d, f**ew**	t	**t**ag, pre**t**end, fa**t**, dress**ed**
ü	r**u**le, tr**u**e, f**oo**d, fr**ui**t	th	**th**in, pan**th**er, bo**th**
u̇	p**u**t, w**oo**d, sh**ou**ld, l**oo**k	<u>th</u>	**th**ese, mo**th**er, smoo**th**
ûr	b**ur**n, h**ur**ry, t**er**m, b**ir**d, w**or**d, c**our**age	v	**v**ery, fa**v**or, wa**v**e
		w	**w**et, **w**eather, re**w**ard
ə	**a**bout, tak**e**n, penc**i**l, lem**o**n, circ**u**s	y	**y**es, oni**o**n
b	**b**at, a**b**ove, jo**b**	z	**z**oo, la**z**y, ja**zz**, ro**s**e, dog**s**, house**s**
ch	**ch**in, su**ch**, ma**tch**	zh	vi**s**ion, trea**s**ure, sei**z**ure

Aa

ab·rupt·ly (ə brəpt'lē) *adverb.* Without warning; suddenly. *The game ended **abruptly** when the rain began.*

ab·sorb (əb sôrb') *verb.* To soak up or take in. *This sponge will **absorb** the spilled juice.*

ac·cess (ak'ses) *verb.* To get at or into something. *We can **access** our garage through a side door.*

ac·com·plish (ə kom'plish) *verb.* To do something successfully; complete. *If we prepare and practice, we can **accomplish** the task more easily.*

ad·ap·ta·tion (a'dap tā'shən) *noun.* A change made to make something more suitable for its environment. *Some owls that live in the prairie nest underground, an **adaptation** that protects them from predators.*

ad·vance (ad vans') *verb.* To move forward or progress in development. *After passing the test, I will **advance** to the next level.*

af·fect (ə fekt') *verb.* To make something happen; to have an effect on. *The hot weather will **affect** how far we can run.*

af·ford (ə fôrd') *verb.* To have enough money to pay for. *After winning the cash prize, he could **afford** a new computer.*

ag·ile (aj'əl) *adjective.* Able to move and react quickly and easily. *The **agile** monkey climbed and swung between trees.*

ag·ri·cul·tur·al (ag'ri kul'chər əl) *adjective.* Having to do with farming or farms. *We studied the **agricultural** impact of the flood during planting season.*

al·ly (a'lī) *noun.* A person, nation, or group that joins with another for a common purpose. *I knew my classmate was my **ally** when he stood up for me against the bully.*

am·bi·tious (am bish'əs) *adjective.* Having a strong desire to succeed at something. *The **ambitious** dancer rehearsed every day before the show.*

an·al·y·sis (ə nal'ə sis) *noun.* A careful examination and study of something. *The doctor's **analysis** of the X-ray proved I had not broken my arm.*

an·ti·ci·pa·tion (an tis'ə pā'shən) *noun.* The act of looking forward to something; expectation. *I waited in line with **anticipation** to meet my favorite author.*

anx·ious (angk'shəs) *adjective.* Nervous, worried, or fearful about what may happen. *My father became **anxious** when he heard a noise under the car's hood.*

ap·pre·ci·a·tion (ə prē'shē ā'shən) *noun.* An understanding of the value of something. *Because of my mother's **appreciation** of music, we attend concerts regularly.*

ap·prox·i·mate·ly (ə prok'sə mit lē) *adverb.* Nearly correct or exact; about. *Our house is **approximately** halfway between the library and the stadium.*

ar·chae·ol·o·gist (är′kē ol′ə jist) *noun*. A person who digs up remains of ancient cities and towns and studies the ways humans lived a long time ago. *The archaeologist concluded that the tools she had found were used for cooking.*

ar·ti·fi·cial (är′tə fish′əl) *adjective*. Made by people, not by nature; not natural. *Plastic is an artificial material developed for its flexibility and strength.*

as·sem·ble (ə sem′bəl) *verb*. To come or bring together. *The band will assemble in the lobby before the concert.*

as·sume (ə süm′) *verb*. To take for granted; suppose. *My classmate studied hard, so I assume she will do well on the test.*

as·sur·ing (ə shủr′ing) *verb*. Stating positively; making certain or sure. *We saw a sign assuring us that the water was safe to drink.*

a·stound·ed (ə stound′əd) *verb*. Surprised very much; amazed. *I was astounded when my little brother rode a bike without any help.*

as·tro·nom·i·cal (as′trə nom′i kəl) *adjective*. Of or having to do with astronomy, the science of the sun, stars, planets, and other space objects. *I looked at the astronomical chart to locate the star.*

at·mo·sphere (at′məs fîr) *noun*. The layer of gases that surrounds a planet such as Earth. *The rocket shot up into the atmosphere to record weather data.*

Bb

bar·ren (bar′ən) *adjective*. Not able to produce anything. *The landscape was so barren that only a few trees could survive.*

be·hav·iors (bē hā′vyərz) *noun, plural*. Ways of behaving or acting. *We watched the behaviors of the frogs as they gathered at the pond.*

blares (blârz) *verb*. Makes a loud, harsh sound. *The car alarm blares in the street and wakes us up.*

blurt·ed (blûrt′əd) *verb*. Said suddenly or without thinking. *I blurted out the answer before he had finished asking the question.*

break·through (brāk′thrü) *noun*. A sudden, important advance. *The doctor had a breakthrough when he found a new way to treat the disease.*

bul·le·tin (bủl′i tin) *noun*. A short announcement of the latest news. *The bulletin before the game noted that the start time had changed.*

---

at; āpe; fär; câre; end; mē; it; īce; pîerce; hot; ōld; sông; fôrk; oil; out; up; ūse; rüle; pủll; tûrn; chin; sing; shop; thin; this; hw in white; zh in treasure.

The symbol ə stands for the unstressed vowel sound in about, taken, pencil, lemon, and circus.

Cc

cache (kash) *verb.* To hide or store something out of reach. *We will **cache** our camp food where the bears can't find it.*

cal·cu·la·tion (kal'kyə lā'shən) *noun.* The act or process of determining something using mathematics. *By my **calculation**, we will arrive in one hour if we stay at this speed.*

cap·ti·vat·ed (kap'tiv āt'əd) *verb.* Influenced by charm, art, or skill. *The cute baby birds **captivated** the onlookers.*

cir·cu·lates (sûr'kyə lāts) *verb.* Moves around in a circular coarse back to the starting point. *Blood **circulates** from the heart through the body and back.*

cir·cum·stanc·es (sûr'kəm stans ez) *noun, plural.* Conditions, acts, or events that exist with other things and that may have an effect on them. *The police asked about the **circumstances** of the accident.*

cite (sīt) *verb.* To mention as proof or support. *My uncle can **cite** information from his passport to show where he has traveled.*

civ·i·li·za·tion (siv'ə lə zā'shən) *noun.* A society in which agriculture, trade, government, art, and science are highly developed. *We searched for buildings, tools, and other signs of **civilization** on the island.*

claimed (klāmd) *verb.* Declared as one's own. *I **claimed** my gloves at the lost-and-found.*

col·lab·o·rate (kə la'bə rāt') *verb.* To work together on something. *The writer and composer decided to **collaborate** to create a musical.*

col·lid·ed (kə līd'əd) *verb.* Crashed against or into each other. *The players **collided** as they both tried to grab the ball.*

com·menced (kə mensd') *verb.* Began, started. *Last year, classes **commenced** promptly at 8:00.*

com·mit·tees (kə mit'ēz) *noun, plural.* Groups of people chosen to do certain work. *We assigned two **committees** to plan and manage the bake sale.*

com·plex (kəm pleks') *adjective.* Hard to understand or do. *I spent hours on the **complex** puzzle but never figured it out.*

com·pli·ment·ing (kom'plə ment ing) *verb.* Expressing praise or admiration. *The director was **complimenting** the actors for another great performance.*

con·cealed (kən sēld') *verb.* Put or kept out of sight; hid. *I **concealed** the gift to keep from ruining the surprise.*

con·fi·dent (kon'fə dent) *adjective.* Having trust, sure; trusting in oneself and one's own abilities. *After studying the words, I am **confident** I will do well on the quiz.*

con·flict (kon'flikt) *noun.* A long fight or war; a strong disagreement. *The **conflict** between the countries began when one government tried to expand its powers.*

con·grat·u·late (kən grach′ə lāt′) *verb*. To give good wishes or praise for someone's success or for something nice that has happened. *My grandmother wrote a card to my sister to* **congratulate** *her for winning the spelling bee.*

con·nec·tion (kə nek′shən) *noun*. Relationship; association. *Doctors have found a* **connection** *between eating well and staying healthy.*

con·serve (kən sûrv′) *verb*. To keep and protect from harm, loss, or change. *My brother will* **conserve** *his energy today for the big race tomorrow.*

con·sid·er·a·tion (kən sid′ə rā′shən) *noun*. Careful thought before making a decision. *After careful* **consideration,** *the President signed the bill into law.*

con·sults (kən sults′) *verb*. Goes to for advice or information. *Before going on a trip, the traveler always* **consults** *guidebooks.*

con·tact (kon′takt) *noun*. A touching or meeting of persons or things. *I developed a rash after coming in* **contact** *with poison ivy.*

con·tra·dict·ed (kon′trə dik′təd) *verb*. Said the opposite of; disagreed with. *My parents* **contradicted** *my claim that I deserved a raise in my allowance.*

con·tri·bu·tions (kon′trə bū′shənz) *noun, plural*. Acts of giving money, time, effort or the like to a cause. *We thanked the parents for their* **contributions** *to the school carnival.*

con·ven·tion (kən ven′shən) *noun*. A formal meeting for some special purpose. *I met my favorite illustrator at the comic book* **convention.**

coun·ter·point (koun′tər point) *noun*. An opposing opinion or viewpoint. *The* **counterpoint** *to buying the item would be saving the money instead.*

cri·te·ri·a (krī tîr′ē ə) *noun, plural*. Rules, standards, or tests by which something or someone can be judged or measured. *My entry was accepted once it met the* **criteria** *for the contest.*

crit·i·cal (krit′i kəl) *adjective*. Finding something wrong with things. *The coach was* **critical** *of the goalie's performance but offered good advice for improvement.*

cul·ti·vate (kul′tə vāt) *verb*. To plant and help grow; to improve or develop. *The block party will* **cultivate** *community spirit among our neighbors.*

cul·tur·al (kul′chər əl) *adjective*. Having to do with the arts, beliefs, and customs of a group of people. *Storytelling is an important part of my family's* **cultural** *history.*

---

at; āpe; fär; câre; end; mē; it; īce; pîerce; hot; ōld; sông; fôrk; oil; out; up; ūse; rüle; pùll; tûrn; chin; sing; shop; thin; this; hw in white; zh in treasure.

The symbol ə stands for the unstressed vowel sound in about, taken, pencil, lemon, and circus.

cy•cle (sī′kəl) *noun.* A series of events that happen one after another in the same order. *The **cycle** of rainy weather ended with five days of sunshine.*

Dd

da•ta (dā′tə) *noun.* Individual facts, figures, and other items of information. *The scientists checked their **data** against other findings to see if they were correct.*

de•bate (di bāt′) *verb.* To argue about or discuss at a meeting. *The community will **debate** the new library hours at our next town meeting.*

de•bris (də brē′) *noun.* The scattered remains of something; trash or litter. *Yesterday's wind storm blew a lot of **debris** into the streets.*

de•cays (di kāz′) *verb.* Rots; decomposes. *The old tree stump **decays** even faster in hot, wet weather.*

de•ci•pher (di sī′fər) *verb.* To figure out the meaning of something difficult to read or understand. *I could not **decipher** my little sister's handwritten notes.*

de•clined (di klīnd′) *verb.* Became less in amount or growth; weakened. *The strength of the wind **declined** as the storm passed.*

de•di•cat•ed (ded′i kā təd) *verb.* Devoted or gave totally or earnestly; set apart for a special purpose or use. *The students had **dedicated** the afternoon to decorating the classroom.*

deeds (dēdz) *noun, plural.* Acts; actions. *The officer won an award for the many good **deeds** that helped our town.*

de•fy (di fī′) *verb.* To resist boldly and openly; to refuse to obey. *The bad dog will **defy** any efforts to get him inside.*

des•ti•ny (des′tə nē) *noun.* What happens to a person or thing, especially when it seems to be determined in advance; fortune. *The talented singer felt that becoming a superstar was her **destiny**.*

de•tect•ed (di tek′təd) *verb.* Found out or noticed; discovered. *The family hurried outside when they **detected** a smell of smoke in the house.*

de•vi•ces (di vī′səz) *noun, plural.* Things that are made or invented for a particular purpose. *My father uses many **devices** to keep him from getting lost on trips.*

de•vise (di vīz′) *verb.* To think out; invent; plan. *When we found out we could not hold a car wash, our team had to **devise** a new plan for raising money.*

di•a•me•ter (dī a′mə tər) *noun.* The length of a straight line passing through the center of a circle or sphere, from one side to another. *We checked the **diameter** of the balls to make sure they would fit through the hoops.*

dis•ap•pear•ance (dis′ə pîr′ens) *noun.* The act or fact of vanishing or going out of sight. *The warm day resulted in the **disappearance** of our snowman.*

dis·dain (dis dān′) *noun.* Contempt or dislike for something or someone thought of as unworthy. *Our **disdain** for the team changed after they played a great game.*

dis·or·der (dis ôr′dər) *noun.* A sickness or ailment. *The doctor told the patient his vision **disorder** was caused by an allergic reaction.*

dis·tract·ed (di strakt′əd) *verb.* Drew one's attention away from what one was doing or thinking. *I was **distracted** from my homework by the ringing phone.*

di·ver·si·ty (di vûr′si tē) *noun.* Great difference; variety. *Our school celebrates **diversity** with a cultural food fair.*

dor·mant (dôr′mənt) *adjective.* Not active. *The flower bulbs are **dormant** in winter but will grow again in the spring.*

draw·backs (drô′baks) *noun, plural.* Things that make something more difficult or unpleasant; disadvantages. *Writing with a pen has some **drawbacks**: marks cannot be erased and the ink can run out.*

Ee

e·merg·ing (i mûr′jing) *verb.* Coming out or into view. *We videotaped the butterfly **emerging** from the cocoon.*

em·pha·sis (em′fə sis) *noun.* Special force used when saying a particular word or syllable; stress. *The teacher read the spelling words louder than the other words for **emphasis**.*

en·coun·ter (en koun′tər) *noun.* A usually unexpected meeting. *Our dog's **encounter** with a skunk resulted in his need for a bath.*

en·er·get·ic (en′ər jet′ik) *adjective.* Full of strength, eagerness, or energy. *I raced to keep up with my **energetic** teammates.*

en·list·ed (en list′əd) *verb.* Joined the armed forces voluntarily. *My uncle **enlisted** in the Navy after reading about the conflict.*

en·thu·si·as·tic·al·ly (en thü′zē as′ti klē) *adverb.* In a way that shows great interest or excitement. *We clapped **enthusiastically** to have the band perform another song.*

en·ti·tled (en tī′təld) *verb.* Gave a claim or right to; qualified. *You are **entitled** to go backstage only if you have a special pass.*

en·vi·sion·ed (en vi′zhənd) *verb.* Imagined something that could or would happen in the future. *He **envisioned** his performance before he even got the part in the play.*

e·ra (îr′ə) *noun.* A period of time or of history. *The 1800s began an **era** of growth in the United States that lasted over sixty years.*

---

at; āpe; fär; câre; end; mē; it; īce; pîerce; hot; ōld; sông; fôrk; oil; out; up; ūse; rüle; pu̇ll; tûrn; chin; sing; shop; thin; <u>th</u>is; hw in white; zh in treasure.

The symbol ə stands for the unstressed vowel sound in **a**bout, tak**e**n, penc**i**l, lem**o**n, and circ**u**s.

e·rode (i rōd') *verb*. To wear or wash away slowly; eat away. *The rising water may* **erode** *the riverbank and cause a collapse.*

er·rand (er'ənd) *noun*. A short trip to do something. *My father made a quick* **errand** *to buy extra food for the party.*

e·val·u·ate (i val'ū āt') *verb*. To judge or discover the value of something. *My teacher asked me to* **evaluate** *how much I had learned this month.*

ex·ag·ger·at·ion (eg za'jə rā'shən) *noun*. An instance of making something seem larger or greater; overstatement. *It was an* **exaggeration** *to claim that my sister was as fast as a cheetah.*

ex·change (eks chānj') *noun*. The act of giving one thing for another. *My friend and I liked each other's backpacks so we decided to* **exchange** *them.*

ex·pec·ta·tions (ek'spek tā'shənz) *noun, plural*. Reasons for expecting or looking forward to something. *After the first win, the team discussed their* **expectations** *for the coming season.*

ex·port (ek'spôrt) *noun*. The act or process of sending goods to another country to be sold or traded. *The pineapples were packed in boxes for* **export** *to nearby countries.*

ex·pres·sion (ek spresh'ən) *noun*. The act of putting thoughts or feelings into words or actions. *His range of* **expression** *made him a wonderful actor.*

Ff

fash·ioned (fash'ənd) *verb*. Gave form to; made; shaped. *The clever boy* **fashioned** *a fishing pole out of sticks and string.*

flex·i·ble (flek'sə bəl) *adjective*. Able to bend without breaking; not stiff. *I stretched the* **flexible** *rubber band around the envelope to keep it closed.*

flur·ry (flûr'ē) *noun*. A sudden movement of many things at once. *The final bell always leads to a* **flurry** *of activity in the hallway.*

fo·cused (fō'kəsd) *verb*. Fixed on; concentrated. *If I stay* **focused** *on the task, I will finish it on time.*

for·age (fôr'ij) *verb*. To hunt or search for food or supplies. *We watched the deer* **forage** *in the clover.*

for·ma·tion (fôr mā'shən) *noun*. Something formed or made. *The marching band lined up in a star* **formation** *for the Fourth of July parade.*

frag·ments (frag'mənts) *noun, plural*. Parts broken off; small pieces. *We glued together the* **fragments** *of the broken plate.*

frig·id (frij'id) *adjective*. Very cold. *The conditions were so* **frigid** *that ice formed across the pond.*

func·tion (fungk'shən) *noun*. Use or purpose. *My phone has a* **function** *that lets me take and send pictures.*

Gg

gen·er·a·tions (jen'ə rāsh'ənz) *noun, plural.* Steps in the line of descent from a common ancestor. *Many **generations** came together for the family reunion.*

ge·ni·us (jēn'yəs) *noun.* A person with high mental powers, especially creativity or inventiveness. *My brother must be a **genius** to be able to fix the computer so easily.*

gla·ciers (glā'shər z) *noun, plural.* Large masses of ice in very cold regions or on the tops of high mountains. *Some ice from **glaciers** melts in spring and provides fresh water to the towns below.*

glis·ten·ing (glis'ən ing) *adjective.* Shining or sparkling with reflected light. *The spider web was **glistening** with dew this morning.*

grad·u·al (graj'ü əl) *adjective.* Moving, changing, or happening slowly. *The growth chart shows a **gradual** change in my height over the years.*

grat·i·tude (grat'i tüd') *noun.* A feeling of gratefulness. *We expressed our **gratitude** to the man who helped us fix our car.*

guar·an·tee (gar'ən tē') *verb.* To make sure or certain. *My sister is a great cook, so I **guarantee** you will enjoy her soups and sandwiches.*

guid·ance (gī'dəns) *noun.* The act or process of guiding; leadership; direction. *We followed the **guidance** of locals when we got lost on our trip.*

Hh

he·ro·ic (hi rō'ik) *adjective.* Very brave; courageous. *The **heroic** firefighter received an award for saving the boy's life.*

hi·ber·nate (hī'bər nāt') *verb.* To spend time sleeping or in an inactive state. *Chipmunks **hibernate** underground during the winter and wake up in spring.*

his·to·ri·an (hi stôr'ē ən) *noun.* A person who knows a great deal about the past. *Our town's **historian** can tell you who had once lived in every house.*

Ii

i·den·ti·fy (ī den'tə fī') *verb.* To tell exactly what a thing is; to recognize. *My mother's yellow hat made her easy to **identify** in a crowd.*

im·pact (im'pakt) *noun.* A strong effect or influence. *The coach's advice had an **impact** on the way the team played today.*

---

at; āpe; fär; câre; end; mē; it; īce; pîerce; hot; ōld; sông; fôrk; oil; out; up; ūse; rüle; pùll; tûrn; chin; sing; shop; thin; this; hw in white; zh in treasure.

The symbol ə stands for the unstressed vowel sound in about, taken, pencil, lemon, and circus.

im·press (im pres') *verb.* To have a strong effect on the mind or feelings. *I hope that my creativity will **impress** the judges of the poetry contest.*

in·di·cat·ed (in'di kāt'əd) *verb.* Was a sign of; showed. *The red arrows **indicated** the path toward the exit.*

in·flu·ence (in'flü əns) *verb.* To change or affect the thought or behavior of; persuade. *My report card will **influence** my parents' decision to let me go to the amusement park this weekend.*

in·quis·i·tive (in kwiz'i tiv) *adjective.* Eager to know; curious. *The **inquisitive** boy couldn't wait to see what was in the box.*

in·su·lates (in'sə lāts) *verb.* Covers or surrounds with material that does not conduct heat, sound, or electricity. *My wool sweater **insulates** me against the cold wind.*

in·tact (in takt') *adjective.* Whole; with nothing missing, broken, or injured. *I was lucky that the bowl was still **intact** after dropping.*

in·ter·cept (in'tər sept') *verb.* To stop or take something on its way from one person or place to another. *The girls hoped the teacher would not **intercept** their note.*

in·ter·pret (in tûr'prit) *verb.* To explain the meaning of something. *"I **interpret** your smile to mean you're happy," my aunt said.*

in·ter·vene (in tər vēn') *verb.* To come between opposing parties. *The referee had to **intervene** to find out who had control of the ball.*

Ll

land·scape (land'skāp') *noun.* The stretch of land that can be seen from a place; a region's landforms. *The **landscape** of the park made it an ideal place for rock climbing.*

loan (lōn) *noun.* Money borrowed. *My father gave me a **loan** to pay for the skateboard because I had not earned enough money yet.*

Mm

mean·ing·ful (mē'ning fəl) *adjective.* Having a meaning or purpose. *My grandfather's old watch is one of my most **meaningful** possessions.*

mem·or·ized (mem'ə rīzd) *verb.* Learned by heart. *The speaker **memorized** his speech so that he would not have to look at his notes.*

mi·grate (mī'grāt') *verb.* To move from one place to another. *The birds will **migrate** south when the weather turns cold.*

mim·ic (mim'ik) *verb.* To imitate. *My uncle can **mimic** the hoot of an owl.*

mis·un·der·stand·ing (mis'un dər stan'ding) *noun.* The failure to understand or comprehend correctly. *We did not know there was a **misunderstanding** until everyone arrived an hour early for the party.*

mois·ture (mois'chər) *noun.* Water or other liquid in the air or on a surface; slight wetness. *The **moisture** on the carpet meant the roof was leaking again.*

Nn

na·tive (nā′tiv) *adjective.* Belonging to a place by birth. *My neighbor visited relatives in his **native** Germany.*

nat·u·ral·ist (nach′ər ə list) *noun.* A person who specializes in the study of things in nature, especially animals and plants. *The **naturalist** looked forward to spending a month in the jungle.*

nav·i·gate (nav′i gāt′) *verb.* To sail, steer, or follow a course over or through. *I used the map to help me **navigate** through the park.*

ne·ces·si·ty (ni ses′i tē) *noun.* Something that is needed; requirement. *A library card is a **necessity** for checking out books.*

neu·tral (nü′trəl) *adjective.* Not taking or belonging to either side in a conflict. *Our parents usually stay **neutral** when I argue with my siblings.*

nom·i·nate (nom′ə nāt′) *verb.* To choose as a candidate, as for an elected position. *We will **nominate** the best speaker to represent our club at the event.*

no·tice·a·bly (nō′ti sə blē) *adverb.* In an easily observed or noticeable manner. *Once the sun came up, the air grew **noticeably** warmer.*

Oo

ob·ser·va·tion (ob′zər vā′shən) *noun.* The act or power of noticing. *The doctor made the **observation** that my cut was healing well.*

ob·sta·cle (ob′stə kəl) *noun.* A person or thing that stands in the way or blocks progress. *The runner was able to dodge the **obstacle** that had fallen onto the track.*

ob·vi·ous·ly (ob′vē əs lē) *adverb.* In an easily seen or understood manner. *The largest door was **obviously** the main entrance.*

op·er·a·tions (op′ə rā′shənz) *noun, plural.* Acts, processes, or ways of performing, directing, or working. *We reviewed the basic **operations** of the machine before using it.*

op·tions (op′shənz) *noun, plural.* Choices; alternatives. *Our cafeteria had three **options** for lunch today.*

or·bit (ôr′bit) *verb.* To move in a circle around another object. *The new satellite will **orbit** Earth and take pictures of weather patterns happening around the world.*

---

at; āpe; fär; câre; end; mē; it; īce; pîerce; hot; ōld; sông; fôrk; oil; out; up; ūse; rüle; pùll; tûrn; chin; sing; shop; thin; this; hw in white; zh in treasure.

The symbol ə stands for the unstressed vowel sound in about, taken, pencil, lemon, and circus.

out·come (out′kum) *noun.* A result, end, or consequence. *Our team received first prize at the contest, so we were pleased with the* **outcome.**

out·spo·ken (out′spo′kən) *adjective.* Honest or open; frank in speech. *The* **outspoken** *man had written several letters to the local newspaper.*

Pp

par·ti·cles (pär′ti kəlz) *noun, plural.* Very small bits or pieces of something. *The sunlight made the* **particles** *of dust in the air visible.*

pas·sion·ate (pash′ə nit) *adjective.* Having or showing a strong feeling. *The baseball fan was so* **passionate** *that he bought tickets to every game.*

pat·ents (pat′ənts) *noun, plural.* Papers issued to a person or company by the government that grant the right to be the only one to make, use, or sell new inventions for a period of time. *The inventor applied for* **patents** *to prevent others from copying her ideas.*

per·plexed (pər pleksd′) *verb.* Filled with uncertainty; confused; bewildered. *I was* **perplexed** *when I found all the lights on, but nobody at home.*

per·spec·tive (pər spek′tiv) *noun.* A point of view. *The view from the airplane was like having the* **perspective** *of a flying bird.*

plan·ta·tions (plan tā′shənz) *noun, plural.* Large estates or farms that grow one crop. *The bananas were grown in* **plantations** *in Central America.*

plumes (plümz) *noun, plural.* Big, fluffy feathers or feathery parts. *We could tell the birds apart by the color of their* **plumes.**

posed (pōzd) *verb.* Held a position, such as for a painting or photograph. *The family* **posed** *as a group for the annual photograph.*

pre·cise (pri sīs′) *adjective.* Very accurate or definite; exact. *The carpenter took* **precise** *measurements to avoid mistakes.*

pres·ence (prez′əns) *noun.* The area around or near a person. *He read the speech in the* **presence** *of his mother, whom it honored.*

pre·served (pri zûrvd′) *verb.* Kept from being lost, damaged, or decayed; protected. *She* **preserved** *the photographs in a special album.*

pre·vi·ous (prē′vē əs) *adjective.* Coming before; earlier. *There was still a great deal of snow from the* **previous** *day's storm.*

prob·a·ble (prob′ə bəl) *adjective.* Likely to happen or be true. *Because the player went home sick yesterday, it is* **probable** *that she will not be at the game tonight.*

prof·it (prof′it) *noun.* The amount of money left after all the costs of running a business have been paid. *After the flyers had been paid for, we found we had made a large* **profit** *from our lawn sale.*

pro·pos·al (prə pō′zəl) *noun.* A plan or suggestion that is presented to others for consideration. *We agreed with Mom's **proposal** to spend our vacation at the beach.*

pros·pect (pros′pekt) *noun.* Something looked forward to or expected. *I was excited by the **prospect** of a holiday weekend.*

pros·per (pros′pər) *verb.* To be successful; to do very well. *The new plants seemed to **prosper** in the larger pots.*

pro·tec·tive (prə tek′tiv) *adjective.* Keeping from harm. *She used a **protective** case to carry her computer to school.*

pur·suit (pər süt′) *noun.* The act of pursuing or chasing. *Our **pursuit** of the runaway cat lasted an hour.*

Rr

rea·son·ing (rē′zən ing) *noun.* The process of drawing conclusions from facts; clear and sensible thinking. *I agreed with my brother's **reasoning** that we should arrive early to get the best seats.*

re·ced·ing (ri sēd′ing) *verb.* Moving back or away. *The **receding** water led us to believe that the danger of flooding had passed.*

re·con·sid·er (rē′kən si′dər) *verb.* To think about again. *When I found out the museum was closed, I had to **reconsider** my plans.*

re·con·struct (rē′kən strəkt′) *verb.* To put parts back together again. *We had to **reconstruct** the shed after it collapsed.*

re·cruits (ri krütz′) *noun, plural.* Newly enlisted members of the armed forces. *The general welcomed the new **recruits** to the training base.*

re·ly (rē lī′) *verb.* To trust; to depend. *I had to **rely** on my sense of touch in the darkened room.*

rem·nants (rem′nəntz) *noun, plural.* Leftover small parts or remaining traces. *The birds pecked at the **remnants** of the picnickers' lunch.*

rep·e·ti·tion (rep′i tish′ən) *noun.* The act or process of doing again or repeating. *The **repetition** of words in the song made it easy to remember.*

rep·re·sent·a·tives (rep′ri zen′tə tivz) *noun, plural.* People chosen to speak or act for others. *The **representatives** gathered to discuss their groups' views on the matter.*

re·served (ri zûrvd′) *verb.* Set apart for a person or purpose. *The flight attendant led us to our **reserved** window seats.*

---

at; **ā**pe; **fä**r; **câ**re; **e**nd; **mē**; **i**t; **ī**ce; **pî**erce; **ho**t; **ō**ld; **sô**ng; **fô**rk; **oi**l; **ou**t; **u**p; **ū**se; **rü**le; **pu̇**ll; **tû**rn; **ch**in; si**ng**; **sh**op; **th**in; **th**is; **hw** in **wh**ite; **zh** in treasure.

The symbol **ə** stands for the unstressed vowel sound in **a**bout, tak**e**n, penc**i**l, lem**o**n, and circ**u**s.

re·solve (ri zolv′) *verb.* To settle, explain, determine, or solve. *My father took the remote to **resolve** the argument between my brothers over which channel to watch.*

re·source·ful (ri sôrs′fəl) *adjective.* Skilled in dealing with new or difficult situations. *The **resourceful** hikers made a shelter out of branches and their backpacks.*

re·store (ri stôr′) *verb.* To bring back to a former or original state or condition. *My father hoped to **restore** the car even though it hadn't worked in years.*

re·trace (rē trās′) *verb.* To go back over. *I had to **retrace** my steps to find where I had left my keys.*

re·veal (ri vēl′) *verb.* To show, display. *The stage curtains were drawn back to **reveal** the performers.*

risk (risk) *noun.* A chance of loss or harm. *She held onto the railing to reduce her **risk** of falling.*

Ss

sat·is·fac·tion (sat′is fak′shən) *noun.* The condition of being satisfied; the act of satisfying. *When I finished the project, I was filled with great **satisfaction**.*

saun·tered (sôn′tərd) *verb.* Walked in a slow, relaxed way; strolled. *We **sauntered** through the park one afternoon when we had nothing else planned.*

sav·ings (sā′vingz) *noun.* Money that is saved or set aside. *Part of my allowance went toward my **savings** for a computer.*

scarce (skârs) *adjective.* Difficult to get or find. *Tickets to the game were **scarce** due to the number of people who wanted to attend.*

seeps (sēps) *verb.* Flows or spreads slowly. *Water **seeps** into our basement after heavy rainfalls.*

sheer (shîr) *adjective.* Steep. *Dad warned us not to sled down the **sheer** hillside.*

short·age (shôr′tij) *noun.* Too small an amount or supply; lack. *Due to a **shortage** of books, classmates had to share copies.*

shud·dered (shud′ərd) *verb.* Trembled suddenly from fear or cold. *I **shuddered** as soon as I stepped outside into the icy air.*

sit·u·a·tion (sich′ü ā′shən) *noun.* A condition or state of affairs; circumstance. *We found ourselves in a difficult **situation** when we ran out of gas.*

sought (sôt) *verb.* Tried to find; went in search of. *The campers **sought** fallen branches to add to the campfire.*

spec·tac·u·lar (spek tak′yə lər) *adjective.* Very unusual or impressive. *She took a photograph of the **spectacular** view.*

spheres (sfîrz) *noun, plural.* Round, three-dimensional figures; globes. *We built our snowman out of three different **spheres**.*

sta·bil·i·ty (stə biʹlə tē) *noun.* The state of being stable or secure. *He improved the table's stability by adding extra support.*

struc·ture (strukʹchər) *noun.* An arrangement of parts. *We designed the structure of the treehouse using toothpicks before building it actual size.*

stunned (stund) *adjective.* Overwhelmed, shocked, or bewildered. *We were stunned when our opponents scored the winning goal in the final moments.*

su·perb (sü pûrbʹ) *adjective.* Very fine; excellent. *The chef is famous for her superb cakes and pastries.*

sup·port·ive (sə pôrtʹiv) *adjective.* Providing approval, aid, or encouragement. *I have a supportive tutor who helps me improve my writing skills.*

sur·viv·al (sər vīʹvəl) *noun.* The act of surviving; continuing to exist. *The survival of our house plants depends on how often we water them.*

sus·pi·cious (sə spishʹəs) *adjective.* Feeling or suspecting that something is wrong or cannot be trusted. *I was suspicious when I heard the neighbor's dogs barking late at night.*

sym·pa·thy (simʹpə thē) *noun.* The ability to feel or understand the sorrows or troubles of others. *I felt deep sympathy for the people who lost their homes in the flood.*

Tt

taunt·ing (tôntʹing) *verb.* Teasing, making fun of someone or something in an insulting way. *The player was removed from the game for rudely taunting the other team.*

tech·niques (tek nēksʹ) *noun, plural.* Ways of bringing about a desired result. *My grandmother knows several techniques to calm a crying baby.*

the·o·ry (thēʹ ə rē) *noun.* An opinion based on some evidence but not proved. *I had a theory that the school bus was always late on rainy days.*

thrive (thrīv) *verb.* To be successful or do well. *The gardener set the plants in the sun and watered them well so they would thrive.*

tor·ment·ors (tôrʹment ərz) *noun, plural.* People or things that cause someone discomfort or pain. *I confronted my tormentors and warned them to leave me alone.*

at; āpe; fär; câre; end; mē; it; īce; pîerce; hot; ōld; sông; fôrk; oil; out; up; ūse; rüle; pull; tûrn; chin; sing; shop; thin; this; hw in white; zh in treasure.

The symbol ə stands for the unstressed vowel sound in about, taken, pencil, lemon, and circus.

trans·formed (trans fôrmd′) *verb.* Changed in shape, form, or appearance. *The stage makeup **transformed** her from a young girl into an old woman.*

tran·si·tion (tran zi′shən) *noun.* A passage from one state, position, condition, or activity to another. *The leaves changed color during the **transition** from summer into fall.*

Uu

un·e·qual (un ē′kwəl) *adjective.* Not the same; uneven. *The slices were **unequal** in size, so I gave my sister some of mine.*

un·ex·pect·ed (ən′ik spekt′əd) *adjective.* Not expected or predicted. *My sister was surprised by the **unexpected** party.*

un·ion (yün′yən) *noun.* Something formed by a joining together; confederation. *The school created a **union** of coaches to discuss the sports program.*

un·sure (un shu̇r′) *adjective.* Not certain or confident. *Because I was **unsure**, I looked up the word's meaning in the dictionary.*

urged (ûrjd) *verb.* Tried to convince or persuade. *We **urged** our cousins to apply for jobs at their favorite summer camp.*

Vv

var·i·a·tions (vâr′ē ā′shənz) *noun, plural.* The extents or amounts to which someone or something changes or varies. *We grew nervous about the **variations** of the dark clouds in the sky.*

vis·i·ble (viz′ə bəl) *adjective.* Able to be seen. *The jet left a **visible** white trail against the blue sky.*

Ww

wages (wē′jəz) *noun, plural.* Payments for work done. *We asked for higher **wages** after the job became more difficult.*

weak·ling (wēk′ling) *noun.* A person who lacks physical or moral strength. *The **weakling** decided to start lifting weights to build muscle.*

wide·spread (wīd′spred′) *adjective.* Happening over a large area or to many people. *The massive storm caused **widespread** damage.*

wring (ring) *verb.* To twist or squeeze forcefully. *I had to **wring** the water out of my towel after dropping it in the pool.*